LIFE & TRADITION
in
RURAL WALES

by J. Geraint Jenkins

with 142 photographs
14 illustrations in text
and a map

D1227628

ALAN SUTTON

First published in 1976 by
J.M. Dent & Sons Ltd

First published in the United Kingdom in this paperback edition
in 1991 by Alan Sutton Publishing Ltd · Phoenix Mill · Far Thrupp
Stroud · Gloucestershire

First published in the United States of America in this paperback
edition in 1992 by Alan Sutton Publishing Inc. · Wolfeboro Falls
NH 03896–0848

British Library Cataloguing in Publication Data

Jenkins, J. Geraint (John Geraint) *1929–*
   Life and tradition in rural Wales.
   1. Wales. Rural regions. History
   I. Title
   942.9009734

   ISBN 0-86299-944-8

Library of Congress Cataloging in Publication Data applied for

Front cover: Llangwm fishwomen at Tenby, *c.* 1900.
Back cover: Harvesting hay with slide car at Dolwyddelan, *c.* 1898.
Photographs: Courtesy of the National Museum of Wales (Welsh Folk
Museum, St Fagans).

Printed in Great Britain by
WBC Print Limited,
Bridgend, Wales.

LIFE & TRADITION IN RURAL WALES

In memory of Melville Richards

Contents

Photographs

Permission to reproduce photographs is gratefully acknowledged to the following: COSIRA, Pls 66, 70; Lt-Col. W. Ll. Evans, Pl. 92; John Field, Pls 111, 112; G. H. Peate, Pls 29, 31; University of Reading, Museum of English Rural Life, Pl. 52; Eric Warrilow, Pl. 124; M. L. Wight, Pls 8, 34, 39, 53, 62, 63, 128, 131, 134, 141, 142; *Y Cymro*, Pls 3, 126.

All other photographs are from the National Museum of Wales (Welsh Folk Museum, St Fagans).

Drawings

HOLYHEAD

BANGOR

CAERNARFON

SNOWDONIA

RHYL

Clwyd

HIRAETHOG

WREXHAM
LLANGOLLEN

PORTMADOC

BALA

DOLGELLAU

CADER
IDRIS

WELSHPOOL

Dyfi

PLYNLIMON
LLANIDLOES

NEWTOWN

ABERYSTWYTH

Ystwyth

LLANDRINDOD

Wye

EPYNT

CARDIGAN

Teifi

PRESELI

BRECON
BEACONS BLACK
MOUNTAINS

BRECON

ST. DAVIDS

Cleddau

ABERGAVENNY

MONMOUTH

HAVERFORDWEST

CARMARTHEN

Tywi

TENBY

LLANELLI

Usk

CHEPSTOW

SWANSEA

NEWPORT

Taff

CARDIFF

COWBRIDGE

WALES

10   0   10   20   30   40   50 MLS.

1 Introduction

'The study of any area which has had a long history of human settlement', said
E. G. Bowen, 'shows quite clearly that the cultural landscape contains many elements besides those associated with the present-day life of the inhabitants. The cultural landscape of such an area has been compared with an ancient manuscript that has been written over on several occasions, yet parts at least of the different writings can still be made out at the present time. Much of the landscape of a long settled country like Wales is thus a veritable palimpsest of culture.'

The keynote to a study of rural Wales is the living past, which still exerts its influence on the daily life of the people. Many features in the cultural landscape and in the social life of Welsh countrymen are of great antiquity. The form of settlement, for example, may be traced back to the tribal system of the Middle Ages and, although the scattered nature of the habitat may be due in part to topographical, climatic and economic factors, in many parts of Wales it cannot be explained without reference to a system of divided inheritance that characterized the society of medieval Wales.

From the earliest times the social order in Wales, as elsewhere, was bound up with the division and occupation of the land. The laws of the medieval king, Hywel Dda, depict a semi-nomadic people with strong tribal affinities, practising a pastoral economy. From the eleventh century the numerous Welsh princes attempted to settle these nomadic pastoralists in permanent homesteads. The unit of landholding in medieval Wales was that of a *gwely* (bed), which was an association of people bound together by blood relationship. They acted together as a family for mutual protection and support, and each individual shared in the common property of his clan. The position of the individual within the *gwely* depended not on his contract but on consanguinity, and his rights, duties and responsibilities were determined by his birth. A permanent base in the form of a family dwelling was set up. Small plots adjacent to the dwelling were enclosed for crop growing, while rather larger enclosures for herding animals were to be found farther away from the homestead. As time progressed, the existing land was subdivided among the kin group, for on the death of a head of family his wealth did not descend to his eldest son but was divided equally among all his sons, and after their day, among the grandsons. When the grandsons were all dead, a final division took place among the great-grandsons and fresh family groups were thus formed. The continued subdivision of property meant smaller and more scattered holdings and this resulted in much confusion.

The pattern of settlement that this medieval system of inheritance brought into being is often quite recognizable in rural Wales today, for hamlets of scattered farms are typical of many districts. In medieval Wales each homestead was called a *tyddyn*, and in the history of the countryside the *tyddyn*, which is synonymous with a smallholding, has been of considerable importance. The medieval laws, more than any other factor, contributed to the existence of small farm units in rural Wales, more especially in river valleys. Uplands and moors were widely used in the Middle Ages for summer grazing; with increasing demand for land, especially in the early nineteenth century, many of these *hafodai* (summer dwellings) became permanent farmsteads.

During that period, too, much of the common land was enclosed and peasant families set up *tŷ unnos* (one-night houses) on the previously unoccupied land. The custom was that if a house of turf was built in a single night and smoke was seen emanating from the chimney at dawn, then the occupier of that temporary dwelling had a legal right to the homestead. An axe thrown from the house marked the extent of an enclosure around the homestead. In time the claims of the occupier were consolidated and a stone-built dwelling was constructed to replace the temporary *tŷ unnos*. In upland districts today may be found the dispersed settlement *par excellence*, with smallholdings dotted evenly over the land.

The existence of a scattered habitat and of so many small farms in rural Wales has had a profound effect both on the social life and on the material culture of Wales. Rural society of the recent past, its character and daily life, were closely associated with the distribution and with the history of settlement. Although with the passing of the centuries wars, conquests and the total replacement of the old tribal system of inheritance have taken place, many aspects of that chapter in the economic and social history of Wales have had far-reaching effects. The past exists in the very nature of the settlement pattern; in the small, irregularly shaped fields surrounding a simple homestead; it persists in the names given to those fields, which indicate that they were named by the occupants of a single farm rather than by a community from a fixed village centre. Each farm has its 'Field in front of the home', its 'Hay Field'; many have 'New Field' and 'Mountain

Field' signifying a stage in land tenure, when the poorer wasteland was incorporated into the farm.

In a less tangible form the medieval inheritance expresses itself in the whole social life of country areas, in the customs and in the character of the people. As in medieval times, most farms in Wales are family farms, and even today the farms of close relatives of the family may be found nearby. Just as consanguinity was all-important in tribal society, so too are blood relationship and the relationship by marriage highly important in the stratification of present-day society, and dominate the social behaviour of the group. The loyalty of any member to his particular family group is always evident, however far removed in degree of relationship he may be. The knowledge of genealogies and the recognition of distant kinsfolk symbolize the importance of family relationships and their part in ordering the lives of the individual members of the group.

In medieval Welsh society the law of Civil Obligation meant that co-aration and co-operation were considered to be the duty of the agriculturist, a duty that survived until recently, when co-aration was widely practised and the co-ownership of an implement by a number of neighbouring farms was common. At harvest time, especially during hay making, and at potato planting or lifting, co-operation was very widely practised, and the individual farmer considered it his duty to help his neighbour, knowing that this favour would be repaid when the need arose.

Strangers who visit parts of rural Wales are often impressed by the great deal of kindness, hospitality and welcome they receive. This again is but a reflection of the tribal past, and owes its origin to the keeping of an open house for those in need.

Although, in areas of dispersed settlement, no village as such may be found, the very way of life and the whole social atmosphere of a district or locality are such that a kind of family feeling, an idea of common destiny and a similarity of purpose in life exist between each family and the whole of the locality in which that family lives. Rural Wales, the land of local cultures, supports a society as tribal in its organization today as that of the early inhabitants described in the Welsh Laws.

The relative isolation of many rural areas from the outside world and the distribution of the homesteads as holdings separate and apart have tended to emphasize individuality of character in members of society. When folk forgathered, it was not on the village green at noon or in the village tavern in the evening as in England, but around the hearth of the individual farmstead at twilight. Each locality continues to possess its numerous houses of call, on whose hearths the inhabitants of the scattered homesteads still meet for conversation and for their entertainment. Much of the informality of the hearth has been transferred to the services of the local places of worship and to the concerts held occasionally in church vestries or parish halls. The latter still possess much of the informality of the traditional Welsh *Noson Lawen* (literally, merry evening), which was once commonly conducted in the farm kitchen.

The age-old isolation, the lack of facilities for formal social events and the long hours of solitude associated with a pastoral life have also had a profound effect on material culture. This is expressed in the products of craftsmanship and in the tools and equipment of the farm and home. Much of Wales consists of inhospitable moorland with narrow valleys leading from the central core of upland like the spokes of a giant wheel. Much of the land is more than a thousand feet above sea level and in many parts is poor and stony, while the climate is damp. Even in the more favoured valleys it is difficult for a farmer to take advantage of the natural condition of his soil if the rain pours down continuously. To obtain a good crop of barley or wheat, sunshine is essential, but when there are mists and rain the farmer must adapt his agriculture to climatic conditions. No part of Wales may be said to be perfectly suited to the growth of cereal crops and, by tradition, Welsh society is a pastoral one; the keynote to its development has been animal husbandry rather than cereal cultivation. Sheep and cattle provided the raw materials for two important industries, those of woollen manufacturing and leather production. Furthermore, livestock farming never needed the elaborate equipment of arable farming, and for this reason specialized craftsmen such as ploughwrights and scythe-handle makers, rake makers and wattle-hurdle weavers, so common in English villages, were a rarity in Wales. All woodwork was carried out by country craftsmen who were able to construct everything in wood from fences to farm vehicles and from coffins to tool handles; metalwork was the province of the general blacksmith and not of specialized families of ploughwrights and scythe smiths and, as in peasant societies the world over, a great deal of the equipment for the farm and home was made by the farmers themselves, rather than by craftsmen. For example, until recently the wheel-less sledges used for harvesting upland fields were built by the farmers. All they required was timber, a hammer, saw and a few nails and they were able to build a perfectly efficient vehicle. In an upland district of dispersed family smallholdings, the making of such things as farm gates, seedlips, baskets, tool handles, rakes and tools was also part of the routine of farming. Farmers often showed considerable artistry in their work and the tradition of the amateur, the tradition of the part-timer, has given us perhaps the greatest expression of our material culture. We can imagine the life of no more than sixty years ago as being far more leisurely than it is today. Entertainment was at a premium, and many of the inhabitants practised some form of craft in their spare time. The things they produced were the utilitarian necessities of the farm and home, but as time progressed the product became purely decorative. It was this tradition that gave Wales its love spoons, its stay busks, knitting-needle sheaths and basketry, products of an upland peasantry that lived in isolation.

To many a hill farmer, life was a constant battle against the gorse, heather and reeds that constantly threatened to take over the limited amount of arable land. The income of the hill farmer in the past was always low, and he could afford neither elaborate and costly equipment nor much beyond a staple diet of home-grown food. Potatoes, oatmeal, milk products and bacon were the main elements in the rural diet, which in many areas was monotonous in the extreme.

Many parts of rural Wales are still isolated from the mainstream of life, and this has had a profound effect on the development of rural industry. Because of distances from the market and large centres of population, rural workshops in Wales have either remained small or have completely disappeared. This is the main reason why an industry like woollen manufacturing, for example, has declined so alarmingly. In the well-populated districts of lowland England, many small workshops, established a hundred or more years ago, that at one time formed an integral part of self-sufficing village communities have, owing to easy marketing conditions, become industries of major importance; but no such development took place in rural Wales. Even in those cases where rural workshops have not developed into major industries, many craftsmen in lowland England have often been able to continue in production because they are within reach of markets. Thus, for example, a Hampshire rake maker still produces willow hand rakes, and is able to make a living because he can sell his products throughout southern England.

2 Life on the Land

Until fairly recent times every rural community in Wales, as elsewhere, was largely self-sufficient, and only on rare occasions did the countryman find it necessary to venture far outside his community and locality to search for the means of life. Most of the inhabitants of rural Wales were born, lived and died within the narrow confines of their own localities, and most realized their ambitions within their own communities, to which they were bound by ties of blood, family and neighbourliness. But the rural neighbourhood was something more than a social entity; it was an economic entity as well.

All the food required by the community could be produced locally; the countryman had animals that could supply him with milk, meat, skins and wool. He had fields, gardens and orchards that supplied him with cereals, root crops, fruit and vegetables. In most parts of Wales, until the end of the nineteenth century, farming depended almost entirely on a wide range of hand tools, a large labour force and the co-operative effort of relatives and neighbours during the busy periods of the farming year. This mutual assistance in farm work was the central theme of neighbourhood feeling. On the one hand there were co-operation and the co-ownership of implements, such as a mowing machine or seed drill, between farmer and farmer. Each farm saw itself as the focus of a small group of perhaps seven or eight other farms with which it had frequent dealings. On the other hand, there was co-operation between farmers and a large number of non-farming cottagers and smallholders, many of whom possessed less than five acres of land.

In an era when the tools and implements of agriculture were few and simple, and farming was a manual art rather than a series of mechanical processes, no farm could exist as an independent and separate unit. For example, few farms of less than eighty acres in size (and that meant eighty per cent in Wales) kept a bull. But since the income of all medium-sized farms, especially in north, mid and west Wales, depended very largely on the sale of store cattle and butter, the bull was an essential farm animal. The breeds of cattle that were most popular in the late nineteenth century were the Castlemartin Blacks and Welsh Blacks, and these always calved in the spring months, thus ensuring a high milk yield in the summer. Since only one farm in five possessed a bull, eighty per cent of the farms were dependent on the other twenty per cent for this essential service. There was a constant traffic of cows from one farm to another throughout the summer months, for without this co-operation between the large farm and its smaller neighbours the economic basis of farming would break down. No cash payment of any kind was usually made for the bull's services, but the debt was paid by providing a day's labour in the hay harvest or at some other busy occasion in the farming year. In the same way, only one farm in eight kept a boar, but since bacon pigs were as important as store cattle in the economy of many parts of Wales, boars were a necessity. For the smooth running of a pastoral economy, therefore, co-operation between farmers was essential.

In an area of dispersed family farms, where the labour force on each holding was of necessity small, co-operation was practised at all times. There was a frequent exchange of labour and the constant borrowing of draught animals and implements, while on certain occasions, such as sheep shearing and potato picking, the labour force on many farms attained vast proportions. The co-operative nature of Welsh agriculture was, perhaps, most clearly seen in the hayfields, for not only did neighbouring farmers help one another in harvesting this vital crop, but their wives and serving maids, together with cottagers and their families, were also expected to help. Let me give the example of a farm of seventy acres in the parish of Penbryn, Cardiganshire, in mid June 1896:

Of the seventy-two adults at work in a hayfield on a particular day

> 10 were neighbouring farmers
> 23 were farm labourers in their employ
> 12 were serving maids, also in their employ
> 18 were cottagers
> 9 were the wives and daughters of cottagers.

In addition to this outdoor labour staff, the farmer's wife and the wives of neighbouring farmers were concerned with the preparation of food in the house, for only maid servants and the wives of cottagers were expected to rake the hay in the fields.

While farmers were paid only by exchange of labour, cottagers were always paid in kind: they were given a pat of butter (called 'debt butter' in west Wales), a bottle of milk, a little cheese, a sack of swedes or a sack of corn for their poultry.

On the other hand, a day's labour in the hayfield might pay for carting a load of coal from the local seaport village or market town or for a cartful of manure for the cottagers' gardens. As far as co-operation between farmers was concerned, a dozen or more holdings within a neighbourhood had, since time immemorial, formed themselves into a workable unit to deal with the hay crop. Farmers, together with the one or two male servants in their employ, would assist one another with the mowing, a task that until the first decade of the twentieth century was always undertaken with scythes. To carry the hay, each farm within the group was expected to supply a horse and gambo (a long two-wheeled cart that made an appearance only at harvest time), together with labour both in the fields and in the rickyard. It is clear, therefore, that since the hay harvest in the late nineteenth century was not mechanized in any way, a large labour force was essential, but no single family farm could supply that labour on its own. Owing to the moist climate of most of Wales, too, it was essential that the hay be harvested very quickly, and again to do this a larger labour force was required.

The corn harvest, on the other hand, was a matter for each individual farmer. There was little co-operation between farms in a neighbourhood group on this occasion. Although the economy of Wales is by tradition a pastoral one, surprisingly large acreages were devoted to arable crop. In the parish of Penbryn in 1890, for example, two thousand five hundred acres of a total of just over eight thousand were under the plough. No cereal crops were grown for sale. Wheat was used in the home, oats for feeding horses, and barley, the most important crop of all, for feeding pigs and cattle. The equipment for dealing with these crops was simple in the extreme. Corn was sown broadcast from a basket or wooden lip or linen sheet; it was weeded with a forked stick and weeding hook and harvested with a scythe (Pls 2, 3). In wet years, when rain and wind had flattened the corn crop, and in dry years, like that of 1894, when the corn stalks were particularly short, the scythe could not be used and the whole crop had to be harvested with a sickle. In these conditions, harvesting was an extremely slow and difficult process, but even in normal years it would take an experienced scyther at least a full day to cut an acre of corn and at least another half-day to bind it into sheaves. It was customary to bind wheat immediately after cutting, a task that was always done by women (Pl. 5), but in the case of barley and oats the crop had to remain on the ground for at least nine days before binding. The sheaves were then stooked, and after a number of days the stooks were collected and built into land mows of either seventy-two or ninety-six sheaves. Finally, the sheaves were carried to the rick yard in gambos and built up in rectangular or round stacks which were then thatched. Harvesting, even on a small farm, was a lengthy process, for under normal circumstances it has been estimated that it would take one man working alone at least five days to cut, bind and carry an acre of corn, without counting the period that the corn had to remain loose on the ground, in stooks, and in land mows.

For example, a farm of a hundred and forty-five acres in the parish of Llan-grannog, Cardiganshire, in 1897 grew thirty-five acres of corn: fifteen of barley, twelve of oats, five of wheat and three of rye. If the farmer were to depend on his own labour resources, consisting of himself, his wife, two male servants and one maid servant, harvesting would take at least thirty-five working days. Meanwhile the day-to-day work of the farm had to continue: the ten dairy cattle had to be milked and fed, the thirty-five calves, fifteen pigs, five horses and poultry had to be cared for and food for all the family had to be prepared; clearly, no family farm of this size could possibly cope independently with all the work that was involved at this busy period. Welsh farmers were, therefore, forced by circumstances to look elsewhere for extra labour in the harvest fields. They looked not towards their farming neighbours, who were themselves fully occupied, but towards the non-farming cottagers who lived in the neighbourhood and were largely dependent on the farmer for the means of life.

In order to feed himself and his family, and to provide food for the pig and hens that he always kept at the bottom of his garden, the cottager was allowed to plant potatoes in a neighbouring farmer's fields. While the cottager supplied the seed potatoes, the farmer undertook the preparation of the ground, weeding and hoeing the growing crop and supplying the manure. In payment for this the cottager was expected to work in the harvest field: for each carefully measured potato row, eighty yards long, the cottager worked for a day cutting the corn, or, alternatively, he spent a day and a half binding corn. Since each family required between two and five rows of potatoes, this custom of work debt solved the problem of scarcity of labour during the corn harvest. In the autumn cottagers were expected to assist with picking the farmer's potato crop before they tackled their own, but the farmer undertook the delivery of potatoes to the cottager's home. This custom of the work debt remained in vogue in many parts of Wales for as long as simple equipment was used; indeed it is only within the last twenty-five years, with the advent of modern machinery, that the last vestiges of it have disappeared. Cottagers were indeed a part-time labour force and the rules relating to their rights and duties in a rural neighbourhood were very rigid indeed. In the late nineteenth century there were at least two legal cases where cottagers had obtained the right of planting potatoes in a farmer's field, but had failed to fulfil their side of the contract by working at the corn harvest. In both cases judgment was given in favour of the farmer, mainly on the grounds that he had supplied manure for the cottager's potato crop.

During this period of near self-sufficiency, craft workshops in all parts of Wales were numerous and important, while domestic skills, such as butter and cheese making, beer brewing, pig killing and salting and many others, were widely practised. Produce of the farm—corn, wool and animal skins—could always be taken to a mill or factory for processing. Some of the products of the mills— cloth, tweeds and leather—could be used by one of the many craftsmen of the neighbourhood to make some essential, while other products, such as flour, oatmeal and blankets, could be used directly in the home. In many cases the craftsmen who processed farm produce were not paid in cash, but were allowed to keep a proportion of the produce that a farmer brought in. Corn millers were allowed to keep a proportion of a farmer's quota of corn for their own use, while woollen manufacturers were allowed to keep a proportion of the fleeces that a farmer brought in for making into yarn or blankets. The owner of a small woollen mill in rural Brecknockshire processed wool for local farmers and supplied them with knitting yarn, cloth and blankets, and kept a small proportion of fleeces as payment, which he made up into cloth and sold on his market stall at Builth. Other craftsmen who processed farm produce were tanners and curriers concerned with leather production; charcoal burners and oil distillers producing turpentine who were concerned with processing timber; and maltsters, brewers and cider makers supplying beverages to the rural population. Of course, by the end of the nineteenth century, with the ever-growing influence of the temperance move- ment in many parts of Wales, these last named industries were less common than they had been. In Brecknockshire, for example, a writer in 1911 mentioned a large brewery at Sennybridge where, in the late nineteenth century, 'considerable trading was done in those damning commodities. It is a great blessing', the writer adds, 'that this trade has disappeared and we hope that the day is not too far re- moved when the business will be but history in all our towns and villages.' Even in the nineteen-thirties a Methodist temperance leader took as his theme for a sermon that of 'Brecknockshire—the cider-besotten county'.

The processing crafts usually demanded a range of immovable equipment and often required water power, and for this reason were practised more often than not in small factories or mills. Woollen manufacturing required water power and a great deal of heavy equipment. The Esgair Moel mill from Llanwrtyd, Brecknockshire, had the following equipment when it was dismantled for re- erection at the Welsh Folk Museum in 1951:

A pair of dyeing vats, one equipped with windlass
Devil for intermixing and disentangling wool
A scribbler carder with intermediate feed and carding engine with condenser
Spinning jack of eighty spindles

Twister	Press
Warping frame	Fulling stocks
Three hand looms	Rowing frame
Cutting machine	Tenter frame

A tannery from Rhaeadr, Radnorshire, also at the Welsh Folk Museum (Pls 104, 105, 106, 107), has the following equipment:

A water-driven mill wheel and a mill for grinding bark.
A plentiful supply of clean water for initial washing of hides in a waterpit, 7 feet deep.
Three lime pits for initial immersion of hides before fleshing and unhairing.
Three mastering pits containing a mixture of hen or pigeon manure, or dog dung and water for treating calf skins.
A pit for fleshings and other waste products.
Fifty tan pits containing oak bark and water in varying strength for the actual tanning of hides.
Beams to act as work benches for fleshing and unhairing.
Unhairing and fleshing knives and scudding knives for removal of lime.
A wooden rounding table and knives for cutting up hides into six or eight parts before tanning.
Hooks and long-handled tongs for handling hides in pits. Plungers for mixing oak bark; bark baskets; bark barrows.
A heavy brass roller for rolling tanned hides on a zinc rolling platform.
Horses and striking pins for removing wrinkles from tanned leather.

After rolling and striking, sole leather did not require further treatment before it could be used, but harness and boot upper leather had to be dressed by the currier. The currier's craft did not depend on water power or on any large, complex pieces of machinery but on dexterity in the use of hand tools. Nevertheless, it was an advantage for the currier to locate his workshop either in or near the source of supply—the local tannery.

In addition to processing farm products, every rural neighbourhood had its craftsmen responsible for producing tools and equipment for the farm. Essentials ranging from field gates to horseshoes and from ploughs to shovels could be produced locally by hosts of wheelwrights, carpenters and blacksmiths. Since each craftsman was concerned with producing farm tools specifically for his own locality, and made them to suit local conditions of soil and topography, considerable variation in tool design came into being. For example, if a farmer required a plough, local craftsmen were quite prepared to make one that was well adapted to the farmer's need and land.

All the furniture for the home could be made by specialized local cabinet makers and carpenters; all the utensils for the dairy and kitchen could be made by turners, white coopers, blacksmiths and other craftsmen. Horse harness, wearing apparel, boots, clogs, indeed everything the countryman required, could be produced locally. If a locality did not possess all the craftsmen considered essential, then there were always the itinerant craftsmen who could visit even the remotest farmhouse.

Many of the creative crafts of rural Wales came into existence because raw material was available in a locality and they usually met a regional rather than a local demand. The pottery industry, for example, came into existence when there was a plentiful supply of suitable clay close enough to the coalfields to obtain fuel for firing kilns. At Ewenni, near Bridgend, in Glamorgan, at least seven potters' shops existed in the nineteenth century, while the history of the Rumney Bridge Pottery, near Cardiff, may be traced back to the fifteenth century at least. In north Wales clay and coal existed in close proximity at Buckley in Flintshire and a flourishing pottery, brick and tile industry came into being in that town. At Newborough in Anglesey, rush-mat making became an important industry in a region where sea rushes grew profusely; wood-turning became important in the well-wooded Teifi valley in west Wales, while livestock-rearing in mid Wales supported a flourishing leather industry. Other industries supplied strictly local needs, and ranged from saddlery to iron founding. The county of Cardigan in 1831, for example, had 28 saddlers, 1 whip maker, 12 printers, 15 tinsmiths, 17 clock makers, 275 blacksmiths, 6 basket makers, 33 wheel- and millwrights, 393 tailors, 523 carpenters, 8 thatchers and 334 stonemasons. At that time too it had specialized craftsmen who met the local demand of maritime communities, and in 1831 it had 5 sail makers, 13 rope makers and 43 shipwrights.

Some indication of the importance of craftsmen in the life of Wales in the past is provided by the following random examples:

Crickhowell, a small Brecknockshire market town, in 1830 supported 3 joiners, 3 saddlers, 2 tailors, 2 hatters, 3 boot makers, 2 blacksmiths, 2 maltsters, 2 masons, 1 wheelwright, 1 straw-hat maker, 1 tiler.

Brecon in 1830 had 6 wheelwrights, 9 bakers, 5 blacksmiths, 8 boot makers, 4 cabinet makers, 5 tinsmiths, 7 joiners, 4 coopers, 2 hatters, 5 maltsters, 3 millers, 4 saddlers, 3 skinners, 6 masons, 2 straw-hat makers, 13 tailors, 3 tanners, 1 gun maker, 1 iron founder, 1 rope maker, 1 pump maker, 1 bright smith, 1 book-binder, 1 woollen manufacturer, 1 nail maker.

Haverfordwest, the county town of Pembrokeshire, in 1840 had 13 bakers, 13 blacksmiths, 16 boot makers, 5 brewers, 11 carpenters, 3 coach builders, 4 coopers, 10 curriers, 3 glovers, 4 hatters, 10 maltsters, 1 lime burner, 4 corn millers, 5 saddlers, 2 rope makers, 4 masons, 7 straw-hat makers, 15 tailors, 5 clock makers, 1 stay maker, 1 cutler, 1 paper maker, 1 cork cutter, 1 weaver, 1 skinner, 1 um-brella maker.

In rural localities, too, craftsmen were as numerous as in market towns. The small village of Rhydlewis in south Cardiganshire, for example, in 1890 had 9 carpenters, 1 blacksmith, 1 basket maker, 1 tanner, 1 currier, 2 saddlers, 6 boot makers, 3 clog makers, 5 tailors, 1 mason, 8 weavers, 1 pin maker, 2 millers, 1 baker.

In 1894 the remote parish of Newborough in Anglesey had 6 stonemasons, 10 carpenters, 1 shipwright, 2 glaziers, 2 plasterers, 2 blacksmiths, 5 boot makers, 1 woollen manufacturer, together with a considerable number concerned with the rush-mat making industry.

Cilgerran, a north Pembrokeshire village, in 1835 had 9 boot makers, 1 hatter, 4 carpenters, 1 corn miller, 1 tailor, 1 tanner, 5 masons, 3 coopers, 2 blacksmiths.

Defynnog, a Brecknockshire village, in 1900 had a wheelwright, a woollen manu-facturer, 2 corn millers, 1 blacksmith, 3 cabinet makers, 2 carpenters, 1 saddler, a saw mill, 2 masons and 1 tailor.

The period 1900 to 1939 saw a widening of the horizons of the Welsh farmer and a new emphasis on production for the market. In rural Dyfed, for example, acreage under arable crops declined very greatly, while first specialized stock-rearing and then dairying became all-important. The most significant single event of the period was the establishment of the Milk Marketing Board in 1933. Almost immediately the production of butter and store cattle declined, sheep and pigs declined in numbers, and the production of liquid milk became the basis of the economy. The milk-collecting lorry became a vital element in rural communi-cation, for not only did it collect the churns from farms daily, but its driver was also expected to bring daily papers and goods from the nearest market town, while the vehicle was often used as a means of conveying people from one place to another. Throughout the period, therefore, a gradual change in the economy took place, the mixed, largely self-sufficient economy of the nineteenth century giving place to a specialized dairying economy by 1935. In 1900 the hardy native Black cattle were all important, but by 1924 they had been largely replaced by the all-purpose Shorthorn, and by 1939 Channel Island and Friesian breeds were gaining ground at a considerable rate.

This change of emphasis completely altered the pattern of work on Welsh farms. Whereas in the first decade of this century most medium-sized mixed farms kept two or three male labourers, who spent a great deal of time cultivating and harvesting the arable crops, by 1933 the farm servant was a rarity except on the largest farms. By that time arable crops had become relatively unimportant, so that the traditional work of the male labourer had dwindled. But as dairying grew in importance, so too did the work of women on the farms increase. Despite a huge increase in the size of the dairy herds, women were still expected to under-take all the milking, feeding the cattle and clearing out their sheds, together with feeding poultry and preparing food for the family. The farmer, now in many cases without assistance from paid labourers, was fully engaged in the fields—ploughing, cultivating, ditching and hedging, spending far less time in the farm-yard.

Because of this change of emphasis and the introduction of new cultivating and harvesting machinery, the paid labour force on Welsh farms declined rapidly and a large number of labourers made their way to the industrial regions of south Wales, the Midlands and London. The break-up of the large estates in many dis-tricts and the fragmentation of holdings contributed further to this decline. Whereas in 1890 the average size of holding in five parishes in south Cardigan-shire was 55.2 acres, by 1910 the average had dropped to 42.8 acres. A great increase in the number of farms of less than twenty acres meant that holdings in west Wales became family farms in the true sense, requiring no more than the labour of a farmer and his wife to undertake all the work.

Nevertheless, the feature that characterized the period above all else was mechanization: mechanization that not only contributed to depopulation but also affected rural social life in all its aspects. In the early years of the century the horse-drawn mowing machine made its appearance and it quickly replaced the scythe on the larger farms for harvesting hay and corn. No longer were the gangs of farmers and cottagers required to harvest hay and corn, for all this work could be completed very quickly by the farmer himself with little assistance. Nevertheless, the purchase of mowing machines meant an appreciable capital outlay, which few farmers could afford. This problem was overcome by a co-operative effort, where groups of half a dozen farmers pooled their resources to buy the new machines. Each farm within the group was allowed to use this in turn and in a specific order, each one providing extra labour at harvest time for the other farms within the group. By 1910 the reaper binder had replaced the mowing machine on many farms, and its appearance dispensed with the need for extra labour to bind corn in sheaves. Since the cost of the binder was considerably higher than that of a mowing machine, the ownership of those implements was often shared by a dozen or more farms. Once again labour was exchanged for building land mows and carrying the crops. As far as grain harvesting was concerned, there were few technological changes between 1914 and 1950, and through the period co-operation between farms continued. For the hay harvest, however, a large number of new implements became popular in the inter-war period, ranging from tedding machines (known as 'kickers') to mechanical hay loaders. Many of these implements, which were popular for only a very short period, were co-operatively owned and all had the effect of making farmers less dependent on one another and on the co-operation of cottagers.

It is clear, nevertheless, that the early stages of mechanization during the first twenty-five years of the twentieth century led to increased co-operation between farmers that expressed itself in the co-ownership of implements and the exchange of labour at busy periods. On the other hand, mechanization meant that cottagers were less essential to the smooth running of the economy than they were in the past, for the traditional work that they performed—cutting and binding corn— was now undertaken by machines, except on the smaller farms. But the custom of cottagers planting potatoes in the field continued until 1939, and even later in some localities, although the rigid rules of the work debt were not as strictly adhered to. A cottager was still expected to plant and pick a farm's potatoes, he was still expected to work at the hay harvest, for although field machinery had been introduced, manual labour was required in the rickyard. In one aspect of farm work, mechanization contributed directly to co-operation, whereas in previous years every farmer had acted independently; this was in threshing corn. By 1905 agricultural contractors with steam-powered threshing tackle were making regular journeys from farm to farm in the autumn and again in January or February in most parts of Wales, spending little more than one day at each farm in turn. Whereas in the nineteenth century threshing was done with flails (Pls 13, 14), the process continuing on odd days throughout the winter months, with the advent of steam threshing tackle, farms required extra labour for the day—some to feed the machine, others to carry the grain to the barn; some to remove the chaff from the machine, others to build straw ricks, while hordes of small boys fed the engine with coal and water (Pl. 16). It became customary, therefore, for farmers to help one another in threshing, and for cottagers to pay for the right of planting potatoes in the farmer's field by giving a day's work at the threshing. In all other aspects of farm work, however, the advent of machinery meant the dying out of co-operation and the rigid social organization that it brought into being. Nevertheless, until 1939 smallholdings still depended very largely on hand tools, although many could borrow the machines of neighbouring large farms for some of their tasks, the debt being paid by providing a day's work at the hay or potato harvests or on threshing day.

Since 1939 the agricultural economy of Wales has been completely transformed and the technological, economic and social changes, brought into being since 1945, in particular, have completely altered the outlook of the Welsh farmer. One of the most significant social changes which came as a result of technological improvements was the almost complete disruption of the neighbourhood group with its intimacy of association and co-operative organization. Today each farm in a region tends to be an economic unit, almost completely independent of its neighbours. Although few Welsh farms employ paid labour on a full-time basis, a wide range of modern equipment makes it possible for the farmer to complete his work with little outside help. It has been said that in areas where farmers regard the neighbourhood as the main social organization of their lives, clear signs of technological and economic backwardness are displayed. In the hills of mid Cardiganshire, for example, where neighbourhood feeling still persists to a certain extent, there is among the farming population an unwillingness to change attitudes, values and institutions which are out-dated in terms of modern economic and social conditions. But in the south of the county technological progress has led to a weakening of neighbourhood feeling, and economic and social conditions have changed spectacularly.

The introduction of new implements did not initially disrupt the established order. Before 1939, machinery was introduced in an attempt to cut down labour costs, for there was a great decrease in the number of employees on Welsh farms. Since 1945, however, Welsh farmers have experienced great difficulty in obtaining labour. Very few young people are prepared to work on the land after leaving school, whereas in pre-war days a proportion of school leavers did take up work as farm labourers. Between 1935 and 1938 fifty-two per cent of youths leaving school in the Penmorfa district of Cardiganshire, for example, took up agricultural work, but in the years 1955–8 less than five per cent of school leavers became farm workers. The foundation of a research establishment at Aberporth has not only provided work for those who in earlier years could have become farm workers, but it has also robbed the farmers of the service of cottagers, who have ceased to provide voluntary labour in threshing and in the potato and hay-fields. Before 1950, for example, the potato crop on every farm was planted and harvested by hand, but since that date farmers have experienced increasing difficulty in obtaining extra labour and the total acreage devoted to the crop has decreased considerably. A number of the larger farms in the region have purchased mechanical planters which are hired out to neighbouring farmers for a specific fee rather than by exchange of labour. In nearly all aspects of farm work, voluntary contribution has ceased and the co-ownership of implements is no longer practised.

In the agrarian changes that have taken place, rural industry has also declined spectacularly. Local craftsmen have disappeared by the thousand and their products have been replaced by standardized goods produced in the urban centres of Britain. Cardiganshire in 1923, for example, had 72 corn mills, by 1969 it had none; in 1923 it had 114 blacksmiths' shops, today 8; in 1923 it had 77 woollen mills, today it has 3. Brecknock in 1923 had 31 corn mills, 22 woollen mills and 102 blacksmiths' shops; by 1969 it had no corn mills, 1 woollen mill and 3 smiths. Pembrokeshire in 1923 had 54 corn mills, 20 woollen mills and 117 blacksmiths; in 1965 it had no corn mills, 2 woollen mills and 4 black-smiths. Other rural industries—clog making, bowl turning, tanning, currying—have virtually ceased to exist, whilst most of the others are much rarer than they were.

As the result of the decline of rural industry, the countryside has lost something more than economic units producing essential goods; it has also lost an important avenue of expression, for in the social history of the countryside the importance of the craft workshop as a meeting place for a rural community cannot be over-estimated. In many cases the cobbler's shop, the smithy and carpenter's yard were social centres where problems were discussed, where argument was rife and wit at its highest level was the order of the day.

3 Farm Implements and Tools

When country craftsmen or farmers themselves were responsible for making tools and implements for the farms of their own locality, they took into full consideration such features as soil and vegetation, topography and slope as well as the ingrained traditions of their localities. In describing the Irish spade Estyn Evans states: 'The precise requirements of each group of townlands forming a neighbourhood unit, resulted from the balance of many physical, human and economic factors; such as condition of soil and slope, method of digging, type of crop, length of arm and leg—cemented by usage and sanctioned by tradition.' In Wales, as a result of similar factors, considerable regional variation in tool and implement design came into being.

An example *par excellence* of regional variation in design is provided by the distribution of cart and wagon types (see pp. 55–66), but variation can also be seen in small farm tools. Over much of upland Wales the usual type of shovel used is a long-handled, triangular-bladed tool made by such smiths as the Davieses of Aberaeron, Cardiganshire; but in the Vale of Glamorgan and in the broad river valleys of mid Wales, short-handled, rectangular-bladed shovels, of a type used in England, are the only shovels known. Even today the rural worker still insists on the familiar tool of his neighbourhood, and although these may now be made by large-scale manufacturers in the industrial regions, the old pattern and old designs persist.

To quote another example, that of the billhook, used traditionally by countrymen for hedging. In the past, billhooks like other farm tools were made by village blacksmiths for the farming population of their own immediate districts. Since each tool was designed for dealing with a specific type of vegetation and local conditions, many different designs were in existence. Not only the shape and size of blade but also the distribution of weight in each tool and the shape of the handle varied tremendously. The billhooks of Brecknockshire were designed primarily for laying hedges of straight hazel, willow and thorn, and consequently the pistol-handled tool had an almost straight blade. In rural Cardiganshire, on the other hand, where the art of hedging was not nearly as highly developed, the hedgerow vegetation consisted of a great deal of bramble and thorn. Blades of the so-called Aberaeron billhook were distinctly concave with a projection on the back of each tool for pushing cut rods into position. The billhook was equipped with a long turned handle, which kept the worker's hands well clear of the prickles.

In the nineteenth century, particularly during the last quarter, village black-smiths who supplied a distinctly local market with all its metal requirements were disappearing very rapidly and their work was taken over by large-scale manu-facturers in Yorkshire and the English Midlands. Representatives of those manu-facturers travelled widely and supplied market towns and villages with their products. However, in small farm tools they did not produce a standardized product, but clung to traditional local patterns and still maintained the old local names: 'Llanelli', 'Ross', 'Machynlleth', 'Llandeilo', 'Aberaeron', 'Newtown', 'Caergwrle', 'Knighton' and many other billhooks, originally local types, could still be bought. As one catalogue of 1905 states: 'We show only those patterns that are most generally used in their various districts. We still make any pattern hook, and if the pattern which customers have been in the habit of buying is not shown here, we shall be pleased to supply them.'

The technological revolution in agriculture, so often ascribed to the late eighteenth and early nineteenth centuries, did not really reach many parts of rural, upland Wales until the present century. By tradition, Wales is a stock-rearing country and, until the beginning of the twentieth century, farmers never demanded the vast quantity of tillage and barn machinery that the inventive ability of agricultural engineers had devised for easing the farmer's labours. Within the last three-quarters of a century or so, however, the isolation has been broken down, and the vast improvement in agricultural techniques, in tools and in implements has completely changed the pattern of life in the Welsh hills. The application of new scientific methods of farming and the development of rural amenities between the two wars, but especially since 1945, have had a far greater impact on Welsh rural society than all the developments of the previous thousand years. In general, Welsh farming until late in the nineteenth century existed in a state of almost medieval simplicity. There were, of course, some prosperous farmers who for a long time had been ready to adopt new techniques and new machinery, but for a large proportion of the rural population farming depended very largely on a wide range of simple hand tools and one or two sizeable imple-ments, perhaps owned by a number of neighbouring farmers. Thomas Tusser, the sixteenth-century poet and agriculturalist, wrote that the only tools required for full efficiency on the farm were a mattock, spade, pike, flail, weeding tongs and three large implements—a plough, a harrow and a cart or wain. For centuries after Tusser's day, this was the range of equipment found on many farms; indeed even in the more progressive districts it was not until well on into the nineteenth century that the ideas of pioneers in agricultural engineering—ideas of people like Tull and Plenty, Ransome and Small—began to make some impact on farmers and craftsmen generally. It is said that inventions in agriculture are only very gradually accepted and that agriculturalists are the slowest to adopt new methods and new apparatus. Be that as it may, the countless new implements of the past were very slow to take root and for many years after their acceptance by the more progressive, many substantial farmers did not make use of new inventions until their labour forces had been depleted by a drift of workers to the industrial regions.

For smallholders, primitive tools and obsolete techniques persisted at least up to 1939 if not later. Until 1950, for example, on a number of smallholdings in south Cardiganshire it was not uncommon to see a farmer sowing grain by hand in a field that had been ploughed with a locally-made horse plough, rolled with a wooden or stone roller and harrowed with a wooden-framed harrow. The seed could be carried either in a wooden or straw lip or more often a linen bed sheet, and the seed was sown by broadcasting it as evenly as possible as the farmer walked up and down the field, his arm moving rhythmically from left to right (Pls 2, 3). Other farmers used a seed fiddle; the motion of the fiddle bow across the bottom of the box turned a disc that caused the seed to be thrown out on either side of the sower. The hand-carried fiddle ensured a more even distribution of seed than the old broadcasting system, which demanded precision and careful calculation on the part of the sower to determine the exact amount of seed that should be sown in a particular tract of land. Only the more substantial farmers possessed horse-drawn or tractor-driven sowing machines; indeed the co-owner-ship of seed drills was commonplace in many parts of Wales until the late forties or early fifties.

Nevertheless, the late nineteenth and early twentieth centuries did witness some improvement in agricultural implements. In threshing, both hand threshers and travelling threshing boxes had gradually supplanted flails in many parts of the country, while in most districts light horse-drawn swing ploughs, usually locally made, had replaced the clumsy implements of earlier centuries such as those of Carmarthenshire, that Charles Hassall described in 1794 as 'unfit for the purpose of neat ploughing'. 'I do not recollect', he adds, 'to have seen such bad ploughing as is commonly observed in this and the neighbouring county of Pembroke.' Pembrokeshire ploughed fields he describes 'as if a drove of swine had been

2. *Broadcasting seed from a straw lip; Dinas Mawddwy, Merioneth, c. 1910.*

1. *A ploughing match poster of 1901.*

3. *Thomas Williams of Chwilog, Caernarvonshire, broadcasting seed from a sheet adapted to form a seedlip.*

4. *Harrowing at Tower Fa:*
Llanboidy, Carmarthenshire,
1969.

5. *Gathering and binding she:*
in Carmarthenshire, c. 1898

6. *Stooking oats; c. 1900.*

7. *Reaping with hook and crook;*
Brecknock, 1931.

8. *Harvesting with a tractor-*
drawn reaper-binder, 1931.

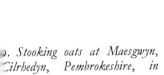

9. *Stooking oats at Maesgwyn,*
Cilrhedyn, Pembrokeshire, in
1968.

10. Raking hay. North Carmarthenshire, c. 1910.

11. Carrying hay on a slide car; Blaencorrwg, Glamorgan, c. 1900.

12. Thatching a rick at Alltwalis, Dyfed, 1969.

13, 14. *Threshers with their flails at Pen-y-garn, Alltwalis Dyfed, c. 1890.*

15. *Winnowing the threshed grain.*

16. Threshing steam power at maen Uchaf, Pant, Bala, in 1916.

17. Awners for removing the 'beard' from barley.

18. Teamwork on sh... ing day at Pennan... Uchaf, Dinas M... ddwy, 1958.

19–21. *Thomas Hughes of Rhandirmwyn, Carmarthenshire, making a rush halter. Preparing the rushes; trimming; the finished halter.*

22. Removing the turf to expose the peat Cwmhesgen, Llanfachreth, 1968.

23, 24. Using the special spade to cut the peat blocks.

25. A view of the cut peat bog, Bwlch-y-gro Cynllwyd.

moiling them'. Of course in many parts of Wales until the mid nineteenth century a team of oxen was used for ploughing and in the Vale of Glamorgan they persisted until late in the nineteenth century. In Welsh society both the ploughman and oxherd were important personalities, and on the substantial estates of such districts as the Vale of Glamorgan, it was their duty to care for the animals, by both day and night. Usually they had their beds in the ox shed, and when they were at work the oxherd acted as a second ploughman, whose duty it was to walk alongside the plough team, with a whip in his hand, singing a traditional song and exhorting the animals to greater effort. Many of these songs of exhortation are known, especially in the Vale of Glamorgan. The final call assumed a variety of forms, the most popular being '*Ma Hw*' and '*Hw, Mlaen*' ('Woo forward').

For example, a Glamorgan ox song says:

Mu fuo i lawar blwyddyn	For many years
Yn canu gyta'r ychin:	I sang with the oxen:
Bara haidd a chosyn cnep	Barley bread and a lump of cheese
Dim tishan lap, na phwtin, Ma hw,	No cake, no pudding, Ma hw,
Ma hw.	Ma hw.

It is often forgotten that for nigh on two thousand years the ox was by far the most common draught beast in Britain, and it was not until comparatively recently that horses replaced oxen in ploughing and carting around the farm. Long before the arrival of the Romans, the Celtic people possessed small and rather weak oxen that they used for a variety of tasks. According to some, the general lack of strength of the prehistoric ox team and the poor design of early ploughs explain why the so-called Celtic fields were small in size and square in shape. Be that as it may, the average height of oxen in Roman and pre-Roman Britain was no more than forty inches. It was the Romans who first introduced the practice of shoeing working oxen, and as long as oxen were used on British farms they were always shod with two crescent-shaped pieces of iron on each hoof. By the Middle Ages oxen had increased in size and strength and various breeds were widely used for drawing ploughs and carts. A plough team usually consisted of six, eight or more often, twelve oxen, yoked in pairs. The yoke consisted of a thick bar of oak or hornbeam, carefully carved into shape and well polished and oiled. The bows by which the yoke was attached to the necks of the oxen were made of ash, steamed and bent into shape (Fig. 1(1)).

In medieval Welsh law a fully grown ox was valued at five shillings and a working ox was yoked to a plough team at three years of age and remained at work for six or seven years. Until the eighteenth century, in many parts of Wales, horses were regarded as noble and valuable animals, and although they could be used for light carting, riding and harrowing, they were not subjected to the drudgery of ploughing. This may explain why in the early twentieth century Welsh horses were given names suggesting nobility and not the homely names usual for cattle; it explains why in many Welsh farms the stable was the building nearest the dwelling and why on the more substantial farms, the chief male servant (*gwas mawr*) was responsible for horses and for nothing else.

The number of ox teams on Welsh farms had already declined by the mid eighteenth century. A great controversy reigned during that century and agricultural writers argued and debated as to which animal was the better for ploughing, the slow, steady ox or the faster, more nervous horse. Although the general opinion of writers rather favoured the ox, horses became far more numerous and gradually supplanted the age-old ox team. Champions of the ox pointed out that oxen were far cheaper to keep, for they required only two meals a day, while horses required at least three. When the ploughman ate his midday meal in the shade of a hedge, the oxen would quietly sit in between the furrows chewing the cud, until it was time to restart work; whereas horses required oats to eat, oxen were quite content with little more than chaffed straw. The ox team could plough about an acre a day, perhaps not quite so much as a team of horses, but the steady, plodding action of the ox team was particularly valuable in ploughing hilly areas. Although the working life of the ox was no more than seven years at the most, when it was killed its meat provided food for the farming family for many a day; the skin could be made into leather; the horns furnished handles, combs, spoons and lanterns. Even its dung was useful as fuel when firewood was scarce. The dung was also mixed with clay, straw and other materials for making daub for the walls of buildings. Yet despite their many advantages, ox teams disappeared very quickly in the eighteenth and early nineteenth centuries. Better and stronger breeds of horses, and lighter, more efficient ploughs hastened their end. By 1890 ox ploughing had disappeared completely in all parts of Wales, the last team being used in the Vale of Glamorgan in 1889.

Welsh Black cattle were regarded as particularly suitable for ploughing duties and for centuries there was a steady trade in cattle driven on the hoof from Wales to south-east England. Welsh cattle were preferred for ploughing by Sussex farmers, for example, and these were driven on a journey of twenty days or more from Wales to Barnet and Smithfield fairs. For the journey the cattle were shod, often on the forefeet only, by blacksmiths who accompanied the droves; if necessary they replaced worn out or loose shoes on the journey. The drovers themselves were a romantic and hardy body of men, who carried a great deal of responsibility. In addition to financing the cattle trade, they executed duties for their fellow countrymen in London: they conveyed rents to absentee landlords in the metropolis and paid local taxes to the Exchequer. In addition they acted as unofficial bankers for the people, and many actually founded banks with such eminently appropriate names as the 'Bank of the Black Ox'.

According to medieval Welsh law twelve oxen, yoked in pairs, were necessary to pull the heavy wheeled ploughs of the period, and indeed later. Many of these ploughs were so inefficient in turning the soil that men and women armed with mattocks or wooden beetles had to be employed to cut up the furrows even further. The real advance in the design of ploughs came with the patenting of Stanyforth and Foljambe's famous Rotherham plough in 1730. This worked on completely new principles; it was a light wooden plough without wheels, equipped with an iron share, mouldboard and coulter. Only one pair of horses or oxen was required to draw it, and the draught animals and plough could be controlled by one ploughman. Gradually the design of the Rotherham swing plough spread to all parts of the country, adapted by blacksmiths and ploughwrights to local conditions of soil and slope, although the old heavy ploughs were still being used in some parts of the country until well into the nineteenth century.

The efforts of the county agricultural societies in promoting improved farm equipment cannot be over-estimated, for they encouraged the adoption of the Rotherham plough among other improved implements. One of the first Welsh craftsmen to build an all-iron plough was Thomas Morris (*Twm Gôf*) of Login in Carmarthenshire, who began to build all-iron ploughs in the eighteen-thirties. By the end of the nineteenth century a large number of ploughwrights' shops had been established in Wales, all producing local variations of the light Rotherham plough. For example, in west Wales a notable craftsman was Josiah Evans of Pontseli, Pembrokeshire, whose 'Number 6' and 'Number 7' ploughs became popular throughout west Wales, Brecknockshire and Radnorshire, and were taken by emigrants to Australia and North America. The Pontseli plough was specifically designed for ploughing sloping fields, and its mouldboard, made at the Carmarthen foundry, was regarded as particularly efficient for cross ploughing. Ffransis Payne in his *Yr Aradr Gymreig* points out that mouldboards of the Pontseli type were used as recently as 1935. 'This casting, considerably improved ... is still in use on scores of ploughs today and is still cast at Brecon', said a correspondent in the *Western Mail* in that year. He continues: 'This type of casting will never be ousted from the hillside farms of mid and west Wales, and it is not uncommon to see smith-made ploughs fitted with this casting win all the

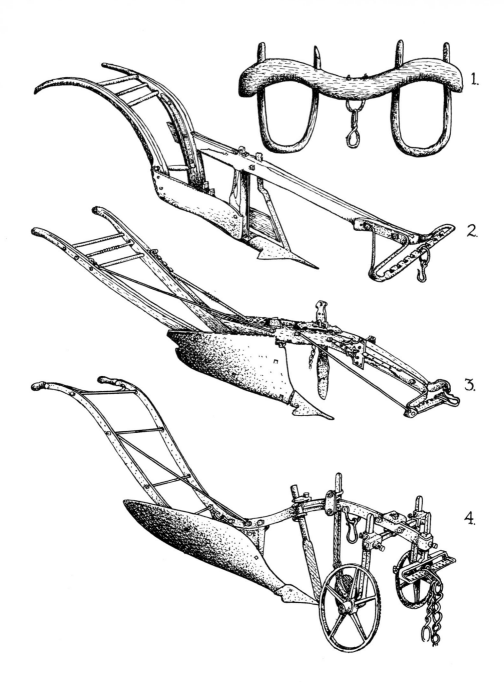

1.

2.

3.

4.

prizes in the championships (swing plough) class in certain districts.' Some plough mouldboards such as those used on the Dyffryn, Cardiganshire plough, were designed by farmers for production by local blacksmiths; others used parts that were based on the design of plough parts produced by large-scale manufacturers. Until 1939, and even after, locally made swing ploughs were still being used in many parts of Wales, and these together with mass-produced implements bought from local agricultural ironmongers were responsible for ploughing most Welsh land.

The greatest innovation of all in Welsh agriculture was the widespread adoption of tractors, but in most parts this did not take place until the late nineteen-thirties (Pl. 8). Although tractors were imported into Britain from America during the First World War, it was not until the nineteen-thirties that they became commonplace. In rural Wales the availability of light tractors and mounted equipment of the 'self-lift' variety revolutionized the mechanization of farm work. From 1939 onwards tractors were used less and less to pull horse-type equipment, and as far as ploughing implements were concerned the 'self lift' tractor plough was a most significant development. These ploughs were the products of an industry located in such places as Uttoxeter and Ipswich, and their popularity spelt the eclipse of the village blacksmith who was concerned with providing farm equipment for his own community. By the end of the nineteen-fifties even a Welsh smallholder was able to afford a light tractor and some of its associated equipment.

In the sequence of preparing the ground for seed, hand tools were at one time used instead of harrows. With spades, mattocks and clodding beetles, men and women followed the plough, breaking up the surface, when the plough had failed to turn the soil. As farming methods improved during the nineteenth century, particularly with the use of the Rotherham plough, the methods of hand cultivation were suspended except on the smaller, more isolated farms. Although in nineteenth- and early twentieth-century Wales there was a variety of local types of plough, there was no multiplicity of harrow types, and there was no real attempt at improving this instrument, which had remained virtually unchanged since the tenth century. By far the most common type of harrow consisted of a rectangular wooden frame, carrying perhaps fifteen tines at intervals of eleven inches or so. Harrow tines had to be re-sharpened at regular intervals, and in rural west Wales this was regarded as one of the minor tasks that country blacksmiths undertook

Fig. 1. PLOUGHING
1. Ox yoke; Glamorgan. 2. Eighteenth-century plough; Gelligaer, Glamorgan. 3. Late nineteenth-century plough; Llanegryn, Merioneth. 4. Plough of 1903–4; Penllwynrhaca, Llan-non, Carmarthen.

without making a money charge for the service. Instead, by tradition, payment was in the form of a small rick of oats or barley presented by the individual farmer to the blacksmith for his poultry, and perhaps a pig or cow. The corn was known as *llafur golym*. Although during the nineteenth century, attempts were made to improve harrow types, the most important being the patenting of the all-iron, zig-zag harrow in 1830, the older variety of harrow persisted in many parts of rural Wales until approximately 1914 and indeed later. In 1964, for example, a rectangular wooden harrow was taken to a blacksmith's shop in a village in Montgomeryshire for re-tining. Another primitive type of harrow used for harrowing grassland was the so-called *drainglwyd* (*drain*—thorn, and *clwyd*—gate). This consisted of hawthorn bushes tied to a gate or a wooden frame, with a heavy log fastened across it to give it weight. Harrows of this type were mentioned in the medieval laws and until the late nineteen-thirties they were widely used in parts of Wales for harrowing pasture land.

Seeding by hand has already been mentioned, and an important craft in many parts of Wales was the making of straw seedlips for carrying seed corn to the fields. In the past a great variety of objects for farm and domestic use were made of straw, bound into rolls with bramble strips and coiled into a receptacle. This category of work is known as 'lipwork'. Throughout western Europe the craft of lipwork was widespread and its history may be traced back to prehistoric times. One of the last exponents of this once vital craft is a mid Cardiganshire smallholder and stonemason, Benjamin Evans, who in his spare time and using the minimum of simple tools is able to produce baskets of excellent quality and beauty (Pls 43, 44).

The principal raw material required to make lipwork baskets is wheat straw, which has to be threshed and not bruised in any way. The craftsman experiences great difficulty today in obtaining the correct quality of straw, for not only has wheat-growing declined very greatly in mid Cardiganshire, but the fact that the lip worker insists on using winter-sown wheat of the *Hen Gymro* variety has aggravated the problem of supply even further. Winter wheat is considered much harder and of a better colour than the more common spring-sown variety. To make matters worse, the advent of modern reaping machinery has meant that it has become very difficult to find unbruised raw material. Ideally, the wheat crop should be cut with a scythe or hook, if the straw is to be of use to the lip worker.

To make a straw basket, Benjamin Evans must also have a quantity of bramble for binding the straw rolls. These have to be selected with great care, for if the bramble has too many prickles and side-shoots it is not suitable for the craftsman's needs. The best type of bramble grows in sheltered positions under trees in

forests and plantations, and the craftsman has to walk miles from his hillside
home to the valleys in search of suitable raw materials. Hedgerow bramble is
almost useless for lip making, for it has too many side-shoots and is much weaker
than forest-grown varieties. The bramble must be winter cut, when there is no
sap between the bark and the core.

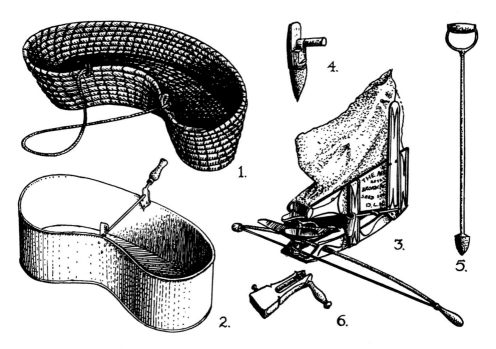

Fig. 2. SEEDING
1. Lipwork seedlip; St Bride's Major, Glamorgan. 2. Mètal seedlip; Pendoylan, Glamorgan.
3. Seed fiddle; Pont-y-pridd, Glamorgan. 4, 5. Seed dibbles; Gwent. 6. Bird scarer; Glamorgan.

Before the bramble can be used for weaving a basket, it has to be prepared very
thoroughly with a sharp penknife. The prickles are removed with a few deft
strokes, but in doing this great care has to be taken not to damage the bark, or it
will be completely useless for the craftsman's needs. Each bramble stalk has
to be split into two sections, the craftsman depending on eyesight and many
years' practice to accomplish this difficult task. The half sections of bramble have
to be smooth so that the ties can be parallel. This is extremely important, for if the
bramble ties are not parallel, the look of the finished basket will be destroyed. The
pith is removed by pressing a knife blade against the bramble and drawing it back

sharply with the line of growth. It is important that all the pith be removed, or the tying material will not be as pliant as the craftsman wishes, and of course its presence would spoil the appearance of the finished basket.

The tools required for the work are few and simple. All that is required are a sharp penknife, an awl and a section of cow-horn for standardizing the diameter of the rolls. Tradition has dictated that the bone awl for opening the weave must come from the hind leg of a horse. It is said that metal awls, similar to those used by osier basket makers, are too hard and pointed, and tend to fracture the delicate wheat stalks. Wooden awls, on the other hand, tend to break easily if they are sharpened to a thin point. One particular type of bone suits the craftsman's needs perfectly: it need not be sharpened or pointed in any way; it is thin, straight and strong enough and it is solid bone, without any marrow.

In the past, the lip worker was as vital to the rural community as the black-smith or carpenter. He made animal-feeding baskets and seedlips; he made bushel measures and bee skeps, baskets for storing feathers and grain, while in many districts he even made armchairs—the well-known beehive chairs. One particular aspect of the trade that persisted until recently in many parts of the British Isles was that of making bee skeps. For this task, rye straw was preferred because of its length and toughness. In many parts of Britain it was common for farm labourers to make their own skeps from straw supplied by their employers.

Today Benjamin Evans is probably the last exponent of this ancient craft in Wales. From the point of view of traditional Welsh craftsmanship he is some-thing far more than a manipulator of straw rolls and bramble stalks, for he re-presents a tradition that is dying: the tradition of the amateur part-time craftsman. Undoubtedly, the amateur craftsman has contributed a great deal to the cultural heritage of Wales.

As an alternative to broadcasting seed from a lip, dibbling was widespread, particularly for sowing large seeds, such as swede or mangold seeds. Holes were made in the ground at regular intervals by a man walking backwards carrying in each hand a pointed wooden or iron rod, or dibbler. Women and children fol-lowed, dropping seeds into the holes.

Although seed drills were widely used in parts of England from the eighteenth century—Jethro Tull patented his famous drill in 1701—few Welsh farmers took advantage of new seeding equipment until well into the nineteenth century, for the farming population as a whole was very slow to adopt new techniques. When horse-drawn seed drills did become popular in rural Wales during the last quarter of the nineteenth century and the first quarter of the twentieth, many were co-operatively owned by three or four neighbouring farmers.

The growing cereal crops had to be regularly weeded with weeding hooks and tongs, a task that in the past was regarded as the special province of casual labourers and junior menservants. Harvesting, especially hay harvesting, was a communal effort in which men, women and children had their parts to play. In general, by the mid nineteenth century the scythe had already replaced the sickle as the implement for corn and hay harvesting. In harvesting corn, however, it was customary to keep a sickle close at hand, so that the ritual of cutting the last sheaf could be carried out. In south Cardiganshire, for example, a small quantity of the last of the season's corn was left standing in the field and tied up carefully. Each reaper would then in turn withdraw to a distance of fifteen to twenty feet, and throw a sickle at the corn until it was cut. The person who managed this feat had the honour of bearing the sheaf into the farmhouse, but it had to be taken into the house surreptitiously for the womenfolk were ready to throw water over the carrier of the last sheaf. A completely dry sheaf had to be taken into the farm kitchen and hung from the ceiling to signify the continuity of the corn harvest from one year to the next. In most parts of Wales, however, except in years when dry weather had retarded growth or the high winds had flattened the corn, the scythe was by far the most common implement for harvesting. The scythe was regarded as being almost sacred, for no one was allowed to touch a scythe except its owner. When reaping, a dozen or more men could be seen at work, slowly making their way in an orderly procession from one end of the field to the other, their scythes swinging rhythmically as they cut a width of crop. Setting the pace would be an experienced scyther, with the other reapers at intervals of about six feet *en echelon* behind the leader. Periodically all would stop and sharpen their scythes with a *rip*: a wooden bar strapped to the waist, smeared with grease and sprinkled with sand kept in a horn. In this way they proceeded until a whole field had been mown. At the corn harvest, it was the men's duty to reap and they would be followed by the women, who were concerned with binding the corn into sheaves. In order to gather and hold the cut corn stalks and facilitate putting them down in neat swaths for the binders, a wooden cradle was fixed to the scythe. This consisted of three or four light and gently curving wooden 'arrows', curving with the blade and reaching to within six inches or so of the tip of the blade. It was held together by cross strips of wood and connected to the scythe snead by wires. For the hay harvest, a bare scythe without a cradle was always used.

Since the First World War, if not before, the farmer has been able to obtain a large variety of mechanical implements to deal with the hay harvest. Horse-drawn wheeled rakes, mechanical hay tedders and swath turners replaced the

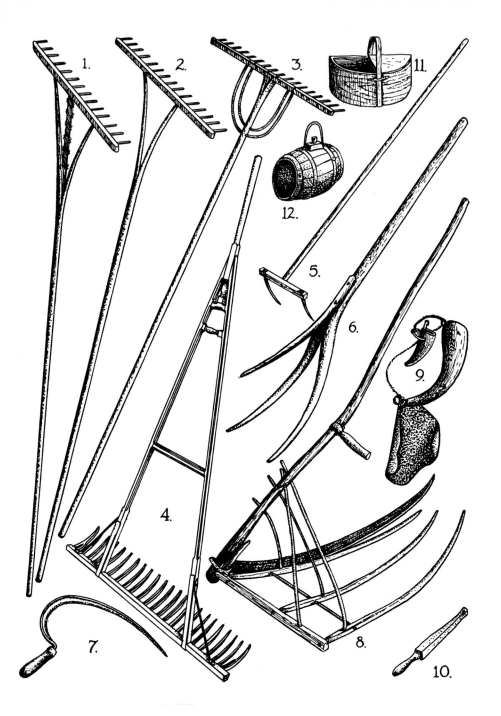

wooden hand rakes and two-tined pitchforks wielded by a large labour force in the past, while in the inter-war period mechanical hay loaders and, later, one-man balers further replaced the human effort once required. Today, every stage of hay making can be done with machine, and as a result the amount of labour needed for the hay harvest has been greatly reduced. One of the most important hay-making tools of the past was the all-wooden hand rake, and there were many country carpenters in Wales who were able to manufacture this important tool. One of the last of the Welsh rake makers was William Thomas of Llanymawddwy, Merioneth (Pls 48, 49).

Hand rakes vary tremendously from one part of the country to the other and there are many variations in the methods of making them. Some are short-handled, others are long-handled; most have wide heads at right-angles to the handle. But those of Glamorgan, designed for raking hay on sloping fields, have short heads at an angle of 45 degrees to the handle. There is a great variation, too, in the type of wood used: English rakes are of tough, springy willow and those of Wales are of ash. In other parts of Britain pine, birch and alder are also used. In northern and western Britain, where hay is often made on sloping fields and is short and springy, the hay rakes are, by tradition, small and well constructed and each one is expected to last for many years. The rakes of southern England on the other hand, designed to cope with the lush grass growth of the water meadows, were much larger and less strongly constructed. Indeed, in the past, the southern farmer rarely expected his rakes to last for more than one season's harvest, and consequently the rakes produced in great quantity by such craftsmen as those of northern Hampshire were sold at very low prices.

To the casual observer the process of making a rake is a simple one, but in order to make a tool that is durable, strong and light, considerable experience and craftsmanship are required. A good rake must be as light as possible, to avoid fatigue during the long hours of harvesting; the handle must be smooth so as to slip through the hands with ease. The teeth must not be set in the head at too sharp an angle, or the tool will not gather the hay efficiently; but on the other hand, if the angle between the teeth and the head is not sharp enough, then the

Fig. 3. HARVESTING
1, 2. Hay rakes; Carmarthenshire. 3. Hay rake by William Thomas, Llanymawddwy, Merioneth. 4. Heel or stubble rake; Cribyn, Cardigan. 5. Sheaf gatherer; Llangwyfan, Clwyd. 6. Barley fork; Ewenni, Glamorgan. 7. Sickle; Caernarvon. 8. Cradle scythe; Broad Oak, Carmarthen. 9. Scythe-sharpening outfit with grease horn, sand horn and rubbing leather; Tudweiliog, Llŷn. 10. Rip for sharpening scythes with grease and sand; Montgomery. 11. Harvesting food box; Caernarvon. 12. Cider costrel; Raglan, Gwent.

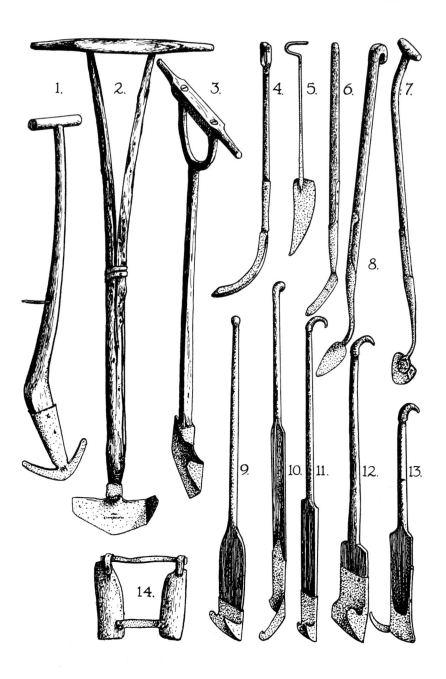

tines will tend to stick in the ground and are quite likely to break off. With no pattern or measurement and no guide but that of long experience, the craftsman has to ensure that his rakes fulfil all these conditions.

The first task in making a rake is to shape the handle. The craftsman takes an ash plank and, with a bandsaw, saws it up into a number of six-foot-long strips some three inches square. Clamping each piece of wood to his bench, the craftsman takes a small rounding-plane and shapes the handle until it is round and perfectly smooth. The ash for the head is sawn out from a solid plank and the positions of the fifteen or more tines are carefully marked at a distance of no more than two inches from one another. The tine holes as well as the four holes for the rake bow are bored out with a brace and bit.

Billets for the teeth are shaped on a driving-stool. A piece of wood is driven through the cutting iron with a mallet. When the peg is almost flush with the cutting edge another one is placed on top of it, thus pushing the first right through to the basket placed underneath. The tines are next fastened into the head and pointed with a draw-knife, and the rake assembled. Finally the intricate process of making and fitting the semicircular ash bows is undertaken. These are shaped with the spoke-shave and gently fitted into place to connect the head and the handle to make an extremely strong and durable tool.

The hay mowers that became popular on the large Welsh farms before 1914 were really a by-product of the search for a machine to cut corn. Their adoption by Welsh farmers made the introduction of tedding and swath-turning machinery easier, for the mowers left the hay in straight, neat swaths which were easier to handle mechanically than the swaths left by the scythe.

For harvesting corn, horse-drawn reaping machines, many of them co-operatively owned, had begun to make an impact on Welsh farms during the first two decades of the present century; many simply cut the crop, laying it in swaths for binding by hand. But the most important development of all was the binder. In 1878, McCormick Deering of the International Harvester Company of America put a string-tying binder on the market. By 1910, this machine was known in many parts of Wales and was the usual machine used for corn harvesting almost in all parts until the adoption of the combine harvester in the fifties and sixties.

Fig. 4. PEAT CUTTING
1–3. Push ploughs for removing turves and top soil to expose peat bed: 1, 2, North Wales. 3, Glamorgan. 4. Marking iron; Brecknock. 5. Peat spade; Staylittle, Montgomery. 6. Marking iron; Abergwesyn, Brecknock. 7. Paring iron; Abergwesyn. 8. Paring iron; Staylittle. 9–13. Peat spades: 9, Montgomery; 10, Llangeitho, Cardigan; 11, Laugharne, Carmarthenshire; 12, 13, Llanwrtyd, Brecknock. 14. Breast shields used when operating push plough; Brecknock.

In many districts, the various steps in dealing with the corn harvest until the adoption of the combine harvester still remained a series of mechanical processes. In a south Cardiganshire parish until the early nineteen-sixties, for example, no machinery at all had been introduced to deal with the processes in between cutting and transporting the crop to the farmstead. Little attention was paid by farmers to the calendar, for it was sufficient to know that oats should be cut 'when the colour of wood pigeon' (*lliw'r sgythan*), barley when the beard was almost dropping off and the field appeared almost white in its ripeness. A field of wheat had to be a rich gold colour (*lliw'r aur*). As soon as the reaper-binder had cut the corn and delivered it in sheaves, stooks of four or six sheaves were built and then were left standing for a number of days for drying in the breeze. Barley was often carried loose without binding, but all stooked sheaves had to be built into field ricks or mows (*teise* or *sopine*). There were two types of field rick—a *tâs penglin* (knee-made rick) and a *tâs llaw* (hand-made rick). Two men were required to build a *tâs penglin*, one passing the sheaves to the other, who intertwined one sheaf with another, pressing them with his knees as he moved around in a clockwise direction. For this type of field rick the number of sheaves varied between seventy-two and eighty. A *tâs llaw* or *sopyn llaw* on the other hand could be built by one person and it was rarely more than six feet in height, compared with the eight or nine feet of the larger variety. An old method of counting sheaves adopted in west Wales was by the *drefa*, a *drefa* being twenty-four sheaves. Two *drefas* equalled a *sopyn llaw* and three *drefas* equalled a *tâs penglin*. Careful building of field ricks ensured that the crop would be perfectly dry and sound in the fields, until Christmas if need be, for in the moist atmosphere of the Welsh hills it is sometimes difficult to find a dry day for carting sheaves.

More will be said in Chapter 4 on the types of vehicle used for transporting the crops from fields to the farmstead, but in the days before combine harvesters, corn sheaves had to be carried very carefully to the stack yard. There on most farms well proportioned stacks had to be built (Pl. 12). By tradition in some parts each stack should contain eight cartloads of sheaves carefully built into a stack (*helem* or *helm*) of traditional shape. In west Wales, oat stacks were built to an acorn shape with a full body and rounded head; wheat was stacked in a *helem* with almost vertical sides and a long pointed head. Stacks of barley and mixed barley and oats, on the other hand, had sides gradually going outwards as the stack was built up, the last row before beginning to draw it into the head projecting about six inches beyond the previous row.

Thatching a corn rick with rushes or wheat straw was a craft that required much practice and patience, for the thatch had to be completely waterproof and safe enough to withstand the power of the winds. In coastal areas in particular, where high winds are commonplace, the thatch had to be weighted down by a network of ropes. In north Pembrokeshire, for example, thatching began with making a long narrow point at the top of the stack, called a *copsi*. The thatcher then moved down from the apex, planting and intertwining the thatching material in a broad yealm, known as a *gwanaf*. The process was then repeated from the apex to the bottom of the head a number of times until the stack had a thick cap of protection. The thatch was then made secure by passing over it a network of ropes. In the past these were home-made straw ropes made by twisting bunches of straw in a twister, but in more recent times binder cord was used. The first series of ropes, known as *cwile*, ran parallel to one another at intervals of ten inches or so all around the stack head. From the *copsi* and intertwined with the *cwile* another series of ropes ran down the side of the rick. Attached to the bottom of these ropes were the *angorion* (anchors), large stones that made the thatch completely secure against gale force winds.

Threshing was done in a variety of ways, with or without implements, but except when straw had to be kept unbroken for thatching purposes, the flail was the main implement until it was displaced by the threshing machine (Pls 13, 14). Usually threshing was the responsibility of the individual farmer and he and his male servants would thresh small quantities of grain throughout the winter as needed. For flailing, the floor of a barn had to be of beaten earth, or a movable wooden threshing floor could be used, but in all cases reasonable headroom for the manipulation of flails had to be provided. The jointed flail with handstaff (*droed-ffust*), beater (*yel-ffust*) and a joining band (*cwplws*) has a history going back to late Roman times. The handstaff was usually of ash while the slightly longer beater or swinger was made of ash, holly, blackthorn or some other hard, heavy wood. The joining bands had leather cappings; grooves, holes or pins could be of a variety of materials: thongs of leather, dried eelskin, snakeskin, willow, hemp yarn or straw rope. Flails were never mass produced and distributed from any particular centre, so that there was ample scope for differences from one area to the next. To thresh corn with a flail, the beater was swung round in the air on the swivel, above the head of the thresher, and was brought down with a chopping blow upon the ears of corn. Although by the mid nineteenth century flailing had been replaced by barn threshers in many parts of Wales, flailing did persist until the present century in some districts, more especially for threshing barley. Ears of barley are less easily knocked off than ears of oats, so that the persistence of the flail in some districts well after threshing mills had become common indicates the importance of barley as a field crop.

As early as 1636 an attempt was made to devise a threshing machine, consisting of a number of flails revolving rapidly in a box, and from that date until the mid nineteenth century hundreds of machines were devised. They ranged from a type of implement used in ancient Babylon to an outsize coffee grinder, but no inventor succeeded in devising an efficient implement until Andrew Meikel invented the threshing drum about 1786. It was this machine that became popular on Welsh farms in the mid nineteenth century and most farmers of substantial holdings were able to buy a drum. This machine separated the grain from the straw by a crude form of drum fitted with oak pegs revolving within a box. Early threshers were driven by water or horse power and sometimes by hand and they were often built into the barn. With the addition of mechanism for cleaning and grading grain and an increase in the size of drums, this was the type of machine, driven by steam power, that became almost universal in Wales during the first quarter of the present century (Pl. 16).

Before the threshing machine became commonplace, many barns, especially in the eastern counties of Wales where threshing was performed, were equipped with two opposite doors through which a draught would blow. The threshed grain was flung up in the air with shovels so that the breeze carried the chaff, while the grain fell to the ground (Pl. 15). When the wind was not strong enough for winnowing, it was produced artificially. Some of these machines consisted of nothing but sacks attached to a revolving wooden frame, but towards the end of the eighteenth century the wooden winnowing box (*blwch nithio*) was devised. This became very common despite the objection of a Scottish Presbyterian minister who preached a sermon 'on the wickedness of the farmer who produces wind for his own particular use instead of waiting till it pleases the Lord to send one'. But even a Presbyterian minister could not arrest progress and soon winnowing boxes were common on almost every farm.

After barley had been threshed, it was necessary to take off the awns, or 'beard', that was injurious to animals. This was done with a 'hummeller' or 'jumper' (*colier*), a tool with a short handle set vertically in a square iron frame which contained a set of blades, parallel to one another and an inch or two apart

Fig. 5. FODDERING
1. Eighteenth-century gorse mill; St Dogmaels, Pembrokeshire. 2. Gorse hook; Pwllheli, Llŷn. 3. Gorse hook; Llangwyryfon, Cardigan. 4. Gorse chopper; Aberystwyth, Cardigan. 5. Gorse beater; Denbigh. 6. Wooden 'gloves' for pushing gorse into cutter; Merioneth. 7. Box chaff cutter; Peterston, Glamorgan. 8. Hay knife; Welsh St Donats, Glamorgan. 9–11. Straw-rope twisters: 9, Merioneth; 10, Monmouth; 11, Caernarvon. 12. Hay carrier; Rhyd, Merioneth. 13, 14. Hay cratches: 13, Carmarthen; 14, Radnor.

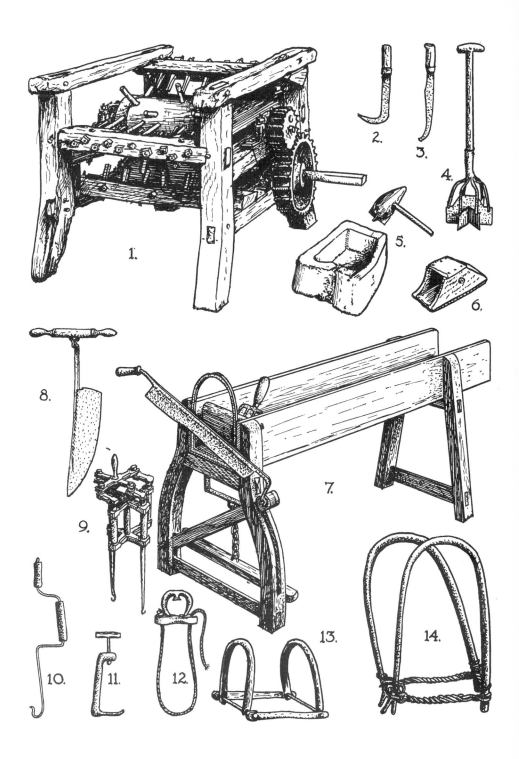

(Pl. 17).Barley after threshing was spread out on the floor and struck with the frame.

Within the last sixty years or so farming has been almost completely transformed from a manual art into a series of mechanical processes. Whatever the task the farmer has at hand, whether it be in the fields or farmyard, more and more pieces of machinery have become available to assist him. Perhaps the greatest single innovation was the introduction of the internal combustion engine soon after the end of the First World War. A stationary engine now took the place of hand, horse or water power on many farms, to drive machinery in the barn, to drive the chaff-cutter, root pulpers and flour mills. In the earliest days, barn machinery was operated entirely by hand. For example, to chop gorse as feed for horses a variety of devices was used. The simplest method of cutting was to place gorse in a stone trough and beat it with a wooden beetle until soft. Nevertheless by the late eighteenth century, hand-operated chaffing boxes had become common. Gorse, or possibly a mixture of gorse and straw, was placed in the wooden trough of the chaff-cutter and clamped in place with a wooden block. The guillotine knife attached to the box was operated by hand. In order to push the gorse along the trough, it was usual in parts of north Wales to wear a wooden 'glove' or box over the hand, a device known as *drynolen bren*.

The custom of feeding animals, especially horses and calves, with gorse remained in vogue in some parts of Wales until the present century, and gorse mixed with straw, hay or bran was regarded as very nourishing for animals. The gorse, known as *eithin Ffrengig* (French gorse) or *eithin bras* (coarse gorse), was grown especially for feeding purposes, and on some farms a field of gorse was regarded as being as valuable as a field of hay. In Pembrokeshire, for example, children were given the task of collecting gorse seed and in that county 'gorse sales' were commonplace in the nineteenth century, high prices being paid for fields of one-year gorse. In all areas, not only were chaff or gorse cutters known, but specialized gorse beaters were also commonplace. These resembled a large mallet, but two crossing cutting knives were inserted in the wooden head to cut up the gorse on a wooden floor. By the end of the nineteenth century, water-, horse- or donkey-driven gorse mills were to be found in all districts. Many of them resembled barn threshing machines with beaters turning rapidly in a wooden box to bruise and cut the gorse placed inside it. In some cases these mills became so large that they had to be accommodated in special buildings.

Water power was also widely used on Welsh farms before the introduction of the oil engine for driving barn machinery. Power was harnessed by a large, cast-iron wheel (*rhôd ddŵr*) which revolved in a rectangular pit in a field close to the barn. Leading from a storage pond (*llyn y rhôd*) at a higher level, some distance away, was a narrow trench which carried the water to turn the wheel, once the wooden door was lifted. From the hub of this wheel a connecting rod led through a series of cog wheels and thence into the barn and the machinery within it. On farms where no water was available horse-driven machinery (known as 'horse works' or *part mâs*), located usually in the centre of a cobbled track in the middle of the farmyard, was used. The horse was led around the 'works', a monotonous task usually performed by a junior servant. In some districts donkey-driven treadmills were used, while in others, especially for such tasks as churning butter, a dog was used for driving a wheel, which could be as much as ten feet in diameter. The dog, or a pair of dogs, was secured to a beam above the wheel by leads or chains and 'climbed' the wheel, which was then kept in continuous motion. In passing it may be noted that dog-wheels were also commonplace in farm kitchens for turning such equipment as roasting spits (see page 130).

Cattle and sheep have always figured prominently in the economy of all regions of Wales. Animals provided the raw material for the once important industries of woollen manufacturing and tanning. Until the formation of the British Wool Marketing Board in 1950, woollen manufacturers in Wales were in direct contact with wool growers and wool merchants in their own immediate regions, and obtained all the raw material they required from local suppliers. In many parts, the wool was short-stapled wool from Welsh mountain sheep; it varied greatly in colour and included a great deal of grey. In some districts it contained quantities of kemp, but it was always soft and possessed good felting qualities. In other districts much of the wool was obtained from Border breeds—Clun and Kerry; this had a longer staple and it was much whiter and crisper and finer than that of mountain breeds. Other districts, such as the Llŷn peninsula and the Epynt foothills, had their own local breeds, but on all upland farms sheep shearing was one of the most important events of the farming year.

Shearing day was a great social occasion attended by farmers or their representatives from many miles' radius (Pl. 18). In the past it was essential that the farmer himself, rather than a servant or other representative, attended a neighbour's shearing, for although no money payment of ny kind was made, the upland farmer depended entirely on voluntary co-oper. ion to complete his work. Smallholders and non-agriculturalists, too, had their part to play, for although they might not have been the owners of sheep flocks, they worked at the shearing to pay for the right to cut peat on the large farmer's mountain, or to pay for the right to plant potatoes on his land.

Although mechanization has meant the end of co-operation in the hay, corn and potato field, in some corners of Wales shearing is still a vast co-operative affair, and the atmosphere of festivity in the shearing shed is still in existence. In 1969 I visited an upland farm near a village famous in the history of Welsh non-conformity, that of Llanbryn-Mair in Montgomeryshire. By tradition, this particular farm of nearly 1,500 acres had been allocated the last Friday and Saturday in July to shear a flock of over 2,000 hardy Welsh mountain sheep. A week prior to shearing day, the farmer with no assistance but that of a sure-footed mountain pony and four well-trained sheepdogs had collected the sheep from the unenclosed mountain for washing in a mountain stream.

On shearing day, when twenty-five neighbours had congregated in the shearing shed, the sheep were brought down from the moor to a field near the farm in the valley and the great annual task of shearing began. Two young boys were given the task of catching the wild, unruly sheep and carrying them in to the shearers, who sat astride low, narrow benches in the shed. With the hand shears, the shearer began the task by cutting a strip of wool down the belly of the animal, but before beginning to remove the fleece from the back the animal's legs were tied with a piece of string. After each sheep was completely fleeced and the shearer prepared for the next, a boy rolled each fleece into a bundle, while the sheep itself was taken to the owner of the flock, whose task it was to inspect every animal. He marked each one with its mark of ownership, marked its ears if necessary, treated wounds, clipped its hoofs and then allowed the shorn sheep to return to the rest of the flock in an adjacent field. For two days this process was continued until the whole flock was shorn and treated.

Shearing time is still a festive occasion characterized by a great deal of bantering between the shearers, but in the past, shearing day often ended with an impromptu concert in the shearing shed, for every locality had its folk singer, story teller or raconteur who made a point of attending all shearings in the district. One of the

Fig. 6. SHEEP AND PIGS
1–6. Shepherds' crooks: 1, Brecknock; 2, Llandeilo, Carmarthenshire; 3, Radnor; 4, West Glamorgan; 5, East Glamorgan; 6, Montgomery. 7, 8, Sheep dipping paddles: 7, Caeo, Carmarthenshire; 8, Llanfihangel Glyn Myfyr, Clwyd. 9. Ram yoke; Tywyn, Merioneth. 10. Sheep shears; Glamorgan. 11. Pitch pot used for sheep marking; Llangwyryfon, Cardigan. 12–14. Sheep markers: 12, Radnor; 13, Carmarthen; 14, Chwilog, Caernarvon. 15. Sheep fetters; Gower. 16. Grease box; Preseli hills, Dyfed. 17. Identification tags for sheep; Chwilog, Caernarvon. 18. Ear punch; Glamorgan. 19. Hand-powered shearing machine; Dingestow, Gwent. 20. Pig stopper, put around animal's neck; Cynwyd, Merioneth. 21. Pig ringing key; Llangwm, Clwyd. 22–24. Pig bristle scrapers (for carcase): 22, 23, Crug-y-bar, Carmarthen; 24, Llanafan, Cardigan. 25. Pig ringer; Llangadog, Carmarthen. 26. Gambrel for hanging pig carcase; Llanafan, Cardigan. 27. Pig belly spreader; Llantrisant, Glamorgan.

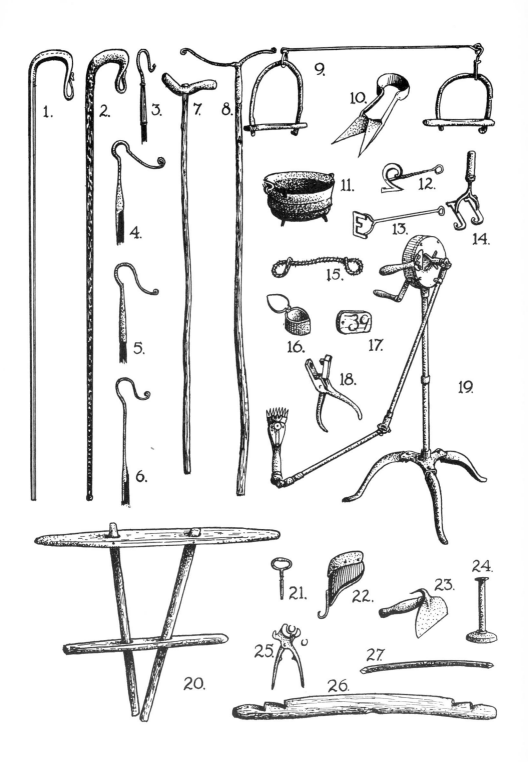

most famous in Montgomeryshire was a certain Evan Edwards, *Ifan Clown*, who until 1939 spent most summers visiting farms on shearing day. On some farms too the end of shearing was celebrated by games of quoits, played with horse-shoes, in the farmyard.

Sheep shearing by hand as it is still practised on some of the upland farms of Wales is a vestige of the past, when co-operation between farmers was a necessity and when a local community looked no further than its own boundaries for its entertainment. Alas, the shearing contractor is becoming far more common even in the most remote farms of Wales and the sheep shearing as I witnessed it in Montgomeryshire will very soon be a thing of the past.

4 Sleds and Wheeled Vehicles

In this age of speed and mass travel, when continents are no more than a few hours' flying time from one another, it is surprising that in many parts of western Europe primitive vehicles have survived to this day. In Britain, sleds, hand barrows and primitive wheeled vehicles that resemble man's earliest attempts at easing his labours may still be seen in constant use particularly in the remote, hilly districts of western and northern Britain. These crude home-made vehicles have survived, not because no more advanced method of transport is known to the inhabitants of those regions, but because the long experience of generations of hill farmers has proved that those simple devices are the best suited to local needs. A smallholder in Snowdonia, for example, still clings to the age-old method of harvesting hay with a burden rope, which has remained by far the quickest and most economical method of harvesting a steeply sloping field invariably in close proximity to the farmstead. A Breconshire farmer in 1960 carried all his hay from a field in a sack although a tractor and trailer were idle in his barn at the time.

The simplest of all the carrying devices that has persisted to this day in Britain is the hand barrow, a vehicle similar to the funeral bier. This consists of two parallel pieces of timber, joined together by a number of cross-pieces which form the carrying surface. The barrow was designed for carrying by two men and was widely used in the nineteenth century, particularly in hilly or marshy districts where no animal-drawn vehicle could go. In the Llanuwchllyn district of Merioneth, for example, all dung was carried to the upland fields in hand barrows no more than a hundred years ago. Each farm in that mountain-locked locality specified a day for manuring its fields, and on that day neighbouring farmers and their families met at the specified farm with a large number of barrows. The carrying was performed in a relay service, the barrow changing hands many times before it reached the upland fields. Hand barrows may still be seen in use in hilly districts, particularly in those areas where peat harvesting is still an essential annual occurrence. Recently, for example in the Hiraethog district of north Wales, the hand barrow was in constant use for carrying peat blocks for a considerable distance from the peat beds to the nearest trackway. The barrow, a simple home-made affair, measured some eighty inches long and consisted of two slit timbers joined by a number of flat wooden slats. The peat was placed on the cross pieces and the barrow was carried across the boggy ground by two men.

Hand-drawn sleds are not unknown in present-day Wales either, simple vehicles that must date back in type to man's first attempt at providing some vehicle to move goods from one place to the other. At the Welsh Folk Museum is a sled seventy inches long and twenty-seven inches wide, which was used until recently for carrying peat from the upland peat beds of the Dinas Mawddwy district of Merioneth (Pl. 26). By removing one of the cross-wise slats a man could carry the sled on his back on the long, steep journey to the moor. After being loaded with peat blocks the vehicle was taken down, and being a dead weight it was self-braking on the steep slopes, whereas a wheeled vehicle would soon overturn.

Animal-drawn sleds, too, are still widely used in the upland districts of Wales. They have persisted because they are still the most efficient method of transport in those districts where any form of wheeled vehicle would be difficult to operate, and also because they are cheap to produce. Unlike the lowland farmer, who in the past was able to call on the services of numerous craftsmen to make and repair the tools and implements of the farm, the upland agriculturalist, often living in an isolated homestead, was some distance from the nearest village, and thus forced by circumstances to make a great deal of his own equipment. To this day simple transport devices made by farmers for their own use may still be found in Wales.

No vehicle, perhaps, shows the adaptation of design to local topography more than the sled, a simple wheel-less vehicle which has been known since Neolithic times. When harvesting hay from an upland field it is customary in Wales to rake the crop for loading into parallel rows that run across the slope. A wheeled vehicle taken along this slope would be at a perpetual tilt, and on loading would almost certainly overturn. A sled on the other hand clings to the surface of the upland field, it is stable and can be turned easily at the end of a row, while on the long descent to the farmstead the dragging action provides an efficient brake.

Perhaps the simplest of all sleds is the slide car, a vehicle that has persisted not only in many parts of western and northern Britain but also in the remote districts of France, Spain and Mediterranean Europe. This vehicle consists of two stout side timbers some twelve feet long, joined together for about half their length by a number of cross-bars which carry the load (Pl. 28). The side pieces project at the front to form a pair of shafts, which are attached to the horse high up on the collar. For this reason the vehicle is dragged along the ground at a tilt so that it is necessary to fit a wooden framework or ladder at the back to prevent the load falling out. A smaller ladder is fitted at the front, while the load can be made more secure by tying it down with ropes, a necessary procedure when carrying ferns, hay or wood on the steep slopes of the Welsh mountains (Pl.11). The dragging ends of the slide car are protected from wear by wooden shoots, each some eighteen inches long. These wear out quickly but can be easily replaced. In the late eighteenth century that noted writer on Welsh agriculture, Walter Davies, described the hay harvest as a vast communal affair, where it was 'not uncommon to see half a dozen slide cars carrying from the same field. A stranger', he adds, 'will hardly credit the alacrity with which a large quantity will be carried in a short space of time by this simple method.'

The sled, which differs from the slide car in that the whole body of the vehicle is dragged along the ground, has persisted mainly in the mountains of central and north Wales. Unlike the slide car the sled was in the past not limited to a mountainous terrain, for it was equally well known in marshy districts.

In Wales the harvesting sled used for carrying hay and ferns from upland fields consists of two side pieces about seven feet long joined together by eight or more cross pieces. Chain traces for hauling are attached to a pair of iron brackets at the front of the side frames, and the vehicle is equipped with fore and tail ladders, and in some instances with side rails. Welsh harvesting sleds are usually tilted forwards on runners, the length of the runners being adjusted according to the slope of the fields. It is necessary to replace these runners at regular intervals. The sled is of course a self-braking vehicle but on the very steep slopes of Snowdonia it is customary to harness two horses to a sled, one in front, the other behind.

The tumbril sled consists of a simple box on runners and is mainly used for carrying manure and lime to the fields; as such it is similar to the slide butt that was used for the same purpose on Cornish farms until recent times. Some farmers, even on valley farms, considered the tumbril sled superior to the box cart or tractor trailer for liming. With a wheeled vehicle, they say, the lime has to be shovelled out at the level of the worker's eyes, but since the body of the sled is no more than a few inches from the ground, there is no danger to the worker's face when this vehicle is used.

The general purpose sled is similar in construction to the harvesting sled, but differs from it in that it does not have side rails and end ladders, but it is equipped with four corner poles (Pl. 29). These are usually fitted to pairs of rings butted at the top and bottom of the side frames. This type of vehicle is mainly used in Merioneth and Montgomeryshire for carrying such things as ferns for animal bedding, gorse for feeding, timber and peat. In some districts, sleds have been improved by adding a pair of cast iron or solid wooden wheels at the back (Pl. 31). With a heavy load the runners at the front of the vehicle act as a brake on a downhill journey, while the wheels are locked with a chain passed around them.

One of the simplest of all wheeled vehicles is the truckle car, which was particularly prevalent in the Gower Peninsula of south Wales. This very simple horse-drawn vehicle, a typological ancestor of all Welsh wheeled vehicles, is basically a slide car placed on an axle and a pair of wheels. In some cases these wheels are spoked, but most of the Gower truckle cars were equipped with solid, tripartite disc wheels. These simple wheels, rarely more than two feet six inches in diameter, bound with an iron tyre two and a half inches wide, are of great antiquity, having been invented in the Near East somewhere around 3500 B.C. Although the disc is certainly earlier than the spoked wheel, the earliest wheeled vehicles represented in the archaeological records north of the Alps already had spoked wheels. It may be imagined therefore that although disc wheels were perfectly strong and durable for the carriage of heavy goods they were far from efficient at times when speed and manoeuvrability were required. From around 2000 B.C. spoked wheels are represented in the archaeological records of Mesopotamia and by 500 B.C. the technique of building both disc and spoked wheels was known to people from China to Western Europe. Until recent times solid-wheeled carts remained in vogue in many isolated districts of the world, particularly on carts and wagons designed for carrying heavy goods locally. It has been suggested that the occurrence of disc wheels has influenced the shape and design of the spoked wheel. Spoked wheels fitted to post-nineteenth-century truckle cars in Gower are rarely more than two feet six inches in diameter, and are never more than two and a half inches wide and display hardly any dish.

The axle of the truckle is either made of iron, sometimes encased in a wooden bed, or consists of a wooden axle bed with iron arms no more than two inches in diameter. This is bolted to the side frames, while the wheels, the centres of which are bored to accommodate iron bearings, are fastened to it by a linchpin. The wheels are usually of softwood, consisting of three planks mortised together, rounded and bound with iron.

The frame of the body is a rigid extension of the shafts, giving the whole vehicle a length of some thirteen feet. One example preserved at the Welsh Folk Museum consists of nothing more than a pinewood pole split down the middle to form the side pieces, the distance between them decreasing from four feet at the back to two feet six inches at the front. The carrying platform simply consists of a number of wooden slats nailed to the side frames. Like its predecessor, the slide car, the truckle is equipped with a tail ladder. A pair of side ladders run from the front of the carrying platform at an angle of forty-five degrees to be bolted to the tail ladder.

In many ways the so-called Irish car (*Car Gwyddelig*) is a close relative of the truckle car, and like the truckle it was mainly used in south Wales, more particularly in the Vale of Glamorgan and in Brecknockshire. Walter Davies, writing in 1815, describes the Irish car of Brecknockshire as 'convenient to carry grain to market or mill or small loads of any kind. In peculiar situations they are recommendable for harvest work on account of the expedition and lightness of roping. We have seen it', he adds, 'used as a sociable covered with a tarpaulin and chairs placed inside it by a farmer conveying his family to town in rainy weather.'

The Irish car is equipped with two stout, slightly dished, spoked wheels no more than thirty-six inches in diameter (Pl. 30). The tyre is either two and a half inches or three inches wide. Characteristically the shafts of the Irish car continue from the side frames of the body in the manner of a slide car. On some of the late Irish cars, however, the shafts are constructed independently of the body framing, but are firmly bolted on the inside of the frames and again project from them. Davies says that in 1815 separately constructed shafts were occasionally replacing the old slide car method of continuing body frames to form shafts. 'The new method was gaining ground on account of timber of short lengths being cheaper to make them.' Nevertheless, on the Irish car as well as on more sophisticated Welsh vehicles the shafts do present the appearance of being part of the body framing, a feature of construction which clearly distinguishes the 'oceanic' cart from the 'continental'. In the latter, as for example in the East Anglian tumbril, the shafts are very clearly separate and removable members.

It has been suggested that the description 'Irish' (*Gwyddelig*) does not of necessity mean that the vehicle originated in that country, but 'may be used as a term to indicate anything old fashioned, native or strange to the present generation'. The Irish car may therefore be an indigenous development of the slide car which has been in existence in Wales from time immemorial; on the other hand it is almost certainly an improved version of the truckle car, a vehicle well known not only in Wales but in Ireland as well. The existence of the truckle in both countries may even indicate that the Welsh and Irish vehicles have a common origin in Ireland, but there is no literary evidence to prove or to disprove this.

The wheel car is a long-bodied two-wheeled vehicle unknown outside Wales (Pl. 27). Until recently it was widely used on the hill farms of central Wales, particularly in the county of Radnor. It may be regarded as the direct successor of the sled, rather than in the same category as the truckle and Irish cars. Unlike the simple wheeled sleds of central Wales, the Radnorshire wheel car is equipped with spoked, dished wheels of relatively large size placed in the middle of the vehicle's body. In the early nineteenth century these wheel cars or long bodies were equipped with small, possibly solid, disc wheels attached to an axle placed underneath the body. The more recent versions of it are equipped with larger spoked wheels with the axle placed above rather than underneath the body framing. The horse is attached to the vehicle by chain traces, not at the lighter, but the heavier end of the body. When loaded with bracken or hay, the load is so disposed that a large proportion of it is accommodated in front of the wheels. This makes the front end even heavier, and since the bottoms of the side frames are bulged and lined with iron the front acts as a brake on descending a hill.

The floor of the vehicle, which measures thirteen feet six inches long and three feet two inches wide, consists of a number of regularly spaced wooden slats mortised to the side frames. As the vehicle is designed for carrying such material as hay or grain in sacks, a solid, boarded floor is unnecessary. At each corner of the vehicle an upright pole is fitted into a pair of staples, and since a great deal is carried in the front half of the car, it is equipped with a short non-removable fore ladder. In addition, a pair of railed ladders or cratches prevent the load from spilling outwards over the wheels.

One of the most distinctive features of the wheel car is the overslung axle, which has the effect of keeping the body low to ensure efficient braking and stability on steep hill slopes. On an example made at Llanbister Road, Radnorshire in 1929, the all wooden axle, five inches square, is firmly bolted to the frame of the car. A metal rod is bolted underneath it to give the axle added strength. Since the arms are only very slightly canted, the wheels display only a slight amount of dish. They can be linked for descending particularly steep hills by means of a chain fixed to the frame of the car. In the traditional manner of the West Midlands and central Wales the wheels are equipped not with one-piece tyres, but with a series of crescent shaped pieces of iron called *strakes*.

The wheel car with its long commodious carrying platform, its large wheels and overslung axle is a remarkable and unique vehicle. Its design owes a great deal to Radnorshire craftsmen, who wished to make a vehicle as easy to pull as a gambo and as stable and controllable on mountain slopes as a sled. Its persistence in Radnorshire suggests that the wheel car is the vehicle best suited by far to the topography of the area.

Ox traction has been well known in Wales for countless centuries and examples of ox equipment and ox-drawn carts from many parts of the country are preserved at the Welsh Folk Museum. The influence of these ox-drawn carts, which go back in time to the prehistoric Middle East, is very clearly seen on the more elaborate horse-drawn vehicles of present-day Wales.

Ffrancis Payne, in his paper, *Cwysau o Foliant Cyson*, has drawn on literary evidence to show the importance of the ox as a draught animal in medieval Wales. Unfortunately, there are only very scanty references to the types of vehicles that these drew. One of the few *cywyddau* which describes a vehicle in anything but fanciful terms is that written by William Llŷn, some time between 1534 and 1580. William Llŷn was either a native of the Llŷn Peninsula or he was a descendant of a Llŷn family. For many years he lived in the Oswestry district, but he also dwelt for short periods in Denbighshire and Merioneth. In his *cywydd* to solicit a wain from Edward ap Huw Conway of Bryneithin, Llandrillo-yn-Rhos, Denbighshire, in 1562, there is an elaborate and fanciful description of the vehicle.

> *Dwy olwyn aur ar dal nant*
> *Drwy oglais yr ymdreiglant.*
> *Certwain arw i sain ar sarn*
> *Cloch cywydd cylchog haearn.*
> *Oes man hwnt sy o'i mewn hi,*
> *A lle i dreiddio llyw drwyddi?*
> *Oes bogel ac ysbigod,*
> *A rhwyll ynghanol pob rhod?*

[Two golden wheels rolling along the brow of the valley. A wain with grinding sound on the paved road, the bell that sings the song of the wain hoop. Has it room beyond to place the draught pole? Has it a navel and axle and latticed spokes in each wheel?]

At the Welsh Folk Museum is preserved an eighteenth-century ox wain of great significance. It came from Wallas Farm, Ewenni, in the Vale of Glamorgan and seems to be very near the design of the medieval ox cart. The vehicle was built between 1750 and 1770 by a certain Thomas Thomas, a Glamorgan wheelwright whose initials appear on the front-board of the wain. Although the wheels are missing, their diameter must have been somewhere in the region of six feet. The body itself consists of light, considerably chamfered side frames to which are mortised a large number of round wooden spindles. The inner top rails curve into arched guards which pass over the wheels, and the whole vehicle very closely resembles the ox carts of Mediterranean Europe. In addition the vehicle is equipped with horizontal sideboards and the floorboards are laid lengthwise, which suggests that the wain was used for other than harvesting duties. The significance of the Ewenni wain arises from the fact that not only does it seem to be the direct descendant of the medieval wain and the wains of Mediterranean Europe, but also to be the immediate predecessor of the well known bow wagon. This remarkable four-wheeled vehicle was known not only in south Wales but also in the west of England. From Cornwall to Berkshire and from Pembrokeshire to Hampshire, the bow wagon was once a familiar sight; indeed wains resembling the Ewenni type were also known throughout this vast region.

Unlike the Ewenni wain, the Cornish wain and the harvesting carts of the West of England, the ordinary harvesting ox carts of south Wales did not have the overlapping sideboards which were curved over the wheels. Like the familiar gambo, these ox carts had railed, open sides though they still retained the draught pole of their English and Mediterranean counterparts. In construction the ox cart showed little variation throughout south Wales, and seems to have been used, particularly in west Carmarthenshire, until the early years of the present century. An ox cart from Whitland preserved at the Welsh Folk Museum is equipped with slightly dished hoop-tyred wheels some sixty inches in diameter. The framework of the cart body consists of two side pieces fixed to the all-wooden axle by a pair of bolts. The builder of this vehicle used a balk of timber with a bulge in it in the necessary position. This was sawn in two, shaped and used as side timbers; the bulge was then bored to take the bolts connecting the body to the undercarriage. This method of construction was also widely practised in East Anglia, where wheelwrights used naturally bulged timber for the pillows and bolsters of four-wheeled wagons, which were pierced by the all important king-pin. The vehicle has a long-boarded floor and is equipped with a draught pole that runs parallel to the side frames. This is bolted to the cross bars. The body itself consists of four upright stakes mortised on either side of the frame. Near the bottom of these uprights is bolted a horizontal rail that runs the whole length of the vehicle, while another parallel rail is bolted some half way up the stakes.

By removing the two bolts that attach the frame to the axle, the whole body of the cart can be removed. This can be replaced by a Y-shaped draught pole (*fforchwan*) and can be used for carrying timber or sacked grain. The Y-body, which resembles the coupling pole of a four-wheeled wagon, can be fixed to the axle and wheels by a pair of bolts that pass through the ends of the Y.

In most parts of Wales the well-known cart, the gambo, was used until recently for all harvesting duties. Not only was this vehicle found in all parts of Wales, but it occurred widely in the border counties of Herefordshire, Shropshire and west Gloucestershire. It is a close relative of the Cornish wain, the Scottish harvest cart and the north of England long cart, and undoubtedly is a development from the Mediterranean cart.

The harvesting vehicle used in the Gower Peninsula and occasionally in south Pembrokeshire is virtually the same vehicle as the Cornish wain, although it is still known as a 'gambo'. The body of the Gower gambo consists of a flat platform some eight feet in length and five feet two inches in width at the front. The dished spoked wheels, some four feet in diameter, are set in the body, so that the width of the carrying platform is no more than four feet behind the wheels. Above the wheels a section of a hoop or a curved piece of wood is fitted to act as a guard, preventing the load of hay or corn from spilling over the wheels. The top of this arch is connected to the side frame by a bar of iron or timber bolted to the frame and hoop. A wooden slat which runs the length of the arch is also fitted to the carrying platform acting as a side plank. At the back a small windlass is fitted to the crossbar and this is used for tightening the ropes passed over the load.

Like the wain, the Gower gambo could be used for horse or ox traction. When oxen were used (and they were used in Gower until the third quarter of the nineteenth century), the gambo, like the wain, was equipped with a central draught pole firmly bolted to the frame of the cart.

The gambo used in the remainder of Wales differs from the Gower cart in that it does not possess the characteristic wheel arches of the latter. In order to prevent the load of hay or corn from spilling over the wheels and clogging them, the gambo is equipped with a pair of side ladders fitted in the body frame in an upright position. Each side ladder consists of two vertical standards two feet high to which are mortised a pair of horizontal rails some three feet long. The ladders either fit into slots in the frame or are mortised to it. In addition, the gambo is equipped with either fore and tail ladders or with four poles, one at each corner of the vehicle. The body itself consists of a flat rectangular platform some ten feet long and five feet wide. The two heavy wheels are approximately four feet in diameter. In early nineteenth-century Wales, Walter Davies notes that many gambos were ox drawn; like the Cornish wain these are equipped with central draught poles.

Throughout western and northern Britain a native development from the simple and ancient harvest cart is the long-bodied cart. In the west of England a cart which may be regarded as the direct successor of the wain is found. This vehicle possesses a built up body rather than a simple platform and it has wide, solid sideboards that curve archwise over the wheels. In the north of England, too, the long cart with its planked sides leaning out over the wheels may be regarded as the direct successor of the ox wain 'with an open body furnished with shelvings'. In Scotland and in Ireland the same development can be traced, while in west

Wales, particularly in the counties of Cardigan, Pembroke and west Carmarthen, the long cart virtually replaced the traditional gambo in the last quarter of the nineteenth century. In south Cardiganshire the side-less gambo is not remembered and it is the long cart that bears the term 'gambo'. In north Cardiganshire, in the Talybont district, the flat gambo was replaced by the long cart some sixty years ago. Here these long carts are known as 'longbodies'. The boundary between the traditional flat gambo in Carmarthenshire occurs along the River Cothi. East of that river most of the harvest carts are of the gambo type, while west of it the long cart predominates.

The framework of the long cart is similar to that of the gambo, the shafts being rigid continuations of the frame. A single width of planking some twelve inches deep caps the frame and this is held in place by three or four pairs of wooden standards or side supports. Each standard is bolted to the side plank, while above each side plank are two railed sideboards which run the whole length of the vehicle.

Both the gambo and its successor, the long cart, are specifically harvest vehicles and, apart from undertaking a few days' work in summer and autumn, they are laid up for the remainder of the year. Like most Celtic carts, the gambo and long cart are light, one-horse vehicles whose origins may be traced back to Mediterranean Europe and to the native slide car.

Over the major parts of Wales, simple sleds and wheeled versions of those sleds have been used for countless centuries to meet all the transport requirements of the farm. Walter Davies, writing in 1815, for example, noted that 'within the memory of a person now eighty years of age, there were only two carts in the parish of Penbryn, near Cardigan; sledges were the only carriages'. This could well apply to many other parishes in eighteenth-century Wales, but nevertheless in the relatively level district of the country there must have been some kind of box cart, in addition to truckles, wheel cars and gambos. These were used for carrying material in bulk, such as loads of dung, sand or gravel.

Unfortunately there is very little evidence to show what pre-nineteenth-century box carts were like. Prints and drawings show very little of their construction and literary evidence is negligible. Davies, however, describes the carts of Pembrokeshire as long and narrow; those of Cardiganshire he describes in the same terms. The wheels of the latter were four feet six inches in diameter, the body five feet ten inches wide and one foot three and a half inches deep. The cart could carry sixteen bushels and had a track of four feet three inches. Little else is known of these vehicles.

Most of the carts that have persisted in Wales are of the Scottish variety.

. Hand-drawn peat sled from Dinas
wddwy.

. A wheel car made by Aaron Lewis of
anbister Road, Radnorshire, in 1928.

28. A slide car from Glyncorrwg,
Glamorgan.

29. A general purpose sled at Llanbryn-
Mair, Montgomeryshire, c. 1930.

30. An 'Irish car' from Llanha[..]
Glamorgan.

31. A wheeled sled used in Montgom[..]
shire.

32. A Denbighshire wagon from Ru[..]
built c. 1880.

Basket panniers and saddle used [on] pack animals.

A pack train carrying limestone, Llanhamlach, Brecknockshire, in 1929.

35. Hedger; Gare
Roderick, Cray, Brec
nockshire.

36. Dry-stone wall
Brecknockshire.

37. *Iron Age turnery excavated at Glastonbury.*

39. *Marram-grass weaving at Newborough, Anglesey, c. 1947.*

38. *A Carmarthenshire turner using a pole lathe, c. 1925.*

40. *Constructing a pottery kiln at Ewenni, Glamorgan, in the 1870s.*

41. *The Ewenni pottery c. 1890. The horse-driven mechanism for the pug mill is at the right.*

42. *A member of the Jenkins family, who have operated the Ewenni pottery since the sixteenth century, at work in 1970.*

43, 44. *Benjamin Evans of Bwlchllan, Cardiganshire, making a lip-work basket, 1970. Detail of thonging; the finished basket.*

45. *Glyn Rees of Dinas Mawddwy, a noted cabinet maker, carving the chair for the Powys Eisteddfod, 1961.*

46. *A country carpenter. Da*
Williams of Broad Oak, Lla
deilo, Carmarthenshire, shapi
the handle of an Aberaer
shovel; 1962.

47. *John Jones, tool-handle mak*
of Pantyblodau, Saron, Amma
ford, shaping a pick handle on h
shaving horse, 1964.

48, 49. William Thomas, rake maker of Llanymawddwy, Merionethshire, at work in 1964. Shaping the handle; assembling the rake.

50. Tom David of Cowbridge long-straw thatching at Llangynwyd, Glamorgan in 1911.

51. Rethatching cottages with Devon reed at St Fagans, Glamorgan, 1961.

52. *Interior of a blacksmith's shop the late nineteenth century.*

53. *A wheelwright and his apprent fitting the felloes of a wheel in a Per brokeshire workshop, 1938.*

54. *Tyring a wheel at Talsar Cardiganshire, in 1933.*

55, 56. *George Scammell of Abergavenny, Monmouthshire, one of the last of the Welsh tinsmiths. His workshop is now at the Welsh Folk Museum. Snipping tin; shaping a meat tin.*

57. *The cooper: Michael Harte, of the Welsh Folk Museum, at work in 1973.*

58. *The top cart for spinning rope, made of hemp, at a Cardiff rope-walk in 1965.*

59. *The sail maker: David Cale of Bango at work in 1968.*

60. *The basket maker: working on a trad. tional* gwyntell, *or potato basket, Ffostrasol, Cardiganshire, c. 1930.*

61. *Gelli Mill, Clunderwen, Pembrokeshire, typical of the larger woollen mills that developed in Wales after 1850, principally along railway lines.*

62. *Tom Griffiths of Middle Mill, Solva, Pembrokeshire, sorting wool.*

63. *Arthur Morgan of the Wallis Mill, Ambleston, Pembrokeshire, washing hanks of yarn in the stream near his mill; c. 1940.*

64. *William Morris of the Esgair Moel M* *winding bobbins.*

65. *Warping a* carthen (*bed cover*) *o* *warping wall at the Esgair Moel Mill.*

6. The modern method of warping: Howard Griffiths of the Tregwynt Mill, Letterston, Pembrokeshire.

7. D. J. Davies of the Esgair Moel Mill weaving a traditional carthen on a hand loom.

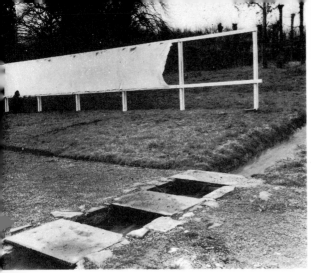

68. *John Abel of the Gwmgwili Mills, Bronwydd, Carmarthen, inserting a length of* carthen *into a fulling machine.*

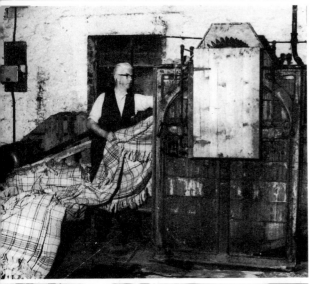

69. *The traditional method of tentering at the Esgair Moel Mill. The material is strained on the tenter hooks on the wooden frame.*

70. *The modern method of tentering at a Carmarthenshire mill.*

Whether these carts are native developments of an earlier type or whether, as in lowland England, that pattern had been imported from Scotland it is impossible to tell. In early nineteenth-century Wales the one-horse cart was established on estates in the Vale of Towy, in Brecknockshire and north Cardiganshire, but they were gaining in popularity only very slowly. Agricultural writers of the time were quite convinced of their superiority over other vehicles. Sir Edward Hamilton, a landowner of Brecknockshire, for example, said, 'My one horse carts . . . are certainly admirable things . . . the general introduction of these would be both an improvement and a great saving.' In England and in Scotland too, agricultural writers were equally enthusiastic about the virtues of the one-horse cart.

Whatever its origin, the one-horse box cart has been well known in Wales for the last hundred years and occurs with little variation in design throughout the country. The box cart is a relatively light vehicle, usually equipped with all iron axles and slightly dished wheels some forty-eight inches in diameter. In many cases the slight dish is compensated by the fact that the spoke mortices are staggered. The wheels are usually narrow tracked and shod with hoops rather than strakes. On some vehicles the shafts are rigid continuations of the body framing but, in the later examples, the whole body is designed to tip, and in this case the shafts are continuations of the underframing. This is fixed to the axle. The body consists of one or more planks, often of deal, which on many carts are bolted to one or more upright ribs. The sides of the cart in this case present a panelled appearance. When the cart is required for harvesting, a wooden framework can be fitted to the top rail, thus greatly enlarging the carrying surface of the vehicle. In addition, on some carts a pair of solid sideboards can be slotted into the top rail, particularly for carrying root crops. On some carts the width of the floor at the front is less than the width at the back. This facilitates the tipping of loose material.

Over much of Wales the four-wheeled wagon is unknown for it is unsuited for work in a hilly country and on high moorland. It does occur, however, in those districts which from time immemorial have acted as geographical and cultural extensions of the English plain. In the south, the Vale of Glamorgan—that region of trim, thatched villages—represents an extension of English lowland culture into Wales. As an element in this cultural extension one finds a bow wagon of superb design and elegance which is closely related in type to the panel-sided wagons of the Vale of Berkeley and Wessex. The broad eastern face of the Welsh Massif overlooks the wide curve of the Severn Valley and is entered by several broad vales. Along these valleys of the Wye, the Usk, the Severn and others, countless invaders have made their way and countless ideas from the English plain have passed, penetrating the very heart of the highlands. Along the Severn

Valley, for example, cultural elements like the short-handled shovel and the half-timbered house have penetrated almost as far as the shores of Cardigan Bay, as has the four-wheeled wagon based on Shropshire design. In the north too, wagons of west Midlands design occur as far westwards as the county of Anglesey.

Wagon types in Wales, therefore, must be regarded as intrusions into the country from the English plain. In the south there is an intrusion from the west of England along the valleys of the eastward-flowing streams and in the north intrusion from Shropshire as far westwards as Anglesey.

Welsh farm wagons may be divided into six distinct types:

(a) The Glamorgan Bow Wagon, which is a panel-sided bow wagon related to the wagons of Wessex and the Vale of Berkeley (Pl. 11).
(b) The Monmouthshire Wagon, which is a simplified version of the traditional Hereford box wagon.
(c) The Radnorshire Wagon, which is also closely related to the box wagon of Hereford.
(d) The Montgomeryshire Wagon, a medium-sized box wagon closely related to the Shropshire wagon.
(e) The Denbighshire Wagon, a heavy vehicle closely related to the box wagons of the north Midlands (Pl. 32).
(f) The Trolley, which is widely used in the southern Border Counties of Radnor, Brecon and Monmouth, is a type that has been known in the west Midlands from at least the mid eighteenth century.

5 Using Local Raw Materials

Amongst the creative crafts of rural Wales there are many that came into existence because there was raw material available to provide the basis for that craft or industry. In rural Anglesey, for example, there was an important group of crafts that utilized sea reed (*môr hesg*), which grows so profusely on the sand dunes of the island. Reed provided the raw material for such industries as mat making at Newborough and broom and besom making at Rhosneigr, Valley and Aberffraw. Itinerant clog sole making developed in the alder groves of rural south Wales and Anglesey, while bowl turning and spoon carving developed in the river valleys of west Wales where there is a profusion of sycamore. In this category of industry dependent on local raw materials may be considered the woollen industry and tanning (described elsewhere in this volume), but it also included such specialized industries as paper making that developed in isolated valleys such as those of rural Monmouthshire and Brecknockshire. These now defunct paper mills were located close to clear, swiftly flowing steams that were essential for power and for the actual manufacture of paper. Linen rags from the industrial areas, and later wood pulp, were easily brought to the mills.

One of the best known of all industries dependent on local raw materials was that of wood-turning.

In many parts of rural Wales the sycamore tree is a very conspicuous element in the landscape, for although it rarely grows in plantations, coppices and natural forests, it occurs everywhere, especially in west Wales, in farm hedgerows, as animal shelter belts and on the banks of numerous rushing streams. Indeed, sycamore is one of the few trees that can withstand the great force of the salt-laden winds that blow in from the Irish Sea. For many centuries the sycamore tree has provided the raw material for a number of important woodcrafts, whose fame has spread far beyond the boundaries of Wales. The most important of these crafts were those of bowl-turning, the carving of wooden spoons and the manufacture of all kinds of dairy equipment, ranging from carved butter prints to coopered cheese vats. Sycamore is eminently suited for making many dairy and cooking utensils, as it is one of the few timbers that do not taint foodstuffs. In addition, like beech, it can be turned and carved while still green and it can be immersed in water at frequent intervals without cracking and warping. Its beauty lies in its pale, lustrous colour, for, unlike yew or oak, sycamore has no strongly marked figure or pattern. On the other hand it may be steamed to darken its colour to a pale yellow and should the craftsman wish to produce a coloured article, then sycamore will absorb dyes of any colour without the natural grain being obscured. Above all, it is the timber's quality as a carving medium that made bowl-turning and spoon carving such an important industry in west Wales.

Until the nineteen-thirties a large proportion of the products of the wood-turner's shop were made of sycamore. With the virtual disappearance of domestic butter and cheese making in the thirties, the demand for dairy utensils of sycamore declined very rapidly. Butter making rapidly gave place to the sale of liquid milk from Welsh farms; cheese making disappeared, and even the making of broth, traditionally eaten with a wooden spoon from a wooden bowl, declined. With the availability of mass-produced domestic ware in enamel, tin, china and, later, plastics, the wood-turner ceased to be an essential member of the rural community. In the nineteen-thirties many workshops closed down and the turners who remained in the trade adapted their output from the traditional utilitarian necessities of the farm, kitchen and dairy to products that had some aesthetic qualities. Timbers other than sycamore were used to an ever-increasing extent and decorative bowls of cherrywood, yew, mulberry, oak and even rosewood and teak became the main products of rural workshops.

Today a notable wood-turner, Gwyndaf Breese, uses a great variety of well-seasoned timber for his work at the Welsh Folk Museum, the principal ones being sycamore, elm, ash, yew, apple, cherry, pearwood, walnut and many other lesser known timbers, such as lignum vitae and sapele. The essentials of a good turning wood are a close grain, hardness and absence of kinks; fine texture and attractive colouring and figuration add to the beauty of the finished article. Native timber, which should be winter cut, has to be well seasoned before it can be used for turning; indeed it was believed by many craftsmen that a piece of wood should be seasoned at the rate of one year for every inch of thickness. Thus a piece of wood ten inches thick ought to season in a well aired but dry store for ten years.

The craft of wood-turning is of great antiquity, for bowls and spoons excavated from prehistoric sites, as at Glastonbury in Somerset (Pl. 37), differ but little in shape and workmanship from those made by twentieth-century craftsmen in rural Wales. In describing the turned ware excavated from the Glastonbury Lake

Villages of two thousand years ago, the excavators described their finds as 'exhibiting such accurate workmanship, excellent finish and refinement of design, that they apparently fall little short of the work produced by some modern village community'. It is in that ancient tradition that the many wood-turners of Wales worked, producing the essential products of the farm and home. The equipment used by many of them was of the simplest, for until the nineteen-thirties many of the turners of west Wales used pole lathes that differed little from those of Iron Age times.

The wood-turner's chief quality is his ability to make simple things; to make something durable without any unnecessary adornments and decoration. In the wake of this utilitarian purpose there follows pride, the true craftsman's pride in creating something useful, but creating it with beauty and good taste.

In the history of Welsh wood-turning the Teifi Valley in west Wales was by far the most important centre of the industry, and the village of Aber-cuch in north Pembrokeshire was until recently a particularly important venue of woodland craftsmanship. No more than fifty years ago there were at least seven families dependent on the craft; there were others who worked on a part-time basis, combining farming or some other occupation with a certain amount of bowl turning. The fame of Aber-cuch as a centre of remarkable craftsmanship had spread far beyond the boundaries of Wales, and even in the mid thirties the prospects of the industry were regarded as excellent. A guide issued in 1935, for example, said 'the growing recognition of the aesthetic beauty of the well turned bowl is creating a new demand for the products of the wood-turner'. Yet by 1962 the last representative of a long line of craftsmanship was dead, and it is only in recent years, as a result of the impetus given to rural crafts by the tourist trade, that wood-turning has been revived in Aber-cuch. In the past, the Aber-cuch craftsmen visited all the markets and fairs of west Wales and the turner's stall was a feature of most fairs and markets in the region. Today, two members of the Davies family, who were the principal turners of Aber-cuch, are still engaged in that trade; the one craftsman is concerned with producing decorative ware, the other with the manufacture of tool handles on a large scale.

Both aspects of turnery, the production of domestic requirements and the production of farm tools, have always been the concern of the Aber-cuch craftsmen; specialization in one aspect of the work or the other only came in the nineteen-thirties with the decline in demand for utilitarian ware. The notable brothers, John and James Davies, who later in life specialized in decorative woodwork and farm tools respectively, were in their younger days concerned with producing a very wide range of turned ware. Dr I. C. Peate, writing in 1935, said that the

wholesale prices per dozen charged by the Davieses before the First World War
were:

'Wooden spoons, small pointed: 1s. 6d.; Ordinary Welsh pat: 1s. 9d.; Pickle and
pudding: 3s. to 6s.; Butter scoops: 3s. to 6s.; Ladles: 3s., 6s., 8s., 10s.; Bowls:
3s., 4s., 5s. 4d., 6s.; Plates or trenchers: 3s., 4s., 5s. 4d., 6s.; Handled bowls: 12s.;
Butter beaters, turned in one piece: 13s., 9-inch: 15s.; Cream skimmers: 8-inch: 7s.,
9-inch: 8s.; Milk plugs: 2s. 6d.; Cream stirrers: 6s.; Stools: 12s., 15s., 18s., 21s.;
Turned cheese vats made to order; Rakes: 13s. and 11s.; Corn cradles: 24s.; Corn
handles: 18s.; Welsh shovel handles: 9s.; Mattock handles: 7s.'

Further up-river from Aber-cuch another notable craftsman, William Rees of
Tre-turnol, Aber-banc, Henllan, practised a trade that had been in his family for
generations, until his death in about 1950. William Rees, unlike the Aber-cuch
turners, specialized in the production of domestic ware and his workshop never
developed into a 'factory' producing implements for outdoor work, which James
Davies's workshop became.

'The Henllan turner', says Peate, 'specialized in butter "clappers" (*claper*) sold
at 1s. each before the war but which now cost 4s. 6d.; milk skimmers (*sleten*):
6d. each, now 2s.; bowls (*ffiol*): 3d. each, now 2s.; trenchers (*trensiwrn*): 3d. but now
2s.; cheese vats, from 2s. 6d. to 10s., but almost completely out of date; ladles at
6d. each but now from 9d. to 2s. according to quality and size; and spoons.
When his father was in his prime', adds Peate, 'spoons were sold at a penny each;
they were sold before the War at 1s. 6d. per dozen and are now disposed of at 5s.'

Although the Henllan workshop closed its doors many years ago, something of
the spirit of the wood-turners' craft still lives on in the neighbouring village of
Tre-groes, where Ieuan Evans has gained a considerable reputation as a wood-
carver of note. He is above all a carver of spoons and ladles, and his products are
in great demand far beyond the confines of west Wales.

To produce a bowl, well-seasoned tree butts are cut into logs, which vary in
diameter according to the girth of the tree and vary in depth according to the
type of bowl that is being made. The sapwood is removed from each log and the
blocks are then stacked under cover to dry out and season before they can be used
by the craftsman. The length of seasoning may vary from a period of six months
to a year.

The process of bowl-turning begins with the shaping of the outside of the bowl,
and for this the craftsman uses a one-inch gouge to reduce the roughly octagonal
block into a rounded form. The lathe used by craftsmen today is electrically

powered but until recent years the older type of treadle lathe was widely used by such turners as the Davieses of Aber-cuch. Here the driving power was provided by the craftsman's foot, which caused the bowl to revolve continuously. An even older type of lathe, used by the Aber-cuch craftsmen until 1938, was the pole lathe. The driving power for this piece of equipment was supplied by a horizontal ash or larch pole anchored firmly to the ground at its butt. A piece of string joined the free end of the pole to the foot treadle, being passed around the lathe chuck first. When the treadle was pressed, the pole bent and the chuck turned, only to spring back again as the foot was removed. On each forward motion of the block of wood, the gouge or chisel was applied (Pl. 38).

After shaping the outside of the bowl, the craftsman again takes a gouge and carefully shapes the inside, removing the core at a considerable speed. Smaller gouges and chisels are then applied until the inside of the bowl is quite smooth. At this stage only a thin pillar of wood connects the inside of the bowl to the lathe centre. Taking a little beeswax the craftsman applies it to the rapidly revolving bowl until it is fully polished. Excess wax is removed with wood-shavings, the lathe is stopped and the bowl is removed for final trimming. The pillar of wood which connected the bowl to the centre screw of the lathe is scrapped and the chuck marks cleaned off with a knife. The bowl turner is in the full sense of the term a creative craftsman, and uses no written measurement or templates, for he has the shapes in his head and hands, shapes that have remained virtually unchanged from the dawn of civilization.

Another important aspect of the turner's work was the making of wooden spoons. In the past wooden spoons were used in Welsh households for a great variety of purposes. Small ten-inch spoons were always required for eating *cawl*, that unique broth of bacon, leeks and other vegetables, the recipe for which seems to have been limited to the western counties of Wales. *Cawl* still remains extremely popular in Welsh farmhouses and many people will not eat it with anything but a wooden spoon. The spoon carvers in addition to making broth spoons also make a variety of large spoons and ladles, ranging from butter scoops for use in the dairy, to kitchen spatulas and stirrers. All these are made by hand and with a few simple tools.

The process of making a spoon begins with the felling of suitable timber in the winter months. There is a tradition that sycamore for bowls and spoons should be winter felled as this ensures a pale lustrous wood free of all blemishes and stains. After felling, the sycamore butts are cut by means of a cross-cut saw into logs, each one approximately twelve inches long. With the aid of a small cleaving iron and hammer each log is cut in two and the process of shaping the spoon begins. Sitting on a three-legged stool, the craftsman rests the sycamore log on the chopping block in front of him, and with a short-handled axe cuts the log to the approximate shape of the spoon. With a few deft strokes the handle is shaped and for this process the craftsman depends entirely on eyesight and long experience, for the shoulders have to slope at the same angle and the spoon has to be perfectly symmetrical. No written measurements or patterns of any kind are used by Welsh spoon carvers.

After roughing out with the axe, the half-finished spoon now needs hollowing and this is done with a peculiarly shaped knife known as a *twca cam*. This tool, which has a handle some eighteen inches in length, has a small curved blade, usually made by the craftsman himself from an old file or chisel. It is kept extremely sharp, and to use it the handle is tucked under the user's right arm and tightly against the body, while the blade is grasped firmly in the right hand. With the tip of the handle acting as a fulcrum, considerable power is applied to the blade, and with a few short sweeping movements the core of the spoon is removed cleanly. The convex side of the spoon and the handle have to be smoothed next and this is done with an ordinary, small-sized spokeshave, held in the palm of the hand. Finally the tip of the handle, the edges of the spoon and the shoulders are cleaned and finished with a short-bladed knife. The whole process of making a broth spoon takes little more than fifteen minutes from the moment when the sycamore log is cleft to the final stage when the spoon is cleaned with the knife.

To make the large ladle which is used for a number of tasks in the home and dairy, the process is rather different. Since the ladle will be at least fifteen inches long, the logs have to be larger. Each one is roughed out in the same way as the broth spoon, except for the fact that the tip of the handle has to be shaped into a hook, necessary for hanging the ladle on the edge of the milk bucket or shelf; it is shaped during the first stage of roughing out with the axe. Since the bowl of the ladle is considerably wider and deeper than that of the broth spoon, something stronger than the *twca* is required to shape it. The roughed out ladle is therefore clamped in a vice and a short-handled adze with a $1\frac{1}{2}$-inch gouge is taken. This adze, known as a *bwyall gam*, is a unique tool that like the *twca* has remained unchanged for many centuries. All that is required to clean the top part of the ladle are a few sharp knocks with the adze, but since it cannot be used to clean the lower end, nearest the handle, a gouge and mallet are used for this. A large-sized *twca cam* is then taken and the inside of the base cleaned exactly in the same manner as in the smaller broth spoon. Finally, with spokeshave and knife, the ladle is completed.

The wooden spoon, despite its simplicity, has been an article of great importance in Welsh peasant life. Although many villages had their full-time craftsmen, the carving of wooden spoons as a pastime in the long winter evenings became very popular on Welsh farms. Some of these spoons were undoubtedly designed for use, but from the seventeenth to the end of the nineteenth century, the highly decorated spoon presented by the maker as a token of love became a very common feature of rural life. These were not designed for use and most of them were very intricate and elaborate in design with slotted handles, chain links and carved patterns and initials. The aim wherever possible seems to have been to carve an intricate pattern out of a single piece of wood, and since the donor of the love spoon was also the maker he tried to emphasize the feeling and care that had gone into its making by elaborating the design as much as possible. The origin of the custom is very obscure, but undoubtedly in remote country districts, where entertainment was at a premium, young men carved their tokens of love to beguile the tedium of the long, dark winter evenings. It must be remembered, however, that the carving of love spoons was never part of the bowl turner's and spoon carver's work; they were the product of an amateur tradition rather than that of the professional craftsman. Generally love spoons were made and presented by young men to the girls of their fancy, as a token of love, but in some parts of the country, notably the Teifi valley, presentation was to the girl's parents. The spoons then were not so much a token of love but test pieces that proved a suitor's competence as a craftsman, the assumption being that he would be able to provide for the girl after marriage if the spoon proved that he had dextrous hands (see page 135).

The county of Anglesey attained considerable fame as the only county in Wales where marram grass growing on sand dunes provided the raw material for an important industry. This peculiarly tough reed, known in Anglesey as *môr hesg*, grows profusely on the west coast of the island, particularly in the parishes of Llanddwyn and Newborough. For many centuries, no one knows exactly how many, the inhabitants of Newborough have made a scanty living by plaiting this material into mats for the farmer's haystacks, barn roofs and cucumber frames as well as into nets and cordage for the fishermen.

In the mid nineteenth century Newborough was described as 'the most miserable spot in Anglesey' and it was the abject poverty of the village that struck all travellers to the county. Its menfolk worked long hours for a miserably low wage on the limited amount of agricultural land, while the women attempted to eke out those low wages by making mats in their homes.

Undoubtedly, the mat-making industry of Newborough came into existence as an antidote to poverty, in an area not well blessed with natural advantages.

> '*I'w llenwi oedd lluniaeth*
> *Ond trist gynhaeaf y traeth.*'
>
> [To feed them there was no food
> But the sad harvest of the beach.]

Although mat making was traditionally women's work, in the palmy days of the industry in the mid nineteenth century, when the demand for Newborough mats was heavy, men, women and children were engaged in the craft, and every house was a little factory supplying not only the district around, but even parts of distant Caernarvonshire, Denbighshire and Flintshire. The industry never extended far beyond the village of Newborough and the reason usually given for this was the fact that the craft of mat making required 'traditional skill, which is either hereditary or acquired in early childhood'. It was said that a girl coming into the village older than fourteen years of age could never learn to make the mats as quickly or as well as a native.

The reed was cut in the summer months, usually in late August or September, and although scythes were occasionally used, the most common tool for harvesting was a broad-bladed reaping hook. The best raw material was two-year-old reed, for the growth of the first year was considered too weak and that of the third year contained too many withered stalks (*môr hesg llwyd*) to be of use to the mat maker. One writer in the nineteen-twenties noted that 'The cutting of grass has been carried on for so long by each family, that now every woman goes to her own particular area of the sand dune and claims it as her own property, from which no one else is allowed to cut any sea reed.'

The method of harvesting was as follows:

(i) A bunch of grass was grasped with one hand and cut with a sharp stroke of the hook. A bunch of grass was described as a *fres* or *frecsan* and each bunch consisted of four or six stalks growing from a single root or stool. Each stalk, with a pointed end, measured from twelve to thirty-six inches in length. The plant was cut as near the stool as possible, usually some two inches below the level of the sand. With careful cutting, the stool would continue to bear its crop of usable reed for many years. Since the reed was always cut while green, it had to be left in the open air to ripen for some weeks before it could be used.

(ii) Four or five handfuls of cut stalks were heaped together and in the evenings, before leaving the dunes, the harvesters carried the crop to dry, sheltered positions in the dunes. The reed was spread out to dry and ripen under the mellowing influences of sun and wind until it was hard, dry and white in colour.

(iii) The reed (*taenfeydd*) was then gathered into bundles, known as *geifr*, and stooked, with their roots at the bottom. Again they were left at this stage for some days, or even weeks, depending on the weather.

(iv) The unusable grey stalks were then shaken out and two bundles of reed placed together, the head of one against the root of the other, and bound tightly with a reed rope some four feet long to form an *ysgub forhesg* (reed sheaf).

(v) After further ripening and the shaking out of all grey stalks the bundles were again bound, but this time with the roots all facing the same way. The sheaves were then placed in water to soften before they could be used.

Harvesting usually took at least a month, depending on the weather, and the crop was then brought to the house. Each woman provided herself with enough material for her own use, but some of the older women who were unable to gather their own raw material bought reed from their neighbours. In the nineteenth century they could buy reed 'in bundles from Aberffraw paying about one shilling for each bundle'. At that time 'the younger girls form into groups of half a dozen and go to work together in some empty house, thus keeping their homes tidy. As most of the houses have only one living room, home work is very inconvenient when the house is occupied by a large family, and by meeting together, the work is less tedious for the young girls. The wives are not able to leave the house and they prefer to work at home.'

The local historian Owen Williamson described the method of working as follows:

'Two or three groups of stalks are inserted into the edge away from the plaiter. As a stalk is inserted it is plaited with the three on the right, using the right hand to plait and the left to hold the work. It is then grasped with the right hand and plaited with the left until the plaited stalk takes the place of that plaited with the right hand. It is obvious that the number of stalks has to be an odd number, and the thumb of the left hand is always used to turn the plait upwards. The number of straws in a plait is eleven, but in order to make the edges rigid, thirteen stalks are used. . . . The mat must consist of lengths of eight plaits, every plait to be eight Welsh yards, each yard being forty inches. After sewing strips of plait to strips of plait—rough side to rough side and smooth to smooth— to make a length of matting eight yards long, the mat is folded and the two sides again joined. The folded mat is opened so that each is sixteen plaits wide and four yards long. A narrow plait of five straws, to sew the edges, is made to prevent unravelling. After folding, the mat is sold to merchants, who keep it dry and safe for the next hay harvest, when they are taken to the markets for sale to farmers.'

The method of plaiting in the nineteen-twenties was considerably simpler than that described by Owen Williamson.

'The grass is two or three feet long. To plait it, six or seven straws of the same size are taken and by knocking the bunch against the knee the worker gets them in order for the plaiting. There are about six of these bunches in each plait and the width of the plait is about four inches. All the plaiting is done by the right hand; the left putting in the new bunches when the old strand is becoming thin, and keeping the plait in position. This method keeps the right edge always smooth, whereas the left edge where the new bunches are joined in, is rough. A leather strap fastened to the ceiling forms a loop to support the plait. When long enough the plaited end is weighted down by a poker or some such object, or kept in position by the foot. In plaiting, the worker is seated and has the work about level with her face.'

The Newborough rush-mat making industry persisted until recent times (Pl. 39), but the advent of corrugated iron sheds for storing hay on farms decreased the demand for thatching mats, which was the main product of the industry. Thatching mats were used for throwing over haystacks until the farmer found time to thatch them, and it is said that these mats kept the hay in better condition than corrugated roofs, since they allowed the sweat to evaporate into the air. Thatching mats measured some three yards long by one yard wide. To make them the plaiter made a four-inch plait some eighty yards long. With a sacking needle and thread of plaited grass, the plait was joined together until it formed nine lengths sewn edge to edge.

In addition to mats, the Newborough craftsman produced considerable quantities of grass rope (known locally as *tannau*), which was widely used for packing glassware, pottery and polished furniture as well as for packing barbed wire for transportation.

Early in the present century the Newborough Mat Makers Association was founded, and a successful attempt was made to search for new markets for the products of Newborough. Horticultural mats, particularly strawberry mats, were made in considerable quantities, as were table mats, floor mats, foot stools and baskets. By the end of the First World War, the mat makers of Newborough were no longer dependent on only two products—thatching mats and grass ropes. The Association too improved co-operation between the craftsmen and had its depot in the village for storing mats. In the nineteen-twenties members of the Association were paid three shillings for each mat they delivered at the depot; a great change from conditions in the late nineteenth century when:

'There was no co-operation among the makers and all trade was done by barter. Each worker made her purchases at the grocer's or butcher's shop, giving the shopkeeper so many mats in payment. These the shopkeeper stored until local merchants came round in early summer to buy them. The merchants took the mats to the fairs held in July at Criccieth and Pwllheli, and here the farmers would buy their annual stock of mats. As a rule, the worker was given food to the value of 1s. 10d. for each mat and the shopkeeper sold them for about 3s. Thus the shopkeeper made a profit both on the mats and on the food given in exchange to the mat maker.'

Nevertheless, despite the formation of the Mat Makers Association, the last thirty years has witnessed the complete disappearance of this once important industry.

Closely related to the craft of mat making was that of making besoms or brooms near the villages of Rhosneigr, Valley and Aberffraw. This was a part-time craft carried out by farm labourers and others who lived near the sand dunes. All the craftsman required was a number of broomsticks and strong cord for fastening the reeds. The besoms were made by tying a bunch of reeds, some three feet long, along the middle, fitting the handle in the middle and tying the tuft of reed firmly to it. In the nineteen-twenties these, which were greatly favoured for such tasks as whitewashing, were sold for threepence each.

In damp river valleys and on marshy land the alder tree grows profusely, and thanks to the heavy rainfall of Wales, the alder is found in almost all districts. The valleys of Cardiganshire, Carmarthenshire and Brecknockshire, as well as the marshlands of Anglesey, are particularly rich in alder. Writing in 1927 Anna M. Jones said:

'In Lancashire, where clogs have always been worn extensively, alder is very scarce; alder from Wales is therefore in great demand and the Welsh themselves prefer their clog soles to be made of it. Being a quick growing tree it is coarse grained and soft, and therefore easy to cut—a great advantage to the cutter. Moreover, being soft, it gives to the shape of the foot and hence it is comfortable. It is supposed also to possess certain medicinal qualities that are good for the feet and is still used by some old people as a remedy for foot trouble.'

Until 1939 gangs of clog sole makers were commonplace in alder groves through-out Wales (Pl. 110). A few were Welsh people, others such as the Dicksons, Barlows, Weavers and Webbs were originally north country families that had settled in Wales, while others were Lancashire people sent by Lancashire firms as journey-men moving from one plantation to the other. 'Breaking up', or clog sole making, was a seasonal industry carried out in the spring and summer months by men who lived and worked in roughly built temporary shelters. Many of these were merely rectangular tents to shelter the clogger from the rain; they were open on one side and the craftsman faced the opening as he worked. The money earned by selling waste timber was by tradition supposed to pay the worker's lodgings while away from home. This craft was distinct from that of the village clog maker (see Chapter 6).

After felling alder trees no more than twenty-four inches in girth, the clogger sawed the tree trunks into logs of fixed lengths, of four sizes—'men's', 'women's', 'middles' and 'children's'. Each log was then split with a beetle and wedge or with axe and mallet into blocks, which were cut with the clogger's knife into the rough shape and size of the clog soles. This process was known as 'breaking up'. If the alder trees used were small nine-year coppice trees, their girth would be considerably smaller, and the splitting process with beetle and wedge was un-necessary.

The work with the clogger's stock knife was highly skilled and intricate. The knife itself was made of one piece of steel, some thirty inches in length, bent to an obtuse angle in the middle. The blade was some four inches deep and thirteen inches long and the whole knife terminated in a hook. This hook was fastened to a ring on a wooden post driven firmly into the ground and forming one of the supports of a low bench. With his right hand the clogger grasped the wooden handle, which was at right angles to the shank, while his left hand held an alder billet, resting on the bench and moving it as required. The large clogger's knife, known as a 'bench' or 'paring knife', is still produced by some large-scale manu-facturers, and with its stout hook and long handle it gives play to the craftsman who wishes to make rapid cuts at different angles; it is still used for some pur-poses in factories along with a variety of modern machinery. The clogger, stoop-ing over the knife, cut an alder billet into the rough shape of a sole with great certainty and speed. A deep notch was cut in the block at a point where heel and sole were designed to meet. The clog blocks were built into small conical stacks which had to remain in the open air for some weeks if not months, and were built in such a way that air could circulate freely between the blocks to hasten the drying process, for 'breaking up' was undertaken while the timber was still green and moist. The rough blocks were then sent to north country clog factories where they were finally shaped in workshops, for stacking marked the end of the clogger's work. It was up to his employer at the clog-making factory to arrange transport to Lancashire and Yorkshire.

A raw material from the Welsh countryside that contributed to the industrialization of south Wales was charcoal; indeed during the seventeenth and eighteenth centuries the actual distribution of iron works depended on the source of charcoal. Gradually, wooded valleys were denuded in an attempt to supply the ever growing iron industry with fuel. Although the last charcoal burner has long passed away, a certain amount of burning was carried out in the Epynt foothills in Brecknockshire until about 1940 and here, as in the Forest of Dean in the nineteen-thirties, charcoal burning was carried out in clamps in the traditional manner. Charcoal burning demanded no special tools or equipment, but it called for considerable skill in the careful erection of the clamp (Pls 127, 128).

Charcoal burning was always carried out in the summer months, and although beech, alder, willow and many other timbers could be used, the best charcoal was obtained from coppice oak. In using oak, however, the craftsman had to be very careful not to include too much bark because this left too much sulphur in the charcoal. The principle of burning was to heat wood in such a way that all the air was excluded, thus preventing complete combustion. Only a very small proportion of the wood in a clamp was actually burnt to ashes, the remainder was just charred. Water and volatile substances such as creosote and tar were driven out, leaving a mass of solid carbon together with a small quantity of mineral ash.

After cutting rough wood into lengths of two or three feet, the timber was stacked for drying for several months before it was ready for burning. It was then carried by means of a wheelbarrow to the burning pit. This pit, which had a level floor of earth or ashes, was some fifteen feet in diameter, and a pole some six feet high was fixed at its centre. Around this were arranged small pieces of wood which would catch fire quickly. The sticks were then piled up, sloping towards the centre pole. Split logs and round sticks were arranged in such a way that the clamp was a dome-shaped erection some six feet high and fifteen feet in diameter. The wood was covered with grass, bracken leaves, turves and rushes and the whole clamp cemented down with damp earth and ashes. The central stake was then removed, leaving a chimney-like hole from the top to the bottom of the pile. A little cold charcoal was then dropped into the flue followed by a shovelful of red-hot charcoal and a few billets of kindling wood. More cold charcoal was used to top up the hole, and as soon as flames began to appear, a turf was placed over the central hole to check the draught. Great care had to be taken in burning, for the clamp had to be checked at frequent intervals. If flames appeared they were damped with water and more sods were placed on any gaps that occurred. The craftsman always attempted to light his fire in a sheltered position, avoiding gusts of wind. A vital piece of equipment was the portable canvas or corrugated iron shelter known as a 'loo' which was erected on the windward side of the clamps. This consisted of nothing more than a rectangular piece of canvas some ten feet high attached to a wooden framework. In the past these wind screens had consisted of wooden frames wattled with bracken and supported by firmer sticks. As the craftsman had to make rounds of the burning clumps every two hours, he and his fellow workers lived in the open air during the summer months. In the past huts of turf, wood and bracken were built. The whole art of charcoal burning lay in the regulation of draughts so that the maximum quantity of wood was charred but the minimum burned.

A rival industry closely related to that of charcoal burning was that of producing oils and acids from waste wood. In the Cothi valley in Carmarthenshire, for example, a Glamorgan craftsman set up a wood distillation establishment in the late nineteenth century. This flourished until the nineteen-twenties, but with bad roads and a haul of six miles to the nearest railway station the cost of coal, essential for power and heat, became excessive and the oil distillation plant was abandoned. Naphtha oil as well as charcoal was produced in large retorts rather than in clamps, and the by-products that would be lost under the old system of burning were regarded as more valuable than the charcoal itself.

While many domestic utensils were of wood, pottery has been known in Wales for countless centuries, but since pottery making was found only in two limited regions—on the fringe of the south Wales coalfield and in north-east Wales—earthenware crockery was unusual in many parts of rural Wales. Nevertheless, pottery stalls were to be found in most rural fairs during the nineteenth century and pottery for cooking, dairying and general domestic use was effectively distributed to all parts of the Welsh countryside. Buckley in Flintshire and Ewenni in the Vale of Glamorgan were notable centres of pottery manufacture, but along a narrow strip of country stretching from east Monmouthshire to Llanelli, deposits of suitable clay led to the foundation of dozens of potteries. All were in close proximity to coal measures, which provided the potteries with fuel for firing the kins. In the Ewenni district of Glamorgan alone, it is said that there were fourteen potteries in existence, most of them operating in the mid nineteenth century (Pls 40, 41). Unlike the pottery industry of Buckley, Flintshire, Ewenni's trade was comparatively local and markets at Bridgend, Neath, Maesteg and Pontypridd were attended regularly by the potters. Buckley potteries, however, had a widespread coastal trade in Wales. In the nineteenth century, for example, there were coastal ships sailing from the villages of Cardiganshire to the Dee estuary exclusively, and Buckley pottery was stored in warehouses that were to be found in many of the villages. Representatives of Buckley travelled widely in all parts of Wales and utensils made in that town were to be found in all districts.

6 Meeting a Local Demand

As long as rural communities remained almost self-sufficient, the craftsman who catered for the day-to-day needs of the neighbourhood was essential in the fabric of rural society. Craftsmen who met a local need were the most numerous class in Wales, and since they were specifically concerned with supplying a limited market, they made things that were well suited to the needs of that market (Pls 43–60). As far as tillage equipment was concerned, for example, craftsmen such as country blacksmiths and country carpenters made that equipment to suit local conditions, and for this reason many regional variations came into existence.

It is craftsmen belonging to this particular class — saddlers, wheelwrights, coopers and carpenters—whose numbers have been most drastically reduced, for today all the countryman's needs are met by national or even international organizations. The advent of mass production, mass advertising and mass transport has meant the death of numerous crafts that were dependent on a local market. Many, such as the white coopers that were concerned with making dairy equipment, tinsmiths and specialized horse-collar makers, have virtually disappeared, and others such as saddlers, carpenters and stonemasons are much rarer than they were.

Included in this group of individuals would be the service craftsmen concerned with the repair and renovation of farm equipment and domestic or personal essentials. For example, it includes the joiner, who was concerned with building repair and maintenance; the cobbler, concerned with the repair of boots and shoes; and the agricultural engineer who is concerned with the repair of factory-made machinery. Since 1918 craftsmen such as boot makers and blacksmiths gradually ceased to be the creative craftsmen that they once were and most, within the last thirty years or so, have become service workers. Of course with the modern demand for craft products many, such as wrought-iron smiths, have reverted to becoming creative artist-craftsmen, but no longer do they depend on a market that is strictly local.

The great changes that have taken place in the countryside have affected the blacksmith perhaps more than any other craftsman, for today most are primarily agricultural engineers concerned with repair work. There are creative craftsmen amongst them, but they are concerned with tourism rather than with supplying the needs of a local agricultural community. In the past, when the horse provided the only motive power on the farm, and the equipment and machinery of agriculture remained simple, the blacksmith was a creative craftsman, essential not only for repairing but also for making a wide range of domestic and farm equipment (Pls 52, 53, 54).

The account book of a certain Robert Phillips, a blacksmith of Pen-pont, Brecknockshire, covering the period 1829–50, for example, gives an indication of the type of work carried out by a country blacksmith. Among the entries are the following:

> Horse shoes (2/6–3/6 per set)
> New swing plough (£2.10.0)
> Strake nails (60 for 2/8)
> Gate hinges (12 pairs for 3/–)
> Steeling hammer (6d.)
> Mending poll axe (3d.)
> Altering smoke jack (7/6)
> Scythe blade (4/6)
> New suck [i.e. ploughshare] and mouldboard (£1.2.0)
> Pot hook (1/3)
> Ax (2/6)
> Pitch fork (1/6)
> Put teeth on harrow (no charge)
> Fireback (2/6)

In many cases no cash payment of any kind passed between farmer and blacksmith, and there are detailed accounts of old iron, bushels of grain, and sacks of potatoes being given in lieu of cash. Re-tining harrows was never paid for in cash, but always in farm produce. An account of 1845–7 was as follows: a bill for goods and services was sent to a certain John Evans, Common, in November 1844 for £7 13s. 7d. In May 1845 the bill amounted to £9 12s. 4d. In October 1845, 3 hundredweights of old iron, valued at £3 4s. 0d. and old iron to the value of 9s. 0d. were handed over by the farmer. By the end of November, with the delivery of a new plough, shoeing two horses and supplying horse medicines, the bill had crept up again to £8 12s. 5d. In May 1846, four bushels of wheat, four of barley, and a sack of swedes were given to the blacksmith, and £1 was paid in cash in February 1847.

In addition to supplying farmers with essential ironwork, Robert Phillips was also a horse doctor; he supplied saddlers with irons for harness, clog and boot makers with nails and clog irons, and undertook wheel-tyreing, fixing irons to cart axles and shafts, and supplying cart body standards to local wheelwrights.

Or take the case of John Williams, a blacksmith of Cellan, Dyfed, who between 1856 and 1869 had the following items in his account books:

	s.	d.
Make 4 shoe	0	8
Mend handle Byddegorddi [butter churn]	0	3
Make new pitchfork	1	4
Steeling 6 gimlet	1	0
Iron for pump	1	0
Make new billhook	2	0
Make iron oven	4	0
Dressing plough	4	0
Binding 4 wheels	4	6
Make new hay knife	2	6
Make 4 hog's rings	0	2
Make 4 pert inchis [sic] for door	2	8
Make small tribbet	0	5
Make bottom grate	0	5
Steel pickas	0	9
For nails wood shoes	0	2
Frosty nails	0	2
Make new iron to new cart	4	0
New mattock	2	0
New harrow	6	0
Plating extree	2	0
Iron shafting	1	6
Make new atchet	3	6
Plating carrllysk [sled]	1	2

Some indication of the working week may be obtained from John Williams's day books. For example, between 30 April and 6 May 1883 he completed the following work:

	s.	d.
30th April. David Davies, Blaencwm		
Making shaft irons and tailboard irons	3	8
5½ of iron	0	5½
William Davies, Llwyngwyn		
4 new horse shoe	1	4
8 of hog rings	0	8
David Davies		
Dressing whipple tree	0	6
David James		
Iron 2 Shoe	0	4
John Evans, Glanbran		
Child 1 shoe and nails	0	2
David Davies, Pistillinon		
Binding wheelbarrow wheel and make 2 rods	1	4
1st May. W. Davies, Ty'nycae		
4 New Horse Shoes	1	2
David Morgan, Tymawr		
Wife new shoes	0	8
2nd W. Davies, Pontfaen		
Nailing 4 shoes	0	10
Mrs. Davies, Beiliau		
Mend tea kettle hook	1	0
John Evans, Contractor		
21 lb. stapples at 2d. per lb.	3	6
Daniel Williams Mill		
Iron 2 shoes	0	4
Thomas Davies, Lodge		
Self and 2 of children's shoes	2	8
David Davies, Rhiweisaf		
Self new shoes	0	4

	s.	d.
4th John Davies, Llwynowen		
1 pair horn shoes	2	3
Morgan Jones, Lanlas		
Nailing 1 shoe	0	2½
William Davies, Llwyn Evan		
Nailing 1 shoe	0	2½
Jacob Jones		
Self New Shoes	1	4
Mary Hughes, Glanteify		
1 Shoe and nails		
Mrs. Davies, Beiliau		
Shoe	0	2
5th Mary Jones, Pantypistyll		
New gate fender	1	0
Evan Davies, Blaenwaun		
2 New horse shoe and nailing	1	6½
Mrs. Jones, Tanygroes		
Nailing 2 shoes	0	4
John Owen, Sychnant		
Hind craddle chain	0	8
Thomas Jones, Llanfair Mill		
3 gate hinges	1	0
6th John Davies, Penlan		
Mend pickas	0	9
Wm. Davies, Llwyn Evan		
Mend horn back strap links	0	3
Mrs. Davies, Beiliau		
Mend share and coulter	1	3
Joseph Jones, Llwynfedw		
Making new slate hammer	0	6

	s.	d.
Isaac Jones, Penllain		
Make new grindstone handle	o	1
David Davies, Penpompren		
1 shoe	o	2
Mr. Davies, Pistillinon		
Stalion nailing 2 shoe	o	6

The Aberaeron shovel and billhook have already been cited as examples of implements designed for particular local conditions. The Aberaeron shovel was well suited to the needs of a hilly country, and for beating the earth banks that are so characteristic of Celtic Britain, although its persistence to the present day, not only in Wales but in Devon, Cornwall and the Lake District, may be due to conservatism rather than for any practical reasons. The Aberaeron shovel is still made in Cardiganshire by Griff Jenkins of Cwrtnewydd and the tradition of the Aberaeron shovel works established in 1850 is still being continued.

But in addition to the Aberaeron forge, which attained some national fame, most other country blacksmiths were capable of producing the tools the farmers needed. Harvesting hooks, twelve inches in diameter for women and thirteen inches in diameter for men, were manufactured in considerable quantities, but no Welsh blacksmith was capable of producing totally satisfactory scythes. Plough-shares, mouldboards, coulters and indeed complete ploughs were made in the country smithies in many parts of Wales, and the Cardiganshire villages of Llanfi-hangel-y-Creuddyn, Sarnau, Maes-llyn, Ffostrasol and Betws (Y Lion) attained considerable fame for the quality of their ploughs in the last century. The mould-boards of these ploughs were well designed for ploughing sloping fields. In some cases mouldboards were designed by farmers and made by local blacksmiths. For example, in the eighteen-eighties David Evans of Rhydlewis, Cardiganshire, de-signed a mouldboard for turning a sod in one piece, and this was made by John Owens of Aberporth with mouldboards manufactured at the Bridgend Foundry, Cardigan.

Harrows, often wooden-framed implements with metal tines, were also manu-factured locally, and re-tining harrows or sharpening them was a task undertaken by blacksmiths for payment in kind rather than in money, as evidenced in the account book of Robert Phillips. A small stack of corn, known as *llafur golym*, was often given to the blacksmith in lieu of cash for this task. Payment, too, could be made by the hauling of coal to the smithy from the nearest coastal village or mine.

One of the most important tasks of all undertaken by smiths was that of completing the ironwork for carts. In binding tyres and making hub bands, body struts and axle irons most blacksmiths worked in conjunction with nearby wheelwrights. But in all cases the wheels brought to the forge for tyreing belonged to the wheelwright, who paid the blacksmith in cash for his services. The price of tyreing varied, but John Williams of Cellan in the eighteen-fifties charged six shillings a pair for banding a cart wheel; for making iron arms for attaching to wooden axles he also charged six shillings. A set of shaft irons cost four shillings, cart body irons three shillings, and hub bands two shillings.

Tyreing a wheel was a most complex process and many a tale is told of how country blacksmiths and wheelwrights, with tempers frayed, argued about the techniques of construction adopted by the other. To tyre a cart wheel, an open fire of wood shavings was made in the corner of the blacksmith's yard and wheel bands, cut to size, scarfed, bent and welded, were heated until they were almost white hot. Alternatively, if the forge hearth was wide enough, tyres were heated inside the smithy, while occasionally tall furnaces where four or more tyres were heated simultaneously were used. The wooden wheel was bolted down on the metal tyreing plate—a circular platform which may still be seen outside most smithies. The tyre, grasped with tongs, was dropped on the wheel, so that the wooden rim burst into flames. Before the fire could do any damage water was poured on to it and as it cooled the tyre contracted and became firmly fixed in place.

Not all blacksmiths were good shoeing smiths and farriers, but a large proportion of the time of most blacksmiths was concerned with making horseshoes and with shoeing. In one week in 1873, for example, John Williams of Cellan shod twenty-eight horses, the average charge for a set of shoes being two shillings and three pence. Farriery demands not only dexterity in shaping metal but considerable knowledge of the anatomy of the horse's foot, its diseases, and methods of curing those diseases. When a horse was brought to the smithy for shoeing the old shoes were removed and the hooves filed and carefully measured across. A rod of iron was then taken and a length equal to $3\frac{1}{2}$ times the diameter of the hoof cut off with cold chisel and sledge. Each rod was then heated in the fire, bent in the middle and shaped. With a punch, nail holes were made in the iron and the actual shoeing began. Occasionally a horse had to be felled for shoeing. After several reheatings, fittings and hammerings the farrier made sure that the shoe fitted the hoof. It was then nailed firmly in place. Great care had to be taken that the nails pointed outwards so as not to damage the sensitive flesh of the foot. With the light shoeing hammer the nails were knocked in and their points clenched as they emanated through the side of the hoof.

In the old days the special nails for fastening shoes were also made in the smithy. A rod of iron (*gwialen hoelon*), some eighteen feet long, was heated and cut to the required size on the cutting edge of the *hardy*, which was inserted in the anvil orifice. It was then inserted in the nail-heading tool, which consisted of a flat metal bar fitted at each end with a perforated knob. The perforation complied with the size and shape of the nail shank and was also countersunk to correspond to the nail head. After inserting the red-hot piece of metal in the nail hole, the tool was placed over the anvil orifice and the head hammered into shape. All that remained was to point the nail either with a rasp or on a pointing horse (*ceffyl pwyntio*).

The blacksmith's trade is one that has changed very greatly within the last thirty years. In the nineteen-twenties, for example, Elias Owens, who operated his blacksmith's shop in the north Ceredigion hamlet of Abermagwr until 1971, completed a two-year apprenticeship with Evan Williams of Beulah. Elias Owens was twenty-two years of age when he began this apprenticeship; he was not paid at all except for his board and lodging. A £12 bond was paid to the blacksmith. For the first few months the apprentice began with the simpler tasks, like removing nails from horses' hooves, filing hooves, and dismantling implements, and slowly graduated to other more complex tasks, so that by the end of two years Elias Owens was competent to deal with most of the tasks of a country blacksmith. After a further period of training as an improver at Beulah and as a journeyman with Ben Jones of Tregroes, Elias Owens moved to Abermagwr to work with Mr Jenkins in the Crosswood estate smithy. In 1930 he took over as a master blacksmith at Llanfihangel-y-Creuddyn and in 1934 he also took over the Abermagwr smithy, working three days at Llanfihangel and two at Abermagwr. By 1937 the Llanfihangel smithy had closed and Elias Owens spent all his time at Abermagwr.

The thirties were difficult times for country blacksmiths and many of them were forced to close, but 1939 and the war brought a new prosperity, although the nature of the work had changed considerably; most of the work now was repair and renovation of agricultural implements. In the twenties and thirties blacksmiths were concerned with such tasks as making gates, ploughs and harrows, with shoeing horses and tyreing wheels, as well as with decorative wrought-iron work. All these tasks were done with the minimum of machinery; the forge had to be blown by hand; iron had to be drilled, welded, and filed by hand; and the craftsman had to work long hours to make ends meet. At Beulah, for example, the working day was from 8 a.m. to 8 p.m., for the craftsman needed these long hours of work in order to complete huge orders from local farmers, orders that took a long time to complete because of the large amount of hand work that had to be done. Since 1945 conditions have changed, for although the blacksmiths draw their customers from a much wider area they complete their work at a much faster rate. Electric power has replaced hand work; the craftsman has electric drills, electric grinders, and screw-making machines; he has electric fans instead of the old hand-operated bellows; he has oxy-acetylene welding equipment and a great deal of other machinery that has helped to make his life less strenuous than in the past.

Another craftsman essential to the rural community was the saddler, and as recently as 1910 there were well over five hundred saddlers' shops in Wales. Indeed, so great was the demand for horse harness and other leather requirements that there were three categories of craftsmen engaged in the work. The first was the horse-collar maker, whose craft was more specialized than that of the harness maker, responsible for the production of straps, bridles and other pieces of harness. But the prince of all leather workers was the saddler himself, responsible for the intricate task of making saddles and little else. After the First World War, however, the work for the individual craftsman gradually declined, and it became necessary for those that remained in the trade to spread their activity and undertake work that once called for the services of three specialists; by 1918 the number of saddlers' shops in Wales had declined to 252. In addition to the saddlers that worked in market towns and country villages, Wales had a large number of travelling saddlers who possessed no workshops except the farm outhouse where they happened to be working during a particular week. There have been changes: the horse is no longer an essential animal on the farms of Wales. Consequently the number of saddlers has declined greatly and is today represented by no more than eight craftsmen. The popularity of horse riding has contributed to a considerable demand for the services of the saddler, but today it is a craft of the market towns—Cardigan, Brecon, Llangollen and Abergavenny—rather than a true rural industry (Pl. 108).

Some indication of the type of work carried out by country saddlers in more recent times may be obtained from the account books of William Edwards of Llangefni, Anglesey, for the period 1920–30. In 1921 for one farmer, a certain Peter Jones of Gwalchmai, for example, he completed the following work:

March	1 jar of black oil	2s.	0d.
	1 pair breeching straps	8	6
	1 halter	1	3
	New whip	2	6

		1 new harness strap	1s.	6d.
		2 new tugs for traces	1	3
		4 new halters at 1/3d. each	5	0
	May	Restitch front and nose band	1	6
		New felt to pad	1	6
		Curry combs 1/6 Dandy brush at 3/–	4	6

Or the account to Mr Evans, Castell, for June 1928:

	New panel to cart saddle	12	6
	New pad to cruper	2	6
	New piece to cruper	1	6
	Restitch cruper and buckle	1	6
	New strap	1	6
	Dec 14 paid.		

In the nineteen-twenties only minor pieces of harness were actually made by the saddler; his work was almost entirely concerned with repair and renovation.

It was not only farm requirements that were produced locally, but also domestic utensils, wearing apparel, furniture and most of the other essentials of day-to-day living. Although most domestic utensils were made of wood or pottery, tinwork has been known in country districts for many centuries, and although tinwork was produced by travelling tinkers the craft of tin smelting was well established in many country districts. Most of these craftsmen worked in the country towns such as Abergavenny, Carmarthen, Welshpool and Dolgellau, and they used tools and equipment that were quite different from those of other metal workers. They required presses and guillotines, heating irons and rollers to produce milking pails, water jacks, cooking dishes and cream separators that were essential in both town and country (Pls 55, 56). Although tinsmiths were to be found in most districts in the early nineteenth century, it was after 1860 that they really became numerous. In many areas the products of their shops replaced the traditional woodware that was so common in farm kitchen and dairy. The tinsmith certainly became a more important craftsman than the 'white cooper', who for centuries had been responsible for the production of milking pails, washing tubs, cheese vats and butter churns. In the industrial regions too, the tinsmith became a far more important craftsman in the nineteenth century, for it was his task to produce such essentials as oil cans and food boxes, tea jacks and milk vending cans, and many other essentials in an industrial community.

Of course, in most country districts, too, coopering was a widespread craft in the past and many wooden utensils were required in the kitchens and dairy

(Pl. 57). A cooper in the parish of Penbryn, Cardiganshire, in the eighteen-seventies produced the following utensils:

> Butter churns (plunger and barrel variety)
> Wash tubs
> Meat salting tubs (*noe*)
> Cheese vats
> Butter prints
> Wooden grain shovels
> Casks—mainly for butter and herring preservation.

Craftsmen of this type were known as 'white coopers', but in many parts of Wales by the end of the nineteenth century they had disappeared completely because of the falling off of demand for coopered utensils. They were of course capable of carrying out the work of the 'wet cooper', who was concerned with making casks to hold liquids. This was the most exacting of all woodcrafts, for not only did the staves in a cask have to fit exactly together so that the cask was watertight, but each cask had also to hold the exact intended contents of liquid. Oak was the only timber used in wet coopering, but for white coopering sycamore was widely used.

A craft that has almost completely disappeared within the last few years is that of clog making. In the past clogs were widely worn by miners and textile workers as well as by most country people in the north of England and in Wales, and in those regions the craft of the clog maker was widely practised. Every village and every rural locality had its own clog maker who was fully employed in making new clogs and repairing the old. Today, with the changes in fashion of the last few years, the clog maker is a rarity and only a few elderly representatives of the craft may still be seen at work in a trade that demands considerable knowledge not only of leatherwork but of woodwork as well.

The origin of the clog is lost in the mists of antiquity, but clogs were certainly worn by rich and poor alike in the Middle Ages. Their great advantage over other forms of footwear is the fact that they are warm and perfectly waterproof in all conditions. The thick wooden soles and iron rims keep the wearer's feet well above the level of a wet factory or dairy floor, while in muddy fields they are ideal. In theory at least, each clog is a perfect fit for the wearer, for the craftsman makes his clogs according to the shape, size and peculiarities of each person's feet. The wearing of clogs in Wales today is a thing of the past and although no more than twenty years ago men, women and children wore clogs habitually, today their clatter can rarely be heard on the roads and farmyards. Village craftsmen who not long ago obtained a livelihood from making and repairing clogs have had to give up work or spread their activity over a much wider field as boot repairers and retailers (Pl. 109).

In the heyday of the clog there were two distinct types of craftsmen engaged in the trade. First, there was the village clog maker, who in the main made footwear for a local market. He made clogs for each individual buyer, measuring the feet and making clogs to fit those feet. More often than not his village workshop was an important social centre of the community, and in Wales the clog maker's shop was regarded as being as important as the ubiquitous smithy or carpenter's shop. In the second category of craftsmen were the itinerant clog sole makers who undertook only the cutting and rough shaping of alder blocks ready for the clogging factories of Lancashire and Yorkshire. Their work of utilizing a local raw material has already been described (Pl. 110).

Although many clog makers were boot makers as well, in some districts the craft of boot making developed into an industry of considerable importance. The most renowned of all boot making centres in Wales was the small town of Llannerch-y-medd in Anglesey, which became the main area of concentration. Very little is known about the origins of this industry, which in 1833 employed as many as 250 workers, but it seems probable that, like the Amlwch tobacco industry, the cobblers of Llannerch-y-medd came into existence to supply the miners of Mynydd Parys and also the quarrymen of Caernarvonshire with footwear. Undoubtedly they were in existence before the beginning of the nineteenth century.

'They attended farms and markets in Anglesey and Caernarvonshire to sell boots that were transported in bags. This gave rise to the phrase "Bag boots" for poor examples. But the cobblers of Llan could produce some excellent boots, according to the evidence of an old man now nearing ninety years of age.'

Until the eighteen-sixties the boot making industry still flourished in Llannerch-y-medd. The craftsmen worked at a trade where only fashion had changed, for the techniques of boot making had altered little in hundreds of years. It was only during the last quarter of the nineteenth century that mechanization entered the boot-making industry and that may explain to a certain extent why it persisted so long in Anglesey. Woollen manufacturing, for example, was highly mechanized by the middle of the nineteenth century, but hand work and simple tools tarried much longer in boot making than almost any other industry. By the eighteen-seventies, however, Northamptonshire-made factory boots were widely available in Anglesey and the craftsmen boot makers of Llannerch-y-medd disappeared very rapidly. 'In praising Captain Pritchard Rayner, the Tory candidate

for the county in 1880, it is said that he provided work for as many as sixty
Llannerch-y-medd and Llangefni cobblers, who were on the brink of starvation
as a result of contraction in their industry.'

By far the most common of the craftsmen that met a local demand were the
carpenters and stonemasons, concerned with building as well as producing
articles made of stone or of wood required by the local community. The country
carpenter, in particular, was by tradition a versatile character able to make almost
anything in wood (Pl. 77). Carpenters were able to make agricultural tools,
furniture and domestic utensils, as well as to contribute to the building of
dwellings and their maintenance in a rural community. For example, amongst
entries in the account book of John Thomas of Rhostryfan, Caernarvonshire, for
1853 are the following entries:

Tresser [dresser]	£3	5	0
Gwely [bed]	1	8	0
2 fwrdd [tables]	1	3	0
Settle	0	7	0
Car Trol [2-wheeled cart]		14	0
Echel newydd [new axle]	1	7	0
Cafn mochyn [pig trough]	0	2	6
Ffram drws [door frame]	0	4	0
Gate		12	0
Coffor [cupboard]		5	0
Berfa newydd [wheelbarrow]		8	0
Trwsio esgyll corddwr [repair wings of churn]		1	0
Cwpwrdd gwydr [glass cupboard]		10	0
3 Cadair fedw [birch chairs]		15	0
Ffenestr [window]		2	6
Cwch gwenyn [bee hive]		1	6
Camogi olwyn [felloeing a wheel]		2	0
Aradr a shell boards [plough and mouldboard]		17	6
Arch plentyn [child's coffin]		7	6
Cryd [cradle]		6	0

Trusio ei dy [repair his house]	£3	10	0
Arch Mary Williams [Mary Williams's coffin]		17	0
. . . . .			
Corddwr [butter churn]	1	1	0
Gosod 3 pladur [fixing 3 scythes]		5	0
Bwrdd mawr [large table]		18	0
. . . . .			
Coedio y tŷ [timbering a house]	1	16	0
Dor y front [front door]		8	0
Dor y cefn [back door]		3	6
Ffenestri [windows]		7	6
Meinser [manger]		6	0.

Workers in stone were also essential in every country district, and quarrymen, who supplied the masons with their raw material, were vital in the economy. In most areas where suitable raw material occurred, there were quarries that provided the raw material for all building requirements in a district. Every type of stone has its own characteristics and in the past the methods of shaping and dressing the different types varied greatly from district to district. Many stone masons were capable of quarrying the stone as well as of dressing it. In most parts of Wales the mason has to deal with a great variety of stone of irregular shape and many different sizes. Unlike the bricklayer, he never deals with uniform blocks of building material; indeed in some districts, such as the Llŷn peninsula and the north Pembrokeshire coast, he may have to deal with rounded boulders of different sizes gathered from the seashore or river valleys. In other districts, such as Merioneth, the building material may be flat slabs of slate of different sizes, while colours may vary considerably from district to district. In rural west Wales, for example, much of the building stone is of a dull brownish-grey colour, considered unattractive to the eye. This led to the popularity of whitewashing the exterior walls of buildings; occasionally bull's blood, coal dust or yellow ochre was mixed with the whitewash to provide a variety of colour. Occasionally too, where fairly regularly shaped building stone was available it became customary to line the mortar in between the stones with whitewash, so that a grid-iron pattern of white stood out in sharp contrast to the dark background of grey stone.

All these craftsmen and many more were concerned with making the essentials of everyday life for a local community that hardly ever looked beyond its own boundaries for the means of life.

7 Woollen Manufacturing

The most widespread and the most important of Welsh rural industries is that of woollen manufacturing; indeed from the Middle Ages until the mid nineteenth century it was the most important single industry in Wales. The textile manufacturer, whether he worked in the home or in a factory building, was as essential to the rural community as the blacksmith or carpenter, for there was hardly a parish in the land that did not have its contingent of spinners and carders, weavers and fullers (Pls 61–70).

In some parts of the country the processing of wool and the manufacture of cloth went beyond the stage of supplying self-sufficient rural communities with essential products, for in those areas manufacturers were concerned with producing flannel and cloth that were exported to all parts of the world. The county of Montgomery in particular possessed the natural advantages of available raw materials and water supply that could have made it into a textile manufacturing region as important as the West Riding of Yorkshire. To understand the character and the personality of certain Welsh towns, a knowledge of their industrial background is essential. Newtown, the old borough of Llanfair-yng-Nghedewain, for example, became a 'new town' in the true sense of the term in the eighteenth century and the whole basis of the new-found prosperity was the woollen industry. It became so important that travellers to the district described it as the 'Leeds of Wales'. It attracted immigrant labour and lost the Welsh language in its rapid development as an industrial town.

To understand the distribution and production of the Welsh woollen industry, and indeed to understand the character of many a textile-producing town and village, one has to look at the past of a craft that is amongst the oldest in Wales. Its history may be traced back for two thousand years but it remains today as it has always been, a rural industry in a rural setting. In the Middle Ages woollen manufacturing was particularly important in the county of Pembroke, where natives and Flemish immigrants spun yarn and wove cloth in their cottage and farmhouse homes. At that time, cloth manufacturing was little more than a domestic activity, and the people of Pembrokeshire worked the wool of local sheep to provide themselves with blankets and rugs, tweeds and flannels. Occasionally there was a surplus that could be sold at one of the many local fairs, or be taken by ship from the nearest creek or bay to Bristol. From Bristol, Welsh cloth was re-exported at considerable profit by traders to Gascony and Brittany, to Portugal and Iceland. Although Pembrokeshire cloth was an important item of trade, its quality was not high; it was thick, rough and drab, being designed for hard wear rather than appearance. Indeed it was so bad that it was given to the poor people of English cities on Ash Wednesday.

By the end of the sixteenth century the demand for Pembrokeshire cloth had fallen off to such an extent that the industry itself almost completely disappeared from the county. But as cloth making in west Wales declined, that of Montgomeryshire, Merioneth and Denbighshire grew very rapidly. By the middle of the eighteenth century Montgomeryshire had attained pre-eminence as an important centre of flannel manufacturing.

In the sixteenth century Montgomeryshire, together with Merioneth and south Denbighshire, became the all-important centres of woollen manufacturing in Wales. Until the end of the eighteenth century, carding, spinning and weaving continued to be cottage pursuits as in previous centuries, but the process of fulling was carried out by machinery at well established fulling mills in all parts of the country. The wide distribution of the word *pandy* in Montgomeryshire place names points unmistakably to the importance of the fulling mill in the life of the county. Spinning on the other hand continued to be practised by women in the cottages and farmhouses of Powys. The only equipment required was a large spinning wheel, which could be bought for a few shillings. The spinners were also responsible for carding the raw wool, but here again the equipment was simple in the extreme, the simplest method being to use teazles or thistle heads. While the poorest cottager could afford a spinning wheel and cards, a loom was a different matter, for in the eighteenth century the cheapest would cost somewhere in the region of £2. Weaving on the farms of the Newtown district became important, and farmers hired servants not only for their skill in the fields, but also for their capabilities as weavers. One or two looms would be kept in an outhouse or lean-to shed known as *tŷ-gwŷdd* (loom house) for use when farm work slackened off in the winter. The loom house and the earlier fulling mills did in fact mark the beginning of the transfer of the woollen industry from homestead to factory.

Around 1800 the carding engine was introduced into Montgomeryshire and water power from an existing fulling mill or corn mill was often adapted for carding. In this manner, many fulling mills developed into small factories where the first and last processes of flannel manufacturing were carried out. The common adoption of this plan accounts in no small measure for the fact that many Montgomeryshire woollen factories were located on farm premises. During the first quarter of the nineteenth century another process, that of willying, the process of disentangling raw wool, also became a factory process with the introduction of the water-driven willy, or willow. The earliest factory in the Newtown district may be considered therefore as a building containing a willy, carding engine and fulling stocks and nothing more.

The next process to be mechanized was that of spinning, for although the spinning jenny was known in Montgomeryshire by the first decade of the nineteenth century it failed to oust the traditional spinning wheel and the age-old method of making yarn. Gradually, by the 1840s, jennies and hand mules were gaining in popularity and were taking their place with carding engines, willies, dyeing coppers and fulling stocks as pieces of factory equipment. Nevertheless, domestic spinning on the wheel continued for as long as woollen manufacturing was practised in Powys.

The highly skilled process of weaving did not immediately join the other processes of woollen manufacturing as a factory pursuit. Its development was somewhat different, for the weaver remained an independent craftsman for almost as long as the industry flourished. In the early nineteenth century it was an advantage for the weaver to locate his shop as near as possible to the source of supply, the carding and spinning factory. Gradually, a factory system entered the industry, and although weaving continued to be practised in remote farmhouses, Newtown, together with Llanidloes, attained considerable importance as centres of weaving. The tall, four-storeyed buildings that are characteristic of the older parts of Newtown bear witness to this day of the importance of hand-loom weaving in the history of the town. A weaving factory occupying the third and fourth floors of a building stretched over many dwellings and could be entered by an outside staircase at the back of the terrace. The owner of a weaving factory was often the owner of a shop at the end of a row, and his office was often behind the shop, which his wife ran. On applying for work a weaver was always asked for the number of persons in his family; the bigger the family, the better were his chances of obtaining work. On being paid on a Saturday night, usually at the average rate of 11 shillings a week in 1837, the weaver immediately bought what he required at the shop, the owner's wife keeping a large proportion of the earnings. This she took to the office, so that the employer needed only a small amount of money in hand to pay all his workers. Weaving factories and the old truck shops may still be seen in Newtown and an attempt is being made to record them, before they are demolished under a town modernization scheme.

In 1837 there were 74 weaving factories in Newtown. These accommodated 710 looms and employed 425 men, 227 women and 35 children. In addition to those employed at the weaving factories there were 245 weavers who valued their independence so much that they were willing to forgo the security of the handloom factory. There was plenty of jobbing work they could do at home, and even part-time weavers found plenty of scope for their activities. The prosperity of Newtown was reflected in the rapid rise in population:

1771 c.	800
1801	990
1811	2025
1821	3486
1831	4550

In 1821 a branch of the Shropshire canal reached Newtown and by 1825 there was a regular service between Newtown and Manchester, the journey taking six days at a cost of 2s. 11d. per hundredweight. The opening of the Newtown–Builth road in the same year made it possible to send flannel by cart and wagon to south Wales. In 1832 a Flannel Exchange was built at a cost of £4,000. This building is now the Regent cinema, but in its architectural style it is still the spacious and elegant public room described by Pigot in his *Directory* of 1835, 'which market is attended by merchants and shopkeepers from London, Manchester, Chester, Shrewsbury and various parts of the kingdom'.

Conditions in the weaving factories of Newtown during the second quarter of the nineteenth century were appalling. In evidence to the Commissioners on Handloom Weavers, who published their report in 1841, one weaver said: 'The weaver's is the most depressed of all trades . . . the men are underselling one another . . . the condition of the weaver is worse than it was some years ago.' Goods at truck shops were dearer than in other shops, masters and men were at variance and 'there is no daily school for the children of the poor'. In 1851 truck shops were still in operation, and the factory proprietors still managed to evade the Truck Act. 'Out of about thirty masters', says a contemporary writer, 'fourteen are directly interested in Tommy Shops and when a person goes to work for any of the above masters he is expected to take out all his provisions from his shop. . . . The masters take care not to pay their men until the market has been closed, thus virtually compelling them to take the whole of the articles consumed at their price.' Since many of the masters were farmers, weavers were often expected to help them with the harvest. 'Our masters can plant potatoes', said one weaver 'without paying anything for the work, except food for the men while they are at the job, and it is very often the case that they are not even allowed this miserable stipend.' It is no wonder that the flannel centres of Montgomeryshire were seed-beds of discontent during the 1830s and 1840s.

The period from approximately 1840 to 1880 was marked by the virtual extinction of the widely scattered domestic industry and a concentration of woollen manufacturing in the towns, Newtown and Llanidloes in particular. This came about as a result of the adoption of steam power to drive mules and looms, an innovation that in itself contributed to discontent and rioting among the handloom weavers of Powys. All the processes of woollen manufacture were amalgamated in single factories, and although the handloom weavers of Newtown struggled on till the 1880s, the mid nineteenth century was really the period of the large urban factory. By the early 1850s steam power was already in use in Newtown, despite the fact that the coal needed for firing the boilers had to be brought by canal and later by railway from the English Midlands. Large factories, all now empty shells, sprang up along the banks of the canal so that this sector of the town had the appearance of a factory estate. When the railway arrived in Newtown in the sixties, the largest of all the factories was built alongside it, but alas, despite the fact that vast sums of money were spent in building and equipping it, the factory was never used and it is empty to this day.

The sixties and seventies in particular were extremely difficult for the flannel manufacturers of Newtown: the handloom weavers were disappearing, factories closed down and the population was declining rapidly. 'The trade', says Worral's *Directory* of 1875, '. . . has declined, so that the production of the district is not one tenth of what it was 30 years ago.' In an attempt to counteract the decline in flannel making, the manufacturers of Newtown attempted to enter other fields, particularly that of shawl making. Perhaps the greatest mistake made by the woollen manufacturers in the mid nineteenth century was to compete with the manufacturers of Yorkshire and Lancashire on their own terms, with the result that there was very little to distinguish machine-made Montgomeryshire flannel from the products of Rochdale. The Welsh manufacturer did not possess the advantages of capital, plant, situation or the scale of production of the Lancashire industry.

The second half of the nineteenth century was dominated by the fact that the villages of the middle Teifi valley—Llandysul, Pentre-cwrt, Henllan, Dre-fach and Felindre in particular—became the main centres of woollen manufacturing in Wales. Although true prosperity was only short-lived, the history of textile manufacturing in the area goes back much further. Before the beginning of the nine-teenth century, flannel manufacturing was merely a domestic industry and con-ditions in the Teifi valley were no different from any other part of Wales. At the turn of the century, however, the woollen trade in Carmarthenshire was given considerable encouragement by the County Agricultural Society, who offered five annual premiums to cottagers, who 'having nothing to depend on but their day labour, who with assistance of their wives and children living with them, such children not being under 12 years old, shall spin the greatest quantity of yarn from the first day of January to the end of the same year'. Almost every year the pre-miums were won by someone from Dre-fach and Felindre in the parishes of Llangeler and Penboyr. Early in the nineteenth century, therefore, the rural parishes of Llangeler and Penboyr were already gaining some eminence as centres of a flourishing domestic industry. Cloth, which was hand woven in the home, could be taken to one of the four fulling mills established in the two parishes some time in the eighteenth century. There is no evidence to suggest that one person undertook all processes. Carding was carried out in the home, using locally manu-factured hand cards, while spinning was carried out by women on large-sized spinning wheels. Local carpenters could build a perfectly efficient spinning wheel for as little as five shillings, but buying a loom was a much more expensive busi-ness. In many cases the weavers were smallholders as well and some of the more prosperous even employed one or two weavers. Thus, some kind of factory system had already entered the weaving industry by the beginning of the nine-teenth century in the middle Teifi valley.

The Ogof factory, in the Esgair valley between the village of Felindre and the hamlet of Cwm-pen-graig, was originally a mud-walled thatched cottage on one floor a hundred yards from the banks of the Esgair. At the north end of the building was the dyeing room, measuring some ten feet square, which accommodated a pair of copper vats. In the centre was the two-roomed dwelling, while attached to it on the south side was the weaving room, measuring some twenty-five feet long and ten feet wide. This was entered by a door at the far end from the tenter field at the south. This weaving room must have accommodated four looms. It was only during the late 1880s that a new factory to deal with all the processes of woollen manufacturering was erected at Yr Ogof, and since the machinery for this mill was water-driven, the new factory had to be built close to the stream. Before that date the factory, in common with many others in the middle Teifi basin, was concerned entirely with weaving and dyeing finished cloth. As recently as 1898 there were nineteen specialized weaving factories in the parishes of Llangeler and Penboyr.

Although handloom weavers continued to operate in many parts of west Wales until the early years of the twentieth century, the greatest innovation, particularly in west Carmarthenshire and south-east Cardiganshire, was the introduction of power looms around 1850. The region entered a period of unprecedented prosperity, but a prosperity that was to last no more than sixty years. It is surprising that, while so many mills in other parts of Wales were forced to close down during the second half of the nineteenth century, such a marked expansion took place in the middle Teifi valley. Mills sprang up along the banks of every tributary of the Teifi and by the 1890s there was 'hardly a spot on any river bank where it would have been convenient to place another mill'. The centre of this new prosperity was again the parishes of Llangeler and Penboyr. A large proportion of the trade was aimed at the mining and metallurgical valleys of south Wales and the major part of the production was concerned with producing flannel for shirts and underwear for industrial workers.

While the introduction of power looms into the Montgomeryshire flannel industry meant its eclipse, the textile manufacturers of the Teifi valley thrived, once power machinery had been introduced. Both textile manufacturers and weavers from other districts migrated to the new industrial centre after 1850, but especially after 1870. As the industry in mid Wales declined, families moved to west Wales and entered the woollen industry. The Goodwin family who ran the Conwil factory at Cynwyl Elfed until 1939, for example, came to the district from Newtown in Montgomeryshire, while the textile machinery manufacturers of Dolgoch, Llanbryn-Mair, started a business in Carmarthen town in the 1880s. Prosperity continued unabated throughout the second half of the nineteenth century and is reflected in the rise in the population of the districts where the industry was located.

	Llangeler	*Penboyr*
1851	1681	1271
1861	1573	1146
1871	1611	1154
1881	1640	1284
1891	1880	1428
1901	1930	1381

The whole life of the villages of the area was tied up with textile manufacturing, and cultural, social and religious life flourished. Nevertheless the textile industry was not without its tribulations for there were pay disputes in 1872, 1873 and 1880, the workers being out of work for seventeen weeks in 1880. In 1891 there was the ever-present dispute of payment of weavers according to the length of warping wall. Manufacturers were anxious to extend the length of wall and their profits, with the result that the weaver's pay was diminished. This led to a bitter controversy, but the matter was never settled satisfactorily.

Many of the larger factories grew up near the railway, which brought coal for driving mill machinery and provided the means of transport for taking the finished products to the markets of the industrial regions. Although the smaller factories were still dependent on water power to drive machinery and all of them were located along the banks of streams, there was a tendency for new, larger factories to be established in villages near railway stations. The Carmarthen–Lampeter line opened in 1864 and within the next thirty years, woollen mills were opened at Pencader, Bronwydd Arms, Llanpumpsaint and Llanfihangel-ar-arth. The line between Pencader and Newcastle Emlyn was not opened until 1895, but a number of factories at Henllan, Llandysul and Pentre-cwrt as well as at Newcastle Emlyn itself were opened soon afterwards.

There was a parallel development in other districts, particularly in Pembrokeshire. At Narberth, for example, there were twelve woollen factories; the largest, Landmill, accommodated as many as forty power looms within it.

In order to sell their goods mill owners paid frequent visits to the industrial areas of south Wales to canvass for orders, but the owners of the smaller mills were often dependent on direct selling to the public at market stalls. Benjamin Jones, Ogof, Dre-fach, for example, attended fairs in the 1880s and 1890s at Llangyfelach near Swansea, Clydach, Llansamlet and Aberdare as well as those held in market towns in west Wales. Llangyfelach fair was considered particularly important and before the railway reached the nearby village of Henllan in 1895, the whole family would travel to Llangyfelach by horse and cart on the Monday, stay at a local inn, sell their wares on the Tuesday and Wednesday and travel back to Dre-fach on the Thursday.

The 1870s and 1880s were a period of great prosperity in the Teifi valley. 'The unhealthy and smoke filled cottages have disappeared', said a contemporary writer, 'and beautiful new houses have been built everywhere; craftsmen in many trades are more numerous and in constant work; the rateable value of the houses is so great that the burden on farmers has been lightened.'

During the second half of the nineteenth century the woollen industry was widespread throughout the counties of Pembroke, Cardigan and Carmarthen. In most cases mills were small, primitive and rural, being mainly concerned with supplying the local needs of an agricultural population. In Cardiganshire, for example, small mills were to be found along the banks of most westward-flowing

streams as well as in all the river valleys leading to the Teifi. In the north of the
county there was some concentration of the woollen industry at villages such as
Tal-y-bont. Along the banks of the Leri five small mills were built to manufacture
flannel for the lead miners of north Cardiganshire some time before 1810. The
Lerry Mills, which are still in production, employed as many as thirty workers
at the end of the nineteenth century.

For a short time west Wales, particularly the middle Teifi valley, enjoyed a
golden era as the most important textile manufacturing district in the whole of
Wales. It was a short-lived prosperity that did not really begin until the 1880s
and was to end shortly after the end of the First World War. During that period
there was a constant demand for the products of the looms; fortunes were amassed
by the owners of mills who could call on an adequate pool of cheap labour. In
such villages as Dre-fach, Pentre-cwrt and Llandysul, children soon followed their
parents to work at the textile mills; indeed mill owners expected that the children
of their employees should work in the textile factories even before their schooldays were over. For example, children in the Cwm Morgan district were expected
to work at one of the local mills as soon as they were ten years of age, mainly to
look after carding machines. The hours of work were from five until eight in the
evening, for which they were paid threepence an evening in 1907. In addition
they were expected to work on Saturday mornings from 8 a.m. until 1 p.m., for
which they were paid fourpence. As soon as schooldays were over, children were
expected to become full-time employees at one of the mills. In the early years of
the present century there are many tales of victimization where weavers were dismissed from employment for refusing to allow their children to work in mills,
which were often cold and damp. 'Very few of the children of weavers were ever
given any secondary education,' said one informant. One mill owner, on being told
that a certain weaver's child would not be coming to work at a certain factory,
said: 'If your boy doesn't come here to work, then there is no room for you. Go
and find another job.'

Apprenticeship as a textile worker lasted for three years and it was customary
in west Wales to have one apprentice to every four experienced weavers. During
the first years, the apprentice did nothing at all except look after the carding
engines and in the early years of this century he was paid at the rate of tenpence
a day for a six-day week. The working day lasted for twelve hours, the workers
starting at 7 a.m. or 8 a.m. Around 1907, when it became customary to work a
five and a half day week, some of the workers were still expected to work a full
six days. Dyeing and washing, for which little machinery was required, were the
usual tasks performed on Saturday afternoons despite the fact that Inspectors of

Factories paid frequent visits to the mills to make sure that no young persons were employed after 1 p.m. on Saturdays. The women were expected to take shawls and blankets to their homes for hemming and fringing over the weekend. In the 1900s there was considerable discontent in the factories of the middle Teifi valley because mill owners refused to start paying their employees until the end of the working week at 1 p.m. on Saturdays and payment was often not completed until 3 p.m. The wages paid to experienced workers were not high: spinners were paid at the rate of eighteen shillings per week rising to a maximum of twenty-five shillings after some five years' service; weavers on the other hand were paid a piece-rate wage, ranging from one penny to eighteen pence a yard according to the factory. Within each factory, except the smallest, there was a distinct division of labour, for as well as spinners and weavers, other people were required for carding, dyeing, fulling and finishing.

In addition to wool brought into the factories by farmers, the mill owners obtained a large proportion of their supplies from wool auctions and from merchants. There was a considerable variation in the quality of wools in west Wales. That bought at Llanybydder and Newcastle Emlyn and the Preseli foothills was considered far superior to wool bought from the mountain district of north Pembrokeshire and mid Cardiganshire, the wool of lowland sheep being less kempy than that of mountain sheep. Wool from the coastal districts of Pembrokeshire and Cardiganshire was not greatly favoured, for it usually contained quantities of sand, which not only added to the weight of each fleece but could also cause considerable damage to carding and spinning machinery.

The woollen industry, with its dependence on the industrial market of south Wales, flourished until the end of the First World War; indeed during the period 1914–18 the price of wool reached a record level. The end of the War spelt disaster; the price of wool fell from 4s. 6d. a pound to 9d. a pound within the space of a few months. This was a fall that the small mills could not face and dozens were forced to close down. The consequences of this situation were reflected in the conditions and appearance of the countryside. Improvements to dwellings were at a standstill, buildings decayed and many were completely abandoned. Bankruptcy faced many mill owners and all were preoccupied with the task of making ends meet. Weavers were dismissed because wages could not be paid and there was a wholesale exodus to the towns and industrial regions. Chapels, grocery stores, public houses and craft workshops closed by the dozen and organizations such as choirs, dramatic societies and brass bands ceased to exist. During the decade 1918–28 fourteen of the factories experienced disastrous fires and only two were rebuilt. In Dre-fach and Felindre alone, out of a total of fifty mills in

1900, at least twenty ceased to function in the period immediately following the First World War.

Since the nineteen-twenties the Welsh woollen industry has steadily declined, with the number of mills decreasing from 250 in 1926, to 81 in 1947, and to 24 in 1974. Within the last twenty-four years the position has gone from bad to worse with even the large and modernized mills going out of production. Although the market for Welsh textiles has been extended considerably, particularly with the introduction of double weave ('tapestry') bedcovers, furnishing fabrics and light tweeds, the number of mills supplying that market has declined alarmingly. One of the main reasons for the decline has been the difficulty experienced by mill owners in recruiting labour, for every factory in Wales, with two notable exceptions, employs less labour than it did twenty years ago. Wages in the woollen industry compare very unfavourably with those paid in other occupations.

At the other end of the scale, when factory owners have wished to retire, they have experienced great difficulty in selling their mills, and consequently for this reason alone a number have ceased production. Within the next ten years at least six or more Welsh mills are in danger of closing because of the advancing age of their owners, and in all cases there is no obvious successor to take over. On the other hand, there are many mills in Wales that are highly successful and have an assured future. Continuity is assured by the presence of young or middle-aged owners who are ready to meet the challenge of changing fashions, by producing and selling well designed goods that are as good as anything produced in Europe.

The so-called 'traditional Welsh costume' has a very short history indeed and that seen at *eisteddfodau* and folk festivals today is almost entirely a creation of fancy; it is the costume of carnival rather than true peasant dress. Ffransis Payne in his paper 'Welsh Peasant Costume' has stated that:

'In all the enormous mass of evidence I have never met with any suggestion of a national costume for either men or women. There is no evidence that Welsh people of position, or of substance dressed differently from those of similar rank in other countries. . . . Down into the eighteenth century, I have never found anything specifically or characteristically Welsh in the garments described. Ordinary folk too, in so far as they were able, followed the fashion, even though they followed it from afar.'

From the second half of the eighteenth century, however, one can see the retention of a form of female dress that was well divorced from contemporary fashion; this was a form of dress popular in many parts of the country including Wales. Payne again, in describing a London tradesman's life illustrated by Wenceslaus Hollar in 1649, says: 'Here we have the open fronted gown, its skirt hitched back displaying the petticoat. Then there is the long apron protecting the petticoat front. The wide bertha or collar covers the low neckline exactly as the neckerchief and small shawls of Welsh costume were to do.'

In 1834 a formidable romantic Englishwoman, Mrs Augusta Hall, Lady Llanover, won a prize at the Gwent and Dyfed Royal Eisteddfod for her essay 'The Advantages Resulting from the Preservation of the Welsh Language and National Costume of Wales'. She upheld the use of heavy Welsh flannel for dresses and deplored the use of more colourful and lighter materials. On her Monmouthshire estates she even set up a woollen mill to produce the 'traditional' heavy flannels of Wales. She and her friends offered prizes in the *eisteddfodau* from the eighteen-thirties onwards for flannel, woollen stockings, cloaks and beaver hats.

'There were', says Payne, 'ten such competitions in the Abergavenny Eisteddfod of 1853. Lady Llanover offered a prize of £5 for the best collection of patterns of Welsh flannels, "in real National checks and stripes with the Welsh names by which they are known ... no specimens to be included which have not been well known for at least half a century. The object of the prize is to authenticate the real old checks and stripes of Wales and to preserve them ... distinct from new fancy patterns. ..." '

It is very significant that no one was worthy of the prize. No one could have won it because there were not any 'real national' checks and stripes. It is to be doubted indeed whether there were many such things in the whole of western Europe.

But even if there were no ancient and traditional patterns, the zeal and influence of this determined lady were such that the country did not mind being persuaded that these patterns did exist. Lady Llanover persuaded her friends from the country houses of Monmouthshire, Glamorgan and Brecknock and elsewhere to dress in this fashion at the *eisteddfodau* and upon other public occasions. Lady Llanover does not appear to have taken as much interest in a national costume for men apart, that is, from some members of her household staff at Llanover. We have in the Welsh Folk Museum the weird and wonderful costume that was fashioned for Grufudd, one of her domestic harpists.

Lady Llanover lost her battle for flannel and wool alone, but her labours left their mark on some other causes. I think it can fairly be said that it was she who turned farm servants' working clothes into a conscious, or rather selfconscious, national costume. Indirectly, too, she left her mark on efforts that were being made to attract tourists to Wales.

By the end of the nineteenth century Welsh costume had become the stereotyped dress of the postcard makers, aimed at a tourist market. Blouse and skirt replaced the bedgown; a paisley shawl replaced the flannel shawl; and the 'models' used by early photographers 'were always ready when the camera called to weave garters, spin wool, collect eggs, knit or draw up their chairs to yet another open-air tea table' (Pl. 99).

Payne sums the history of Welsh costume as follows, 'In the early part of the nineteenth century, the efforts of Lady Llanover and her friends had given new life and a new significance to an old rural costume that had hardly anything specifically Welsh about it and, here, towards the end of the century, we see this later, commercial activity doing much the same kind of thing.' Yet the objects of these two movements were poles apart. The earlier was addressed almost entirely to the Welsh people themselves; but the later movement was directed at the English.

Lady Llanover wished to see all the people of Wales, the rich man in his mansion and the poor cottager who worked for him, Welsh in speech and custom—and costume. On the other hand, all this later business about what were now obsolete customs, phoney costumes, souvenirs and comic postcards was a condition of a sickness, endemic in a bilingual community such as was emerging in late nineteenth-century Wales.

And so, at the end of the century, all over Wales people began to interest themselves anew in a so-called national dress that had disappeared. There was not much interest in the harsh and ugly garments that occasionally survived from earlier in the century. 'It was the false and prettified ones of the studio portraits that were attractive.'

8 Leather Working

The availability of raw material brought into being the most important and widespread of rural industries: that of textile manufacturing. Second in importance to the woollen industry was that of leather manufacturing, a well distributed rural industry that used the skins of Welsh cattle and sheep to produce leather that was exported from Wales to other parts of Britain for use in the boot-making, saddlery and harness industries. Not only did Wales possess the raw material that was essential in the industry, but it also possessed a number of other materials essential for the functioning of that industry. Bark from the stunted oak trees of the Welsh hills was regarded as being particularly rich in tannin, the chemical agent responsible for the conversion of a hide into a piece of leather. Welsh mountain sheep, long regarded as providing the best of meat for the table, provided a plentiful supply of tallow, required for the dressing of certain types of leather. In addition clean water from the mountain streams ensured that the tanned skins were not discoloured by impure water.

As a result of all these natural advantages the tanning industry became as commonplace in Wales as the saddlery and boot-making trades that the tanning industry supplied. The industry became particularly important in Welsh market towns, where there were ample supplies of cattle and sheep in the hinterland to supply the tanneries with raw materials.

The old country tanyards obtained their hides from a variety of sources. In some cases they purchased hides from the slaughter-houses of large cities such as Manchester, the Scotch heifer hides being particularly sought after. In other cases they obtained hides from the fellmongers who bought them from local abattoirs or farms. Sometimes, too, the tanner acted as his own fellmonger and bought hides directly from the butchers. All the hides obtained from these sources were known as slaughter or market hides and they arrived at the tannery in a moist, soft condition, often covered with blood and dirt. From the mid nineteenth century, imported hides were widely used by Welsh tanners. These arrived in two conditions: as dry salted hides or as wet salted hides, tightly packed in large barrels, and before they could be tanned, all traces of salt had to be removed. In addition some tanners also used sun-dried or flint hides.

In many Welsh tanneries it was customary to keep one or two large mastiff dogs, and it is said that as soon as market hides were delivered to the tanyard, each one was pegged to the ground so that the dogs could bite off any fats and flesh that adhered to the skins. The mastiffs were, of course, useful to guard the premises and to keep control of the vast number of rats that always infested tanneries. In addition the dogs' excreta when mixed with hot water was essential for treating certain types of soft leather before tanning.

The first process in the lengthy business of tanning was to cleanse each hide in the water pit. Blood had to be removed from market hides because the presence of blood in leather leaves dark stains and bad grain, while all traces of salt had to be removed from imported hides. The water pit, measuring some seven feet square and nine feet deep, received a constant supply of clear water, while the presence of an overflow pipe ensured a gentle movement of the water. In addition to removing impurities, the water bath had the effect of swelling up the fibres of the hide, bringing them back as near as possible to the condition in which they left the animal's back.

After being washed, the hides were placed in one of three lime pits, each one containing a solution of lime and water. The first pit usually contained a weak solution of old lime, highly charged with bacteria; the second pit contained a less mellow solution while the third contained almost new lime. The length of time that hides remained in lime depended entirely on the quality of leather required, for the softer the leather, the longer the hide remained in the pit and the mellower the solution. For example, hides designed for sole leather had to be hard and tough and eight or ten days in fairly new lime was sufficient. Harness leather, on the other hand, had to be much more pliable and required mellow liming of twelve days or more, while soft shoe-upper leather required anything up to six weeks in old and mellow lime. The skins were either suspended by chains from the side of the pits or were allowed to float in the lime solution, but the main object of liming was to loosen the hair and epidermis of the hide. These were then removed by special knives, leaving the corium, the central layer of skin, which had to be preserved. The craftsman responsible for these cleaning processes was known as a beamsman and he worked in a special building designed for the purpose, known as a Beam House. At the Rhaeadr tannery, now at the Welsh Folk Museum (Pl. 104), this was a low building measuring some twenty feet long. The tanner's beam is a steeply sloping working table of wood and cast iron, convex in section, over which the hide is thrown for dehairing and fleshing (Pl. 130). The unhairing knife is a somewhat blunt, narrow-bladed, two-handled tool which the craftsman used by pushing downwards against the hide. It was considered essential to remove as much as possible of the hair root sheaths and fat glands, which could discolour the leather.

After removal of the hair, hides were thrown into cold water so that they swelled a little, and then underwent the operation of fleshing. This again was done over the beam and the knife used was a double-edged fleshing knife. The concave edge of this was for scraping while the much sharper convex blade was for cutting. Finally, fine hairs were removed with a very sharp butcher's knife.

So far the treatment of all skins, from the lightest glove leathers to the heaviest sole leathers, was similar in principle, but from fleshing onwards there was a great diversion in technique. Lighter hides for boot uppers, for example, were placed in a solution of hen and pigeon manure or dog excreta and water to mellow and soften. Great care had to be taken not to leave them in these mastering pits for too long, for the solution would rapidly reduce the substance of the hides. Other hides were not mastered in this way, but they were again placed on the beam and all traces of lime removed from them with the slate-bladed scudding knife. Before tanning, too, each hide had to be cut up or rounded with a sharp butcher's knife, for the degree of tanning required for the different parts of the hide varied considerably. For example, the butt of a skin is close grained while the offal is loose and coarse. If both were placed in the same tan pit, the best tannin would be soaked up very quickly by the open-pored offal. After rounding, the irregular pieces of hide that were considered uneconomic to tan, together with the fleshings, were thrown into a pit to be taken away as raw material for glue and gelatine manufacturers.

After scudding and mastering and rinsing through water or weak acid, the tanning process proper began.

To make the tanning liquor, the craftsman needed a vast quantity of oak bark, ground finely and mixed with cold water. In the past, oak was especially grown in coppices, and the bark was harvested after some twenty-five or thirty years' growth. The coppicing of oak trees for bark was an extremely expensive process, for vast quantities of bark were required by every tannery. Some eighteenth-century Welsh farmers regarded the production of oak bark as an essential part of the farm economy and the demand for good quality bark at that time was very large indeed. In more recent times, bark was obtained as a by-product of winter-felled oak trees, or of those felled during the spring months. It was far easier to remove the bark from spring-felled oak and the method of stripping was to score the tree at intervals of some twenty-four inches with a hatchet or bark knife.

Vertical slits were then made with the bark knife and large semi-cylindrical plates of bark levered off. As tannin is soluble in water, the plates of bark had to be stacked in such a way that the rain did not penetrate them (Pl. 103). Barking was a task often undertaken by women and children, who sold the bark to the tanneries, and the oaks of Brecknockshire and Herefordshire were considered especially rich in tannin.

One of the most unpopular tasks in the old tanyards was that of grinding oak bark, for the fine dust emanating from the bark mills penetrated everywhere. The large, dried plates of bark were placed in the hopper of the water-driven grinding mill and pushed down between the rapidly revolving cutters of the mill. At the Rhaeadr tannery, the bark shed was a very large high building and in the hey-day of tanning it was kept full of ground and unground bark collected from the forests of mid Wales and the Border counties. The ground bark was carried in large baskets from the mill to the series of leaching pits where the tanning liquid was made by adding cold water to the bark. Occasionally, some other vegetable matter such as gambier, valonia or sumac was added to the oak bark in order to hasten the tanning process. The tanning liquor was then pumped from the leaching pits to the others in the yard and tannage began.

The butts, as unsplit hides are called, were first placed in the suspender pits, a series of eight or ten pits containing the weakest liquors in the tanyard. Each hide was tied to a string and attached to sticks laid across the top of the pit, while a more modern method was to tie the hides to a wooden framework or roller which could be moved gently to and fro to ensure an even flow of tanning liquors. The hides were moved daily from one pit to the other, the liquors becoming progressively stronger from one pit to the next. The tanner had to be very careful that the hides did not touch one another in the suspender pits or they would display touch marks and be of uneven colour.

At the end of the suspender stage, the butts with all traces of lime removed would be soft and porous, and they had to be laid flat to straighten out lumps and creases, before being placed in the next set of pits—the handlers or floaters. Here the hides were laid flat rather than suspended and were moved from one pit to the other at regular intervals of two or three days. Tanneries had twelve or more of these handlers, and each contained stronger liquor than the one before it. A bucketful of finely ground bark was often added to the liquor in these pits so as to increase its strength. A long-handled wooden plunger was used to distribute the bark dust evenly throughout the pit, while the spent liquors were pumped back to the suspenders. In the handling pits the hides were moved from one to the other by means of long-handled tongs or steel hooks (Pl. 105).

Cilewent, a sixteenth-ry long house from ryn Claerwen, Radnor-.

Well maintained long-w thatched roof on a age at St Nicholas, morgan.

Built to withstand the lantic gales: Rhos on Isaf, Davids.

74. North Wales oak d...
from Caernarvonshire, a...
from the mid-eighteenth cen...

75. South Wales oak dresser...
open superstructure and pot...
below; an early eighteenth-ce...
example from the Swansea V...

FURNITURE

76. An oak chest of thirteenth-century type,
although this one was made in the seventeenth
century.

77. Oak mule chest, early eighteenth
century.

78. *Court cupboard, or buffet, early seventeenth century; from Tredegar Park, Monmouthshire.*

THE COLLECTION OF THE WELSH FOLK MUSEUM.

79. *Court cupboard of the first quarter of the seventeenth century, from Monmouthshire.*

80. Cwpwrdd tridarn *of 1677 from Harlech, Merioneth.*

81. Cwpwrdd deuddarn *of 1702, from Blackwood, Monmouthshire.*

82. Tallboy *of the mid-eighteenth century, from Glamorgan.*

83. Panelled oak chair, a direct development from the medieval chest. This dates from the early sixteenth century and comes from Pembrokeshire.

84. Turned oak chair with triangular seat, early sixteenth century, from Wenvoe, Glamorgan.

86. Oak chair bearing many characteristics of the Tudor period but dating from the early seventeenth century; from Nannau, Dolgellau, Merionethshire.

85. Turned oak chair of about 1550, from Tre-gib, Llandeilo, Carmarthenshire.

87. Side table and benches, second half of the seventeenth century; from Bargoed, Glamorgan.

88. Oak bed at Kennixton farmhouse, Welsh Folk Museum.

89. Sampler of 1823. The embroidering of samp was widely practised in Wales until the late nteenth century. Girls were taught the elements needlework and the alphabet in this way.

90. Egg clappers for collecting eggs at Easter, Anglesey.

91. The wren house used in the New Year celebrations, especially in Pembrokeshire. This one was used in the village of Marloes.

92. The Mari Lwyd at Llangynwyd.

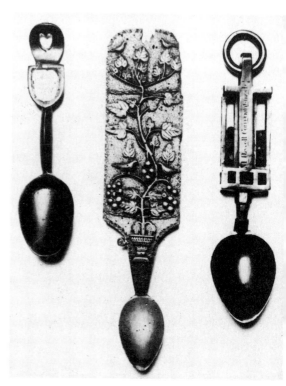

93. *A wassail bowl used in connection with the* Mari Lwyd *ceremony in Glamorgan. This bowl was made at the Ewenni pottery.*

94. *Love spoons*

95. *The harvest knot—*Y gaseg ben fedi—*made from the last sheaf and designed to be hung from a kitchen rafter as a symbol of the continuity of the crop.*

96. *Dog tongs used at Clynnog Church, Caernarvonshire, for removing stray dogs from church services.*

After some weeks of moving through the series of handlers, the hides then passed to the final set of pits, the layers, which contained the strongest liquors in the yard. Each hide was in this case sprinkled with finely ground oak bark so that each one was saturated with tannin as it sank to the bottom of the pit. Occasionally, the liquor in the layer was pumped off, and partially exhausted vegetable matter removed for further extraction. The hides were then returned to a new liquor until they could absorb no more tannin, a process that took anything up to six weeks.

After the last layer, the fully tanned hides were washed in a weaker solution before being sent to the drying sheds. Before drying, the hides were very lightly oiled with crude cod-liver oil and allowed to dry slowly and evenly. When half dry, they were laid out in a pile with sacks in between each hide and then pinned with the striking pin. This is a triangular bladed, two-handled knife, designed to remove all irregular marks from the hide. Once again the hides were dried, and in order to knit the fibres together they were placed over a heavy roller. They were usually rolled three times, with a period of drying between each rolling. The whole process of finishing took at least a fortnight and the craftsman had to take great care with the temperature of the drying shed.

The tanning of leather was a highly complex chemical process and it is surprising how much of these complexities our forefathers knew. A piece of skin would remain in the tanyard for eighteen months and more before it was converted into leather.

Before a piece of tanned leather can be sold to the saddler or boot maker, it has to pass through the hands of another craftsman—the currier, whose task it is to make it more supple and highly polished. While the tanner's craft is one where considerable knowledge of chemical processes is required, that of the currier is a craft demanding a high degree of skill in the use of hand tools that are entirely different from those used by any other leather worker. The tanner could not complete his work without the assistance of the currier, for tanned leather is stiff and badly coloured. Although in more recent times tanning and currying were carried out on the same premises by highly skilled, though separate and specialized craftsmen, in earlier times the craft of tanning and the craft of currying were always independent and separate. At the Rhaeadr tannery in the late nineteenth and early twentieth centuries, for example, both crafts were carried out under the same roof, but before 1850 the currier's shop was situated half a mile away from the tannery. Again, the mining town of Ystalyfera had its currier's shop until the 1920s, but the nearest tannery was at Brecon, some thirty miles away. The peculiarities of the leather trade in Britain were the result of legislative interference which decreed it illegal to carry on together the two trades of tanning and currying. Thus two operations, which are naturally a part of one process, became separated and leather was dried out by the tanner, taken to the currying shop and then wetted again by the currier.

After delivery from the tanyard, the currier's task is to prepare the leather for dyeing or polishing by removing the 'bloom' and the dried tanning liquor that clogs up the grain. The hide is soaked and softened in a hot sumac bath and is then laid on a large mahogany table and scoured with a hard brush, possibly using soap and large quantities of water. To force out the dirt retained just under the hair roots or just below the grain layer, the currier uses a peculiar knife called a slicker, which is simply a flat steel blade some six inches wide and four inches deep set in a wooden handle. The handle is grasped with both hands and rubbed with considerable pressure against the surface of the hide until all the impurities are removed. In modern tanneries, a striking machine is used for removing bloom. After staking and scouring, the hides are partially dried, or 'sammed', by pressing or squeezing between rollers. The sammying machine, with its pair of heavy rollers pressing against each other with considerable force, was an innovation of the late nineteenth century, but the traditional method of sammying, which persisted until recent times in some tanneries, was the heavy brass roller (Pl. 107). This is some fifteen inches wide with the roller some eight inches in diameter and it usually required two men to pull and push it over the rolling platform. The platform itself, usually some eight feet square, had a surface of wood or of sheet zinc and it was a feature of all currying shops.

Perhaps the most skilled and intricate of all the currier's tasks is the hand shaving or splitting of sammed hides. This is done on a heavy upright beam faced with glass or lignum vitae, and is undertaken with the peculiarly shaped working knife. This consists of a heavy, rectangular blade some ten or twelve inches long and six inches deep. It is made of soft steel held by a bar down the centre which carried a handle at each end; one handle is in line with the bar and the other at right angles to it. The knife is first of all ground to a sharp edge and set on a 'Water of Ayr stone' (a whetstone). It is then placed between the knees, with the cross-wise handle resting on the ground, and the edge is gradually turned to a right angle. This is done by rubbing a smooth steel, held with both hands, with considerable pressure against the blade. This is pressed over the edge of the hide, first outside and then down the angle formed by the blade. A thin shaving of leather on the flesh side is then removed and the hide is ready to receive oils and grease.

The process of impregnating leather with grease is known as 'stuffing' and the traditional method is to dampen the leather and then apply a thick layer of dubbing to one or both sides. Dubbing itself is a mixture of tallow, preferably that from mountain sheep, and cod oil, which in the past was imported from Newfoundland in large casks. These are boiled in a large cauldron and allowed to cool before use. The dubbing is applied with a brush known as a 'drumming brush' and the hide is allowed to dry slowly at a moderate temperature. As the water evaporates, the fat becomes thoroughly distributed over the fibres, but the harder fats called 'table grease' are left on the surface and have to be removed with a sleaker.

After drying, the flesh side of the hide has to be whitened with a steel sleaker that has a slightly turned edge to remove surplus grease and smooth the surface. The whitening table itself consists of a sheet of plate glass in a wooden frame, which is placed over the currier's mahogany table; unlike the scouring sleaker, which it resembles in general shape, the whitening sleaker is used with a near-circular motion rather than in an up and down movement.

The tools for softening leather and for the finishing processes vary considerably. If, for example, the leather as it comes from the tannery is very stiff, it has to be softened on a stake. This consists of a thin half-moon knife blade some six inches wide fixed to the top of a wooden stake some thirty inches long. The leather is pulled backwards and forwards over this stake until it is soft and all the irregularities removed. For softening white leather made from horse hide and required for thonging, a T-shaped hand staker, again with a half-moon blade, is used. Finishing processes differ according to the kind of leather that is being processed. For taking marks out of shoe upper leather and harness leather, a stone sleaker is used, while for calfskins finishing is done with a sizing pad—a tool some eight inches long that consists of a wooden block with soft leather nailed to it. Again for waxed goods, particularly calfskin, a grain is raised by boarding with a rectangular cork board. This is rubbed lengthways and across the hide for a considerable period of time; it is then passed from corner to corner so that a pebbled grain of no definite form results. For ordinary shoe upper leather the hide is polished and the grain applied with a rectangular mahogany board, which is rubbed over the hide with the forearm. Indeed many old craftsmen believed that the best polished surface of all could be obtained by rubbing the flabby, bare forearm over the leather. It is said that in the past a good currier often was recognizable by the fact that his forearm was coloured a near-black.

The blacking of waxed goods is done on the flesh side with a mixture of lamp-black and oil, applied to the surface with a circular colouring brush. Smuts are removed with an oval smutting brush, and the hide is smoothed and brightened with the forearm or by rubbing with a smooth, thick glass sleaker. Leather in which the grain side is blacked is brush dyed and the grain raised by boarding.

There are, of course, numerous variations in the currying of leather. True Morocco leather of goatskin, for example, has to be tanned with sumac, oiled, dried and then grained with a cork board and finally stretched on a frame. Oil or chamois leather is freely impregnated with fish oil, pressed and washed in alkaline solutions, while calf kid is glazed with flour, egg yolk and oil.

The currier's craft is a very ancient one, for in prehistoric times primitive man knew all the secrets of treating stiff hides with oils and specialized equipment. Indeed, the technique of currying changed but little in thousands of years and it is only within the last seventy years with the popularity of chrome leather that the requirements of leather dressing have changed to any great extent.

9 Cottage and Farmhouse Homes

The traditional houses of rural Wales owe their design and layout to a complex interaction of geological, geographical, economic and social factors. The nature of the climate, the conditions of local geology and the availability of suitable building materials have their effect on determining the type of house found in a particular region. In the past, the countryman built his home from the materials occurring locally; he often designed his own home; he built it according to his needs; and he considered primarily not architectural beauty of design but the utility of the building. In so doing, the countryman followed no particular style or fashion that was prevalent in other districts at the time. In the Llŷn peninsula, for example, much of the surface of the land is covered with coarse boulder clay and in many parts of the peninsula there is little suitable building stone; from time immemorial, therefore, the peasant farmers of the district utilized earth intermixed with straw, cow dung and other commodities for the construction of the walls and floors of their cottage homes. In south Cardiganshire, to quote another example, mud-walled cottages were commonplace until the mid nineteenth century, but if the countryman lived in close proximity to the sea, well rounded pebbles from the shore were used to construct an uneven cobbled floor. Roofs were thatched with wheat straw or sometimes with heather, rushes or gorse. During the eighteenth century, however, roofing slates were imported by sea and small stone quarries supplied raw materials especially for farmhouses. Although by the beginning of the nineteenth century stone buildings had become fairly common, the cost in labour, money and time of extracting those stones was so great that the poorer section of the community could not afford them. For the cottager, mud-walled homes were still the order of the day until well on into the nineteenth century.

Wales, as has been said, is predominantly a high moorland plateau dissected by deep river valleys that branch out from the central core. Along the valleys that run eastwards, many alien influences entered the Principality. Along these valleys, for example, came the English four-wheeled farm wagon, English short-handled spades and even the English language. Along the valleys too came the vernacular buildings of Herefordshire, Shropshire and Cheshire—along valleys where the oak tree predominates. In these oak-growing river valleys of the Welsh borderland the half-timbered house predominates, and this attractive form of dwelling is found in such valleys as that of the Severn, crossing the watershed almost to the shores of Cardigan Bay; the Wye valley nearly to the heart of the Plynlimon range, and the Dee valley almost to the source of the river at Bala.

Abernodwydd, a Montgomeryshire half-timbered house preserved at the Welsh Folk Museum, St Fagans, is typical of this 'Border' tradition. This is a timber-framed house of the late sixteenth century, the timber framing being placed on a solid stone foundation. The panels of the framework were all wattled with hazel rods, daubed with clay and finished with a coating of plaster.

'The house has two roof trusses, the ridge piece extending from truss to truss, with a hip at each end. These trusses were placed above the two original partitions of the house, i.e. the house was three-roomed divided ... by wattle and daub partitions. There was no chimney, the fireplace being in the centre of the floor of the central room, the smoke finding its way out through the doorway and windows.'

In the seventeenth century a fireplace of the open-hearth type was installed.

Llanidloes, a small Montgomeryshire town, was described in 1798 as a 'town of houses built with laths and mud filling up the intermediate spaces of a timber frame'; and in 1822 as 'a mean town, composed chiefly of lath and plaster houses'. Newtown, too, was dominated by half-timbered houses, while in the surrounding countryside farmhouses, cottages, inns and mansions were until the early nineteenth century often built with timber frames with the intermediate spaces in-filled with wattle and daub.

Just as the valleys of the Severn, Wye and other rivers lead into the heart of Wales, so too does the southern coastal plain, the Vale of Glamorgan, act as a routeway from the English plain into Wales. Along the Vale came the four-wheeled wagon of exquisite design that bears a close similarity to the wagons of Wiltshire and lowland Gloucestershire. Here too was found a technique of thatching far superior to that found in any other part of Wales; here in a vale of trim, white-washed villages one sees a settlement pattern far more closely related to the west of England than to moorland Wales (Pl. 72). Iorwerth Peate in *The Welsh House*, in describing the cottages of the Vale of Glamorgan, says:

'The single roomed cottage, sometimes partitioned, with a loft over all its area is well exemplified in Glamorgan. . . . In the mid nineteenth century, at Peterstonsuper-Ely, the cottage accommodation is deplorable. It consists of old thatched buildings, very low, with one living room, a portion of which is partitioned off as a pantry, and a general garret or sleeping room for the Welsh family.'

Straw from wheat threshed in the normal way, although not favoured by some craftsmen, has been used by many generations of thatchers. However, owing to the increased popularity of combine harvesters and balers, threshed long-straw thatching, as it is termed, is becoming far less common than it was in the days when flails and threshing drums were used. Modern machinery tends to flatten the tubular stems, so that the straw lies less compactly and is less waterproof. In Glamorgan in the past, it was customary to cut the wheat close up to the ear, thus leaving the stems undamaged by threshing. Even in recent years it has been the custom to reserve for thatching the wheat growing around the edges of the harvest field. This was generally cut either with a sickle or with a scythe and cradle in order to open the field for the reaper. Threshed long straw is applied so that the stalks lie along the plane of the roof, which then sheds the water falling on it.

Besides the threshed long-straw method of thatching there is another way of using wheat straw. It is not threshed in the usual manner and the material is known as reed straw or Devon reed, since the custom of using the material in this way originated in Devon. In the past the grain was beaten out over a threshing frame, and in some districts that favoured reed straw, flails were less often used for threshing since their beating action tended to bruise and flatten the wheat stems. The threshing frame, known as a 'webble', was two feet high and three feet wide and had some fifteen horizontal bars joining the gently curving side pieces. A small sheaf was taken and beaten against the bars of the frame, so that the ears were knocked out and the straw kept whole.

A slightly more advanced method of beating out the ears without damaging the stalks was to employ a small threshing drum. The grain was beaten out by the revolving arms inside the drum and the straw was pulled out without damage. The larger combing machines were in more recent times attached to steam threshers. Selected wheat is fed through this machine, which strips the ears and flag from the wheat without the straw going through the drum. The combed wheat reed thus comes from the machine undamaged, and is bundled with ends lying in one direction.

A roof thatched with reed straw has a somewhat different appearance from that thatched with long straw. The object is to present a brush-like surface to the weather; it is coarse but plush-like in texture, produced by the outward facing butts of the stalks. A roof thatched with Devon reed on a forty-five degree pitch generally lasts some fifty years. Since threshed long straw has become less and less suitable to use, the custom of thatching with Devon reed is far more widespread than in the past.

The most durable roof is that built of Norfolk reed (*Phragmites communis*), an aquatic plant that grows in many parts of the country, for example, in the Jersey Marine district of west Glamorgan, where it is harvested annually. Reed, most expensive of all thatching materials, is grown specially for the purpose. When cut with a scythe or sickle it is from three feet to eight feet high. During harvesting great use is made of waterways, for since the reed grows on marshes and river banks, wheeled transport can seldom be used. After cutting, the reed is stacked until needed and much is sold to buyers from far afield. A reed thatched roof, similar in appearance to Devon reed after weathering, has a life of up to a hundred years, provided the roof pitch is of forty-five degrees or steeper.

The design and technique of building cottages and farmhouses in Glamorgan are quite different from those of other parts of Wales. The houses of the slate-quarrying areas of north Wales have a character of their own, while the bleak promontories of the Llŷn peninsula and Pembrokeshire have well built, massive stone houses, as befit an area where the force of westerly gales bearing in from the sea could easily destroy more fragile structures (Pl. 73). On Bardsey and the St David's peninsula in Pembrokeshire local granite was used for the construction of dwellings, and in the latter the houses were influenced by the Norman castle dwellers, one of the features being an adaptation for domestic purposes of the round chimneys of the Norman castles. They possess thick stone walls, deeply recessed windows, arched doorways, massive chimneys, stone staircases and built-in stone benches, strongly reminiscent of Norman castles. On Bardsey Island, too, the houses are equally massive and all farmhouses are built behind the tall, thick walls of a courtyard and resemble fortified settlements.

But both in Pembrokeshire and the Llŷn peninsula the granite rocks were of restricted importance for building purposes; igneous rocks and stones from the glacial drift were utilized for building many a dwelling, especially substantial farmhouses and mansions. 'But', says Peate, 'in Llŷn, clay or mud was formerly used for the small cottages so characteristic of the area. Habitations . . . particularly in Llŷn consist of walls built of . . . cob, that is an argillaceous earth having straw or rushes mixed with it while in a state of paste, and then laid layer upon layer, between boards.' In Pembrokeshire 'the whitewashed cottage, either stone or mud stands out clearly in the mountain landscape on the side of the Precelly range . . . and the prevalent type was described in 1814 as "a mud walling about five feet high, a hipped end, low roofing of straw with a wattle and daub chimney, kept together with hay-rope bandages, the disgrace of the country".'

The major part of Gwynedd—north-west Wales—is stone country; this is a land of dry-stone walls of slate and stone tile roofs. There are dwellings whose walls consist of huge boulders, there are others where narrow slabs of slate are used for wall construction. Many of the cottages are small with walls of great thickness and all windows are at the front of the house. Chimney places are large and capacious and inside them bacon or herrings were dried after salting. Llainfadyn, a one-roomed cottage at the Welsh Folk Museum, is typical of the cottage homes of Snowdonia. The house from Rhostryfan, Caernarvonshire, dates from the mid eighteenth century, and roughly hewn boulders of tremendous size are used in the construction of its walls.

'Welsh cottages', says Peate, 'have belonged . . . to the single room tradition . . . very often the simple form of single room for living and sleeping—and a more developed variant e.g. the *croglofft* [i.e. half-loft] stage could be found at the same time in the same district. . . . The cottages appear scattered throughout the countryside . . . in the corner of a field, on the side of a road, in the shelter of a hillside, under the shade of an old holly tree.'

Conspicuous in the landscape of Snowdonia are the dry-stone walls that surround the cottages and farmhouses. Although no mortar or cement is used in the erection of these walls, they have to be solid enough to withstand the strong force of winds and storms on exposed upland farms. The waller's art lies in his ability to work with irregular material of many sizes, for he must size up the possibility of each stone and judge whether it will fit into a particular gap. The true stone waller does not cut his raw material to size if he can possibly help it. This is particularly true in north Wales where the native stone is hard and difficult to cleave cleanly.

The rocks of Gwynedd have for centuries yielded slate of excellent quality that was exported from such seaports as Portmadoc and Port Dinorwig to all parts of the world. Villages such as Llanberis, Bethesda, Penygroes, Corris and Aberllefenni were famous for their slate quarries; indeed it was the extraction of slate that occupied the majority of the inhabitants of those villages until recent times. These slates varied in colour from blue to purple, and the splitting of slates was a craft that demanded great skill. Slate sizes were referred to as 'Duchess', 'Viscountess', 'Broad Ladies', 'Narrow Ladies', together with many other names referring to female rank.

Much of Wales, of course, consists of a moorland plateau of scattered homesteads. Many of the houses are located on a windy and rather rain-swept upland, where it was important to have access to cattle at all times. For this reason, the long house that accommodated man and beast under the same roof became commonplace in Wales (Pl. 71).

'The long house', says Peate, 'is, as its name implies, a single, long, low, oblong building which houses both the family and its cattle. The dwelling itself is always at one end, generally called the "upper end" (*pen uchaf*) though this depends upon the situation of the house—in some cases the dwelling is the "lower end" (*pen isaf*). The other end (generally *pen isaf*, occasionally *pen uchaf*) is the cow-house. Between the two is the door. In most cases this opens into a passage called *penllawr* (literally, the head of the floor) or *bing*, with another door at its further end. This passage dividing the house into its two parts, dwelling-house and cow-house, generally serves as a feeding-walk. There are however many instances (a) where the feeding-walk does not exist and (b) where it has been modified by the insertion, between cow-house and dwelling, of a dairy, storeroom or calf-box. It is obvious from the houses examined, most of which have been greatly altered and reconstructed during the last one hundred years, that originally the Welsh long-house consisted only of these two parts, dwelling-house and cow-house, upper end and lower end. The upper end, without exception, was always paved, the paving terminating in the passage, the cow-house floor being of earth. The name *penllawr*, "head of the floor", is therefore significantly descriptive. At a later date in several of the houses examined, the dwelling part was partitioned off into two, three or even four rooms, parlour, dairy and bedroom(s). On the other hand, several houses examined were built with provision made for these separate rooms.

'One of the features characteristic of the modern renovation of these houses is that of raising the roof of the dwelling end to make possible a second storey. Consequently from the outside, many long-houses appear as modern dwellings of 19th century type with a central "front" door, two ground-floor windows (one on each side of the door) and two or three above, with a low-roofed out-building attached. . . .

'. . . But despite these reconstructions, the essential feature—that of internal access to the cow-house—has been retained and is an excellent example of the tenacious clinging to the old tradition, referred to by Campbell, by people who, if they so desired, could easily afford separate accommodation for their domestic animals. In the unrestored examples, there is a loft (*towlod, taflod*) for storing wool, cheese and corn and sometimes used as a bedroom for the servants, which is entered in some instances by a staircase from without but generally by a stone staircase from within. The floor of the loft is usually on a level with the wall-plate.'

Of course, not all the traditional homes of the moorland core of Wales were long houses, for rectangular buildings and two-roomed dwellings were commonplace throughout the region.

In west Wales, two-roomed cottages were known as *tai dau ben* (two ended, i.e. two-roomed houses) the two rooms being known as *pen ucha* (the upper end or kitchen) and the *pen isa* (the lower end or chamber). The outside walls, whether they were stone or mud built, were always whitewashed with two small, four-paned windows providing insufficient light to the low-ceilinged interior. In some houses, additional sleeping accommodation was provided by the addition of a cockloft (*dowlad* or *taflod*). While in some houses the cockloft covered the whole cottage, in the majority of cases it covered the kitchen only, the chamber having a much higher ceiling with no loft above it.

A natural development from the *tŷ dau ben* was the addition of a second storey to provide two rooms on the first floor. In the second half of the nineteenth century the conversion of two-roomed cottages was commonplace. All the activities of the family, work and leisure, all took place in the *pen ucha* or kitchen, while the other room on the ground floor was converted from a bedroom to a parlour. In most dwellings this was a prestige room, uncomfortable and unused, into which none but the strangest of callers was admitted. On the rare occasions when the member of a family suffered a prolonged illness, the parlour came into its use as a sick room. On death it was customary to bring the corpse of the deceased to rest in the parlour before burial. Except on those special occasions the Welsh parlour was a museum of forgotten things—family portraits, china souvenirs and furniture of an uncomfortable, unused best. The parlour is like the 'West Room' described by C. M. Arensburg in Ireland:

'It soon becomes apparent that there is something special about the west room . . . the room was a sort of parlour, into which none but distinguished guests were admitted. In it were kept pictures of the dead and emigrated members of the family and all fine pieces of furniture. Nor were my hosts alone in keeping objects of sentimental and religious value in the special room. . . . The general feeling was, that such things belonged there.'

On the more substantial farms, large dwellings were commonplace in many parts of Wales from the late eighteenth century. These were often rectangular houses, usually with four rooms on the ground floor and three or more bedrooms above. In south Cardiganshire, for example, the most common type of farmhouse has a large kitchen, traditionally with an open chimney, a small, unused parlour at the front of the house; and two rooms—a dairy and eating room (*rŵm ford* i.e. table room) at the back. Here the family and its servants traditionally ate all their meals, and it was furnished with a long, rectangular scrubbed table and two wooden benches; it had no fireplace. Most of these farmhouses possessed three bedrooms at the front of the dwelling, with a long narrow *aisle* above the dairy and eating room. In the past this room was used for storing grain after threshing and in many farmhouses it could be entered by a stone staircase on the outside.

FURNITURE

The preponderance of oak in many districts meant that, in the past, a large proportion of Welsh furniture was made of oak; and even when, in the eighteenth century, it became fashionable to use mahogany for the best quality furniture, Welsh cabinet makers still used the traditional oak; often this was coloured with bullock's blood to resemble mahogany.

As with most of the other requirements of the home, furniture was made by craftsmen that were members of the local community. In a moorland community, occupied largely by people who could not afford the luxury of imported timbers, it was customary to use timber that occurred locally, and in the design of furniture, durability and suitability were more important considerations than following fashion. Of course, certain styles were followed, but since much of upland Wales was far removed from centres of fashion, it seems likely that many years were to pass before a piece of furniture fashionable in lowland England became popular in Wales. The results of isolation affected every aspect of Welsh life and it seems that in furniture design Wales was at least a hundred years later in development than England. In the post-medieval period, a distinctly Welsh style of furniture seems to have been evolved. As a result of the Act of Union with England, the aristocratic classes of Wales began to emulate the fashion of the English court, not only in language but also in the material objects of daily life. In the seventeenth century, many of the Welsh gentry were familiar figures in London and they brought back into Wales ideas and styles in furniture which the woodworkers of Wales were quick to emulate. In some cases they even brought back actual pieces of furniture, as when the squire of Plas Llangoedmor, Cardiganshire, brought back a fireplace surround and overmantel with an oil painting by the seventeenth-century painter Thomas Wyck from London on horseback. More often, however, it was the ideas and styles of contemporary designs that were brought back, and these imported styles were modified by Welsh craftsmen to meet local needs and to utilize local raw materials. As a result of this, a distinctly Welsh style of furniture evolved.

To the layman, the dresser is a piece of furniture peculiarly associated with Wales. Examples made in Shropshire, or even as far afield as Yorkshire, are invariably described as 'Welsh' dressers, so much so that the term dresser has unfortunately become synonymous with Wales. The origins of this so-called 'Welsh dresser' were not in Wales at all, but its design was based on that of the medieval 'board' of the English home. This was merely an open framework of shelves for storage and display of ceramics and pottery and it occupied a position of pre-eminence in the halls of the nobility. It became a complex and elegant piece of furniture in medieval England, but shorn of its medieval splendour 'the board' became popular in Wales. It now appeared not in the homes of the aristocracy, but banished as a useful piece of furniture to the farm and cottage kitchen. While it is by no means peculiar to Wales, the dresser exhibits more variety and individuality in Wales than elsewhere. Dressers, most of them made by local craftsmen, perhaps as a dowry for a farmer's daughter when she married, were regarded as pieces of furniture for the general storage of pewter and crockery, especially copper lustre ware. Two distinct types may be recognized. Dressers made in north Wales were generally fitted with cupboard doors in the lower section and possibly on the sides of the upper stage (Pls 74, 75). Examples made in south and west Wales on the other hand, had open understages fitted with apron pieces above (Pl. 75). In most cases they would have two or three drawers between the top and bottom sections of the dressers, while in some cases the shelves of the upper section would be open at the back, while in others they were boarded. Most of the dressers seen in Welsh farmhouses date from the eighteenth or nineteenth century; the later examples often incorporate glass-fronted shelves on each side of the upper stage.

A characteristic of some Welsh dressers as well as of other pieces of furniture is the inlaid decorative work that, oddly enough, persisted down to the late nineteenth century. Scroll pattern in holly and linear pattern in bog oak were commonplace, especially in Glamorgan in the eighteenth century and indeed in the nineteenth; for despite the fact that in much of England inlay had been ousted by marquetry in the late seventeenth century, in Wales the earlier method of decoration persisted. Marquetry of course was known in Wales and this consisted of a veneer of expensive wood placed on a foundation of cheaper material.

A well-known piece of furniture in the halls of noblemen in the later Middle Ages was the buffet (Pl. 78), and from this developed the court cupboard with its lower section enclosed by doors. This piece of furniture usually housed the silver ware used at meals in the homes of the aristocracy. The court cupboard was introduced into Wales in the sixteenth century and became so popular amongst country people that it became known as a *cwpwrdd deuddarn* (two-piece cupboard). Its popularity was maintained throughout the seventeenth and eighteenth centuries into the first half of the nineteenth. The *cwpwrdd deuddarn* had doors at two stages and it developed details of treatment such as the carving of the uprights and the lower rail, generally associated with Welsh oak furniture (Pls 80, 81). It persisted for centuries after the court cupboard had disappeared from England, but by the middle of the seventeenth century the *cwpwrdd deuddarn* showed such an individuality of treatment that another type of cupboard, the *cwpwrdd tridarn* (three-piece cupboard), evolved from it. In the *tridarn* a third stage in the form of a canopy and an extra shelf for the display of pewter and earthenware was added, a development peculiar to Wales (Pls 80, 81). Thus was designed a three-tiered court cupboard that was essentially Welsh in character, the *deuddarn* being popular in many parts of England as well. During the age of walnut and mahogany, many pieces of oak furniture were discarded by the nobility, and the court cupboard was no exception. Many may still be seen in Welsh country homes today, and many may be regarded as discards of the wealthy that found their way to the dwellings of yeomen and farmers. Many have been passed down from generation to generation and the *tridarn* in particular may be regarded as a unique and typical product of Welsh rural workshops in the eighteenth and nineteenth centuries.

The chest (Pl. 76) is a piece of furniture that dates back to the Middle Ages; indeed the chest may be regarded as the most ancient of all pieces of furniture, for from it developed such items as settles, buffets, cabinets and even chairs. It was according to medieval Welsh records the most commonplace of all pieces of furniture, for few homes had the movable furniture that is associated with later centuries. The Welsh certainly possessed beds, tables and chests, but little more, for in the Middle Ages furniture throughout western Europe must have been similar in its essentials. However, in succeeding centuries national or regional styles developed throughout the world. In the Middle Ages, chests were merely hollowed-out logs, possibly banded with metal, but as early as the thirteenth century framed, rectangular chests for use in church and home were fairly common. In time, with the addition of carved decorations of geometric and floral designs, the chest developed into a most elaborate piece of furniture. The chest was regarded as the only article of furniture capable of holding bed linen and clothes, and women on marriage were presented with linen and blankets in a wooden chest that became known as a 'dower' chest. Many of these were elaborately carved and many bore the name of their original owner. The mule chest (Pl. 77), with drawers below, was a later development of the ordinary chest and from it developed chests of drawers that were found in every Welsh home.

Up to the end of the seventeenth century, movable chairs were rare in Wales, with the exception of those used in the homes of the aristocracy. Stools, benches and settles were certainly common and the earlier type of chair found in the homes

Fig. 7. Kitchen of Cilewent farmhouse, a sixteenth-century long house from the Claerwen Valley in mid Wales; now at the Welsh Folk Museum.

of the aristocracy was heavy and 'box-like' in form, panelled, with arms, with a straight back and stretchers. A more commonplace type of oak chair that developed in the sixteenth century was constructed of turned members and was triangular in form and three-legged. The eighteenth century witnessed the influence of designs such as Chippendale, Hepplewhite and Sheraton, and chairs based on these designs began to replace the heavy, crudely designed oak chairs of earlier times. Although usually some years behind contemporary English fashion, Welsh cabinet makers began to copy the styles of the great designers. This was easy, for many of these designers published catalogues in which the designs could be followed by any country craftsman who possessed them. Chairs of coiled basketry, preaching chairs that could be converted into wayside pulpits, commode chairs, double courting chairs and three legged armchairs, long associated with Cardiganshire, were all made in a great variety by country craftsmen, but throughout history one of the features of furniture design in Wales has been the Welsh craftsman's ability to modify and adapt to the simple needs of the countryside those designs which came and went in fashionable centres outside Wales (Pls 83–6). Perhaps Welsh craftsmen were slow in adopting new designs. As Twiston-Davies and Lloyd-Johns say: 'Though there were nearly 600 subscribers to Thomas Sheraton's *The Cabinet Maker and Upholsterer*, published in 1793 there is not one from Wales. This fact shows clearly how isolated the Principality was from current trends of taste and fashion.' For a long time, even until the beginning of the present century, Welsh country people were content to put up with furniture made locally, however out of date it might be, and for many centuries local oak or ash or elm, grown and seasoned in the locality, was the usual raw material for country craftsmen.

In the cottages and farmhouses of rural Wales, the hearth is the centre of family life (Pls 113, 114). A fire of peat or of coal dust mixed with clay—a mixture known as culm—was always kept burning in the hearth. As in medieval Wales, there were until recently in many parts of the moorland fires that were never allowed to die out. As long as a house was occupied, said medieval Welsh law, a fire had always to be kept alive, so that it became a symbol of the perpetuation of family life. The fire as a focus of family life is, according to Estyn Evans, a characteristic of the 'Atlantic' province of European folk custom, as distinct from the 'oven' tradition of Central Europe, where the table and not the hearth is the focus of social and family life. The seat of honour in the house is that nearest the fire, and although the armchair, probably locally made, is usually reserved for the head of the family, that seat will be given up to any visitor that may call.

Fig. 8. BAKING AND COOKING
1. Dough kneading crock; Tregaron, Cardigan. 2, 3. Baking pots; Rhaeadr, Powys. 4, 5. Oven peels: 4, Nelson, Glamorgan; 5, Vale of Tywi, Dyfed. 6. Kneading trough; Glamorgan. 7. Earthenware oven; Llancarfan, Glamorgan. 8. Bottle-jack bracket; Marshfield, Gwent. 9. Bottle-jack; Tredegar, Gwent. 10. Clockwork spit-jack, c. 1700; Merioneth. 11. Meat roasting hook; Monmouth. 12–14. Toasters: 12, Llanwrtyd, Brecknock; 13, Llanrhystud, Cardigan; 14, Mynytho, Llŷn. 15. Toasting fork; Rhondda, Glamorgan. 16. Cleaver; Llangollen, Clwyd. 17. Chopper and chopping bowl; Llanbister, Radnor. 18. Sugar nippers; Tonyrefail, Glamorgan. 19. Beer muller; Aberavon, Glamorgan. 20, 21. Meat beaters: 20, Cefn Mabli, Gwent; 21, Llanwrtyd, Powys. 22. Currant washer; Monmouth. 23. Oven peel; Gladestry, Radnor.

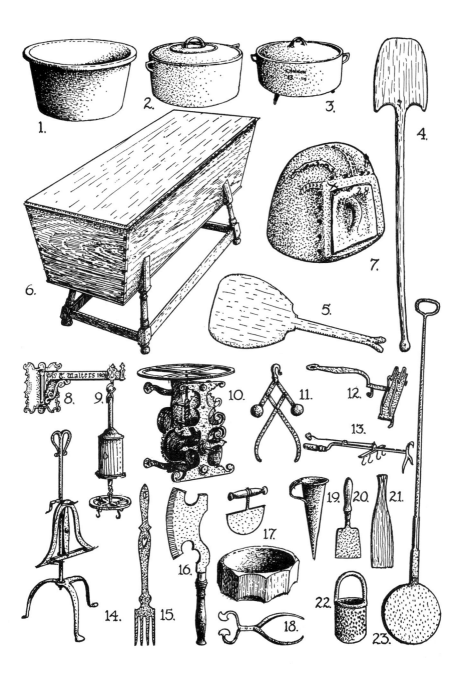

By tradition too, most of the food required by the family was cooked on the open fire. Although in the recent past, the old open chimney and fire at floor level were replaced by more modern grates, many of the accessories of the old open hearth persisted. Above the fire, suspended from an iron bar or from an iron crane, which swivelled from side to side (*y crân*), was a large iron hook from which were suspended the vessels for cooking most of the family's food—a three-legged cauldron (*citl* or *celwrn*) for boiling broth, a large boiler (*paer*) for boiling water for washing, or a pot oven (*ffwrn*) in which bread was often cooked. In bread making, the dough was placed in the pot, the lid put on and the pot placed in the glowing peat which was also placed around the pot and over the lid. In areas where peat was not used, the pot oven was merely suspended over the open fire, but in others dried cowdung, gorse, twigs and fern were used. In some districts cooking was often done outside the house. A hole was made in the ground considerably larger than the baking pot; it was well lined with glowing peat from the house fire, the pot was put in with its lid on and then completely covered with peat.

In many households, however, the baking oven was separate from the main fire and was built into the wall alongside the fireplace. In some districts this was heated to the required temperature by placing lighted twigs inside it, the hot ashes being removed before the dough was inserted; in others the fire was placed in a grate below the oven.

Roasting by means of a spit is one of the oldest methods of preparing meat, and during the Middle Ages the hand-operated spit, which revolved on irons or fire dogs, was in continuous use, especially in the homes of the aristocracy, until the introduction of the roasting oven at the end of the eighteenth century. The work of turning the spit by hand was arduous, especially on hot days when the heat of an open hearth was almost unbearable. From the sixteenth century, therefore, there were mechanical improvements. One was the revolving fan, or smokejack, driven by the heat of the fire; this was built into the chimney and connected to the spit by a series of cogs and chains. Alternatively, a weight-driven spit-jack, operating on the same principle as a long-case clock, became very common, while in the more substantial homesteads the dog-wheel became commonplace in the sixteenth century. The dog turnspit was a miniature tread-wheel, usually constructed of oak. It was secured to brackets high up at the side of the fireplace and was connected by an endless chain to a grooved pulley attached to the spit itself. A dog was then placed inside the wheel and it trod patiently, causing the spit to revolve. The turnspit breed of dog, was, according to Thomas Bewick, long bodied with 'short crooked legs, its tail curled upon its back and is frequently spotted with black, upon a blue grey ground. It is peculiar in the colour of its eyes; the same dog often having the iris of one eye black and the other white. It is a bold, vigilant and spirited little dog.' By the middle of the nineteenth century dogs had ceased to be used for turning spits, although in parts of north Wales dog-wheels were used for churning butter up to about fifty years ago. A round

Fig. 9. Kitchen at St Fagans Castle, Welsh Folk Museum. This is basically a sixteenth-century kitchen with two fireplaces. Note the smokejack for driving the turnspit, the bread rack and, in the second fireplace, the dog-wheel for driving a spit.

wooden platform up to twelve feet in diameter was found in many a farm out-house and this inclined wheel was connected to a butter churn. A chained dog ran on the inclined steps of the wheel and caused it to revolve.

The development of domestic equipment during the last fifty years or so has been so phenomenal that it is difficult to realize that modern labour-saving equipment replaced that which had been in use for hundreds of years, only within the memory of many people. The development of washing machines and driers dispensed with such essential pieces of domestic equipment as mangles. The ponderous box mangle, with its huge chest weighted with stones, was moved to and fro on rollers by turning a handle. This type of primitive mangle was still being advertised during the last quarter of the nineteenth century.

'The laundry woman', says Peate in his *Tradition and Folk Life*, 'has been a well-known figure in the Welsh villages and rural towns and in the smaller industrial centres. Laundering has always been carried out by the household staff of the farms, but it is equally a cottage industry. The washerwoman was certain of a weekly quota of work, and even when the washing was done at home, the mangling was often done by the village washerwoman. Indeed public sympathy for a wife whose husband has been incapacitated or killed, has frequently taken the form of a subscription list to purchase a mangle, with which she may earn a sure if scanty living.'

Smoothing irons varied tremendously, from those in which hot charcoal was placed to irons fuelled with paraffin, while for goffering lace and linen a variety of devices were found. The simplest form of gofferer was a small copper bar (*cwic*), which was heated and then applied to the fabric, while a more advanced version was the box gofferer or 'Italian iron'. In this the heated bar was thrust into a tubular case fixed horizontally on an iron stand, and the material to be fluted was pressed over this. The wooden goffering stand too, was widely used throughout Wales, and in this damp linen was fixed in a zig-zag manner between removable wooden quills placed in slots between two upright pieces of wood (Pl. 123). The loaded goffering stand was then placed in front of the open fire and removed after drying. In this way a semi-permanent creasing was obtained. The small, mangle-like table crimping machines, most of them the product of a Midland metal industry, marked the last stage in the evolution of crimping and goffering equipment. The washing tubs, like the butter churns and cheese vats, were the products of a rural industry.

Not long ago most country households, especially in the more remote corners of the Welsh uplands, were lit by tallow candles and rushlights. The manufacturers of these essentials was very much a part of the routine of most country houses. Rushes were gathered in the height of summer and the peel, with the exception of a narrow supporting strip, was removed before the pith was dipped in scalding grease until saturated (Pl. 126). An inadequate light was provided by the rapidly burning rushlight each one lasting no more than half an hour. Rushes lacking rigidity had to be supported by a special holder. Tallow candles, made by dipping cotton strands in melted fat or by moulding in a plant stalk or tinplate mould, were also widely made in Welsh homes (Pl. 125). Since the cotton wicks did not burn away by themselves they had to have constant attention by snuffing. Snuffers of steel, brass, Sheffield plate, japanned tin or silver were essential in all homes, as were candle-sticks and horn lanterns.

Until the last quarter of the nineteenth century, oil lamps were not widely used in Wales, although open shell lamps for burning fish oil were known in coastal districts. In the Gower peninsula, for example, lamps made from the shells of local oysters were widely used. In these a wick of twisted rag was inserted in the oil or fat placed in the shell saucer. The wick overlapped the edge of the shell to provide a poor light. The crusie lamp, consisting of two metal saucers with a wick overlapping the edge, is said to have been used in parts of Wales, but this was far more common on the west coast of Scotland and may have been imported into Wales.

Mineral oil was imported into Britain from Rumania and Burma before 1850, but it was very expensive and was not widely adopted for domestic lighting. The discovery of rich oil fields in North America after 1859 brought cheap and abundant supplies of petroleum to Britain and rapid developments were made in domestic lighting equipment between 1870 and 1914. Hundreds of lamps were patented and by the turn of the century in the less remote parts of Wales, oil lamps equipped with broad, ribbon-like wicks were widely used for lighting farm and cottage kitchens.

Before the introduction of matches, fire was usually provided by means of a flint, steel and tinder box. The flint was struck sharply against the edge of the steel so that the sparks fell on the tinder, which was charred cotton rag. The tinder was blown until it glowed and a flame was obtained from it with a sulphur match. About 1810 'Instantaneous Light Boxes' were introduced from France and rapidly gained in popularity. In these a wooden spill was dipped in a paste of chlorate of potash, sugar and gum. On drying these were dipped in a bottle of vitriol and quickly withdrawn to burst into flames. In 1826 the first friction match was devised, which was made by dipping wooden sticks in chlorate of potash, sulphide of antimony, gum arabic and water. To strike, the matches were nipped with sandpaper. In 1829 sulphur was added to the mixture to make 'Lucifer' matches and in 1832 phosphorus was included to make 'Congreve' matches. In the 1830s, too, the 'Vesta' with a stem of waxed wood or cotton strands was also devised. In 1855 the first safety match was invented.

10 Folk Custom and Belief

Throughout Britain, urban influences have encroached on the indigenous culture of the countryside and traditional ways of thought and behaviour are rapidly disappearing before the destroying breath of the 'spirit of the age'. Nevertheless, many of the customs practised by a rural community remain, while others are still present in an altered form. Folk customs, though survivals from an ancient day, still have an important role in the life of the countryman and are important because they are closely interwoven with the whole pattern of life.

In a peasant community children are regarded as an asset, and throughout the world rejoicings take place before or soon after birth. In many districts it was believed that, if nuts were numerous, many children would be born in that year. Certain acts were forbidden to the expectant mother, in the belief that her behaviour influenced the unborn child. She might not step over a grave; if she did her child would die. She might not dip her fingers in dirty water, otherwise her child would have coarse hands. If she tied a cord around her waist her child would be unlucky; if she meddled much with flowers, her child would not have a keen sense of smell; children born when the moon was new would be eloquent; those born during the last quarter would have excellent reasoning powers. To be born at night made one open to seeing visions, ghosts and phantom funerals. In some parts of Wales, christening was an occasion for heavy drinking by members of the family who had come to the christening, and in parts of mid Wales special christening glasses were used. Each glass held nearly a pint and those at the christening ceremony were supposed to drink a whole glassfull at one gulp, the object of the toasts being the mother rather than the baby. In almost every country district it still remains a practice for neighbours to visit a house where a child has been born, bearing gifts of clothing for the baby, or a pound or two of sugar as a gift for the mother.

A child born with a caul (a fragment of the amnion) covering the head was regarded as lucky. Since the possession of a caul was supposed to give protection against drowning, there was a considerable demand for cauls from sailors. In addition, the possession of a caul had many magical and medicinal virtues, the ability to see and speak to ghosts amongst them.

Courtship in rural Wales was usually long and surreptitious. In the past 'bundling' or 'courting in bed' was widely practised in country districts and this custom was celebrated in song and poem. The man, after throwing pebbles at the girl's window, would use a ladder from the rickyard to gain admittance through an upstairs window to the bedroom. He would leave by the same means before dawn, unseen and unheard by the sleeping household. An unwanted suitor could find himself drenched with a bucketful of swill as he attempted to gain access to a house. The promiscuity permitted by traditional methods of courtship did, until the beginning of the present century, bring in its wake a high degree of pre-marital pregnancy and illegitimacy, a surprising feature in a rural community that regarded alcohol, gambling and 'breaking the Sabbath' as the gravest form of sin.

A common feature of courtship in nearly all parts of the world is the giving of presents as tokens of love and affection. Carved wooden love spoons (see page 73) (Pl. 94), stay busks, knitting-needle sheaths, lace bobbins and even home-made valentine cards were all associated with courtship in rural Wales. Though no specimen earlier than the seventeenth century has survived, there is no doubt that the practice of giving love tokens was much older. Stay busks can be dated to the period when the corset was essential in the formal dress of women, namely from the early seventeenth century to the last quarter of the eighteenth century. The knitting-needle sheaths were first made by countrymen, but during the mid to late nineteenth century they were also made of ivory, metal and a variety of materials as the knitting-needle sheath was accepted by townspeople in Victorian drawing-rooms. Love spoons, which had begun as a present made by a country worker for his sweetheart, were selfconsciously copied by all wood workers as a vehicle to display their skill. The National Eisteddfod encouraged this prolific copying of traditional patterns by regularly setting them as subjects for competition.

Sixteenth-century spoons were based on the simple lines of the contemporary pewter or silver spoons. Then the wood carver displayed his skill by making the handle hollow with four pillar-like lengths of wood at the four corners of the square section. Within this hollow space, round wooden balls were carved from the core of the handle. These ran free in the hollow. A curved wooden chain was another skilled motif. As the nineteenth century proceeded, the handle was made as a rectangular panel and its surface covered with a pattern, which often involved the piercing of the wood; the effect was to reflect the Victorian preoccupation with intricate patterns and fret-saw type of work.

A variety of objects were added to the original spoon. Knives, forks, anchors, chains were attached as additional decorations, also inset panels on which the dedication was written are often found. All these spoons had a ring or a hole for suspending them on the wall as a decoration.

It is not always possible to date every love spoon, nor is it possible to be precise in every case about the area in which it was made or for a clear type to be distinguished for specific regions. It has been suggested that the single stem with an inlaid glass panel containing the dedication was a Caernarvonshire type. This is probably an eighteenth-century fashion. The dolphin-shaped and ridged handle is another Caernarvonshire characteristic.

In the past when a man and woman, usually after a long surreptitious courtship, had decided to marry, the first step was for the man to approach his father and tell him of his decision. This was known as *retyddia* or *notyddia*. If the father approved of his son's choice, then he, with his wife, relative or close friend, would visit the bride's parents to discuss the wedding arrangements, the dowry (*gwaddol*) and other matters. In west Wales the bride's father was expected to provide his daughter with some furniture, household goods, cows, pigs and poultry, items that in farming are traditionally the wife's responsibility. The man's father on the other hand was expected to grant his son a holding, hay, horses, sheep and wheat. Amongst the farming population these arrangements are still in practice occasionally, and the parents, by giving or withholding the dowry, as the case may be, approve or disapprove of the match.

When the day of the wedding had been finally arranged, invitations to the function were sent out either on a printed sheet or, more often, by word of mouth. The local bidder (*y Gwahoddwr*) was asked to visit all the houses in the neighbourhood and invite the people to the wedding feast (*y neithior*). As recently as the early years of the present century the rural neighbourhood of Pontgarreg in south Cardiganshire still possessed its bidder, who was well known as a humorous character, possessing considerable skill at the composition of impromptu verses. The bidding was a general invitation to the whole neighbourhood to meet at the house of the bride and groom bringing with them presents, however small, to the newly married couple. The *Gwahoddwr* was attired in clothing especially suitable to the occasion, and carried in his hands a white stick of office decorated with ribbons of all colours. On entering a house he would strike the ground thrice, ask for silence and deliver his speech in prose and in verse. Though formal bidding of this kind has long passed away, the inhabitants of country districts still consider it a duty to attend the wedding ceremony, whether it be as guests or as spectators, just as they consider it obligatory to give wedding presents. Some families are paying a debt (*talu'r pwyth*), repaying a gift that they received at their own wedding, while others are creating a debt, which the newly wedded couple will be obliged to repay when the occasion arises. This almost rigid custom of *talu'r pwyth*, or *talu'r ddyled*, is as important in the day-to-day life of the community as it was in the day when the *Gwahoddwr* went from house to house almost demanding repayment.

August 25, 1798.

Having lately entered the Matrimonial State, we are encouraged by our Friends to make a Bidding on the Occasion, on Thursday the 13th Day of September next, at the Dwelling-House of Daniel Thomas, (the young Woman's Father) called Ifcoed-Mill, *in the Parish of St. Ish-mael, at which Place we humbly folicit the Favor of your good Company; and whatever Donation you may then be difpofed to beftow on us, will be grate-fully received, and cheerfully repaid, whenever de-manded on the like Occafion, by*

Your moft obliged humble Servants,

Ebenezer Jones,
Mary Jones.

☞ The young Man's Grandmother, and young Woman's Father and Mother, defire that all Gifts of the above Na-ture. due to them, may be returned to the young Couple on the faid Day, and will be thankful for all Favors con-ferred on them.—The young Man's Uncle *(David Thomas of Ifcoed Ucha')* and young Woman's Sifters, will alfo be thankful for any Favors conferred on the young Couple.

Fig. 10. A bidding letter of 1798.

The damping influence of Methodist Revival destroyed many of the old wed-ding customs. The concealment of the bride, and the pursuit of bride and groom to and from the church by the young men (*y gwŷr shigowts*, i.e. scouts), had dis-appeared by the middle of the last century. Such customs as prevail, for example, the firing of guns and the throwing of confetti and rice, and the tying of old boots, tins and horseshoes to the wedding car, are fairly common throughout Britain. It is customary to hold the groom on his way to the chapel or church by stretching ropes across the roadway, or by tying the church gate, so that he cannot pass without the customary payment for release. In the same way the whole wedding party is held up after the ceremony. The custom is known as *cwinten*, and it seems to be related to the quintain, which was a feat of horsemanship in English tournaments.

The traditional *neithior* has lost much of its significance because of the increasing popularity of the honeymoon, which had no place in traditional Welsh wedding customs. Even today the honeymoon may be limited to a single day at a seaside resort, while occasionally among farming couples it is completely absent. In those cases something approaching the traditional *neithior* takes its place. After the ceremony in the morning the wedding party make their way to the bride's home for the feast, and they remain there for the remainder of the day. Neighbours and relatives are constantly visiting the house, bringing gifts and partaking of the wedding feast. The couple will stay at the bride's house till the following day, when they will move to their own house. For the first few weeks of their married life, visitors are frequent and the gifts received are numerous. If the couple concerned are farmers, and they are starting life (*dechrau byw*) in a holding of their own, neighbours may assist with a day's work in getting the farm into order.

A birth or marriage is a joyful occasion, and the joy that has come the way of a particular family is a signal for neighbourhood rejoicing. In the same way illness brings many callers, for it is considered obligatory for at least one member of each family in the locality to visit (*rhoi tro*) the sick person. They often bring gifts of food or money, and should the person be so ill as to require constant attention, they offer their services to watch (*gwylad*) at night. Should this offer not be made, the family of the ailing person consider it un-neighbourly, even though the offer may not be accepted.

Death brings further manifestations of kindliness, and in the interval between death and burial the bereaved family leaves much of the housework to other people. Male neighbours look after the farm and tidy up the surroundings of the house for the funeral, while female neighbours clean the house and prepare food for sympathizing callers, and for the funeral 'feast'. Experienced female neighbours also prepare the corpse (*troi heibio*), while undertaking and burial arrangements are made by the men. *Gwylad* (vigil) does not cease with death, and it is still customary for neighbours to keep a nightly vigil in pairs until the arrival of the coffin. Two or more candles are lighted in the parlour, where the corpse lies, and it is the duty of the *gwylwyr* (watchers) to see that these candles are kept properly alight. It is possible that the custom of placing candles near the body has some ritual significance, for they are kept alight both night and day, even though other means of lighting may be available in the house. The custom is possibly a survival from medieval times, when Wales was Catholic, for this practice seems fairly general in Catholic countries.

All families in a neighbourhood consider it their duty to visit a bereaved neighbour, and it is considered a serious breach of etiquette not to pay this visit. Gifts of food, especially highly valued tinned food, and money are presented to the next of kin irrespective of their wealth or social status. After expressing sympathy, speaking at length on the good qualities of the deceased, and listening to an account of his illness and death, the visitors are expected to eat a meal, or at least to drink a cup of tea before they leave. They are also expected to pay a visit to the parlour in order to view the corpse, for the coffin is never closed until the cortège is about to leave the house for the interment.

Until 1939 it was customary for a service to be held in the house on the night preceding the funeral. This service was called a *Gwylnos*, and though similar to the Irish wake, in that the visitors ate a meal before they left, there was never any of the feasting and heavy drinking characteristic of the wake. The service itself took the form of an ordinary nonconformist prayer meeting, with two or three elders of the deceased's chapel taking part. No minister or clergyman was ever present, but only neighbours who came to offer neighbourly comfort to the bereaved family.

In the past the *Gwahoddwr* of the wedding feast became the *Rhybuddiwr* (warner) of a funeral. Dressed in sombre black, he would visit all the houses in a locality telling them of the date and time of the funeral. Just as the *Gwahoddwr* asked neighbours to bring gifts to a wedding, so too did the *Rhybuddiwr* invite the people of a locality to bring food and drink to the funeral, or give the family of the deceased a sum of money, if they should be in need.

In north Wales it was customary to make an offering to the clergyman and to the parish clerk on the day of the funeral. The offering (*offrwm*) to the clergyman was made during or at the end of the service; in Llansilin, Denbighshire, a small board specially fixed to the altar rail was used for this purpose and the total was later announced by the clergyman. In another parish nearby the service was interrupted in the middle when the clergyman left the reading desk and, after a short prayer at the communion table, took his stand at a table or desk. At this point, the chief mourner left the pew in which he was sitting and placed a piece of money on it. The other mourners and friends present all followed his example.

Outside the church, at the porch or at the graveside, a second contribution was made, this time to the parish clerk. This was commonly known as *arian rhaw* (spade money) because it was collected on a shovel held over the open grave by the clerk himself. The sum collected varied but was often about one-quarter of the amount given to the clergyman. Like the *offrwm* the spade money became a token of esteem for the deceased and varied accordingly. Only silver or gold was given in this collection in Llangurig, Montgomeryshire, in the middle of the last century. In Merioneth, where a bowl was used for the collection instead of a shovel, the custom was open to abuse when a funeral went from one parish to another and a double offering was collected by the parish clerks at the house and at the graveside respectively. At Llwydiarth, Montgomeryshire, the *offrwm* was a collection made in the church but given to the clerk and not to the vicar—an interesting variation on the custom. The funeral would be kept waiting while the clerk added up the sums given and announced the total. The *offrwm* and *arian rhaw* were probably similar in origin but came to be associated with the particular services rendered by the clergyman and his clerk.

Another form of contribution was found in some parts of north Wales until about 1830. In Mallwyd and Llanymawddwy the 'shot', as it was called, was held at the nearest public house—usually near the church. 'All females, as well as males, were expected to go there and contribute towards the "shot", or, more plainly, for a supply of drink. Beer was brought on the tables in jugs, with small glasses, or earthenware vessels, for distribution. The male portion of the company would generally contribute sixpence, and in some cases, a shilling each; and the females half of that sum. It would not be necessary for any one to stay there to get the value of his money; he or she might take a drop and go. But any one who went home without going in and contributing to the "shot" was looked upon with suspicion. The names and addresses of all who contributed were written down, and the record would be handed over to the nearest relatives of the deceased, who, when an opportunity offered, would pay the same respect to the memory of their departed friends. After the first contribution was expended in drink, tobacco etc., the steward, or person in charge of the "shot" would cry out, *Y mae'r tŷ yn rhydd!* [The house is free!] when those who wished to remain had to subscribe again.'

In addition to the customs and beliefs associated with important events in the life of the individual, there were many customs associated with the calendar. The Christmas season, whether a Christian festival or a season associated with the winter solstice, has been celebrated from the earliest times. In north Pembrokeshire, as a symbol of winter rest it was customary to carry a plough into the table room (*rŵm ford*) of a farm, and as neighbours partook of ale in the farmhouse it was considered obligatory for them to throw a few drops of ale over the plough. This symbolized that the plough was not forgotten and would be brought out once again to plough the fields after the holiday.

Although early morning services (*y plygain*) were held, and are still held in some districts, Christmas Day was less important in the life of Welsh countrymen than New Year's Day. Before the end of the year, however, a number of ceremonies were practised in some parts of the country. Owen, for example, describes the custom of holly beating practised in many parts of Wales on Boxing Day. This was 'a furious onslaught made by men and boys armed with large bushes of prickly holly on the naked and unprotected arms of female domestics and others of like class until their arms bled'. This custom was still being observed in Gower as recently as 1879. In Montgomeryshire the last person to get up on Boxing Day was whipped with holly, and for the remainder of the year he was to perform all the menial tasks for the family.

Another custom associated with the period between Boxing Day and Twelfth Night was that of hunting the wren. A wren was caught and then placed in a ribbon-bedecked box, or wren house (Pl. 91). This was carried on a bier from house to house, those bearing it, 'singing the while a long ditty. . . . The foursome [carrying the house] would then enter the doorway groaning under the weight of their burden'. After singing or reciting verses, the party would be invited into a house for refreshment and possibly a money gift. On New Year's Day from midnight to noon, children would go from home to home collecting *calennig*, a custom that is still practised in some districts. In the nineteenth century it was a common practice for children to decorate an apple or orange by sticking sprigs of rosemary or ears of corn in the fruit and surrounding it with holly. Verses were sung at the doors of houses and a gift of food or trifling amounts of money were handed over to the collectors as they completed the recitation or singing of a stereotyped verse. In Pembrokeshire, *calennig* collectors carried vessels of freshly drawn spring water, with sprigs of box, holly, myrtle, rosemary or any other evergreen plant. The hands and faces of every person they met on their rounds were sprinkled with water in return for money. In each house that they entered, water was sprinkled around the living-room, the sprinkling being accompanied by a verse.

In south Wales, especially Glamorgan, the *Mari Lwyd* (grey mare) made her rounds at the New Year (Pl. 92). A horse's head was draped in white and decorated with colourful ribbons. The *Mari* was led from house to house, a member of the group donning the horse's head. At the head of the procession the leader carried a stick. At each house a request for admittance and for permission to sing was proffered in extempore verse, following traditional rules. The occupants of the house replied in verse and a rhymed dialogue of a set type took place, ending with the admission of the party who were offered food and drink. Quite often a highly decorated wassail bowl (Pl. 93) was passed around the company, the bowls being of wood or of pottery.

In many counties the customs of Easter were associated with the egg. Eggs were decorated and in many districts during the week before Easter, it was customary for children to go around the parish begging eggs. 'Most of them would collect as many as two hundred. The china on the dressers of their homes would then be cleared and replaced by the eggs, the eldest child's collection being placed on the top shelf. On their collecting expeditions, they used wooden clappers which were rattled to the accompaniment of a sung phrase or couplet.' This custom of 'clapping eggs' was particularly prevalent in Anglesey, where it persisted until recently (Pl. 90).

A widespread custom associated with the harvesting of corn was that of cutting the last sheaf (*Y gaseg ben fedi*), said to be a custom 'concerning the personification of a harvest spirit in the last sheaf' (see page 41). Ornaments were made from the last sheaf of corn reaped and, after a complicated ceremony of getting it into the farmhouse dry despite the attempts at wetting it by the womenfolk, it was hung from the rafters of the kitchen until the next harvest (Pl. 95).

In any discussion of folk belief the place of the chapel as a social and religious force in the life of rural Wales must not be underestimated (Pls 100, 101). Although other interests have now become commonplace, destroying much of the simplicity of rural life, religion was the ruling centre and dominating interest of people's lives until quite recently. In my own background in a rural parish in west Wales, for example, religious matters were important. Attendance at all the meetings of the local chapel was obligatory in the nineteen-thirties and forties. The personalities of pulpit and denomination were as well known as the television personalities of today and the standards of morality laid down by the church were the dominating features of life, directing the whole social and individual behaviour of the countryman.

The beginnings of most culture elements are hidden in the shrouds of antiquity, and similarly the dense mists of myth and legend conceal the story of the original conversion of the Welsh people to Christianity. We do know, however, that in the fifth and sixth centuries A.D. Britain, in common with other counties of Western Europe, witnessed a rapid expansion of Christian teaching. In this expansion Wales received its teaching from the missionaries of the early Celtic Church. They utilized the well traversed sea routes of 'Atlantic' Britain and established a large number of religious settlements on or near the coasts of Wales, and the Celtic fringe in general. The prefix 'Llan' in Welsh place names often indicates the location of the early Celtic Church.

Roman Catholicism took a very firm foothold amongst the inhabitants of rural Wales, and the cultural and economic contributions of the faith to the life of the nation were indeed great. Rome gave to the native of Wales a faith which, as Peate has pointed out, was much in accordance with his own natural temperament. Dwelling in the isolation of his own rigidly organized community, the Welsh pastoralist's background was such that he was rarely forced to think for himself on the intricate problems of life. By nature he was Calvinist, other-worldly and fatalistic in outlook, a believer in destiny and always willing to succumb to 'the order'. Rome satisfied the intellectual needs of the people by providing them with a rigidly organized system and a simple doctrine to follow; it supplied them with beautiful carven images and rich colours, tangible elements that appealed so much to the native mind. Above all, Catholicism provided a priesthood that was of the people, a priest whose peasant background was similar to the social background of the people he ministered. The priest lived amongst his flock, he understood their ways, he knew of their problems, and they in turn regarded him as an intermediary between the worshipper and God, exalting him into a position that was almost supernatural. In the shadows of this system Wales became a nation of wealth and prosperity: economic wealth accumulated by the monasteries, cultural wealth expressing itself in such creations as the *Mabinogion*, the *cywyddau* of the *Gogynfeirdd* (court bards), and the countless manuscripts transcribed for all time by the abbots and monks. The Roman church was a patron of the arts, it encouraged the promotion of the Welsh way of life, 'and it brought security within insecurity which was all the people demanded of it.'

In Wales the Reformation was merely a matter of English politics, that failed to arouse any fervour and enthusiasm amongst the native population. During the earlier years of the Reformation, the religious changes were over-shadowed by the Union with England, which in turn brought to an end the old tribal system of inheritance. Isolated by his ignorance of the English language, deserted by the aristocracy who had become anglicized under the Tudors, the Welsh countryman was left to sink into ignorance and want. The Reformation to him meant robbery of land, the desecration of things held dear—the monasteries, the abbeys, and the rich decorations within them. The bulk of the population understood very little of the new faith, preached to them in an alien tongue by priests who were not of their own class. While from outward observance the people may have been forced to turn to Anglicanism, at heart they remained Catholic, clinging tenaciously to their old way of thought and traditions, and they became as it were Catholics without a Pope, without the *gwerinwr* (peasant) who was their priest. It is no wonder therefore that the Welsh nation was plunged into a deep slumber from which the Civil Wars and the religious turmoil of the seventeenth century failed to arouse them. The almost complete absence of literary contributions during this period was indeed a true reflection of the cultural poverty of the nation.

Like the Reformation, the Puritan movement of the seventeenth century failed to arouse the fervour and enthusiasm of the Welsh nation as a whole. It was essentially a product of Lowland Britain, and although it obtained a strong grip on the towns of the eastern borderland, and penetrated to the valleys and plains leading into the heart of the country from the east, yet it was not until the Methodist Revival of the eighteenth century had got well into its stride that the Puritan influences reached the westerly parts of Wales. It is possible that the whole economic and social background of the Welsh peasant was not conducive to the spread of Puritanism, for this was a religion for the independent of mind, it was an appeal to the reason rather than to the heart. It had no rigid system, no set belief, no graven images and no priest whose status was almost divine. It gripped 'the outposts' of the traditional culture of rural Wales, amongst a population unable to afford the conservatism and old ideas of their predecessors. In these areas so much in contact with the English plain, change meant survival, stagnation—destruction. It was a religion where each man had to think for himself, where he had to carve his own salvation. It was a religion for the thinker, the businessman, the practical; for the group who had been rudely awakened from their sleep since the Reformation by the new impetus given to wool production and manufacture, and by the politics of the Commonwealth period. Rural Wales in the eighteenth century may be envisaged as being of extreme languor. Services were irregular; preaching in Welsh was rare in a country whose language was habitually Welsh; the clergy was listless and inadequate, and the upper classes, who had adopted the English language and habits, were indifferent to the religious needs of the people. Education was almost completely absent but for the aristocratic few, and clergy and flock alike had no zeal or enthusiasm for their religion. With their loss of independence the intellect of the Welsh, so very active before the Union, lay dormant and non-progressive. Life continued unperturbed, the people tilled the land, they attended the flocks, paid their tithes, married and died in complete obscurity, without being touched to any great extent by the intellectual movements of the sixteenth and seventeenth centuries. All the elements were therefore there for a sudden intellectual and moral expansion, and the renaissance in Wales came in the form of a religious revival great in its intensity and consequence. It was a religious revival, but it was more—it was a rebirth of a nation, re-creating and strengthening the mental and moral qualities of the people.

The armament of Welsh Methodism was the explosive force of enthusiasm, it was an appeal to the heart, it appealed to the rural temperament with its unhurried, unchanging ways. Howell Harris said, 'We preach to the heart, so that there be faith in the heart rather than enlightenment in the head.' It attempted to bridle fervour and harness emotion to the service of personal salvation, in a community whose thoughts were always towards their fate in the world to come. In this respect Methodism contrasted sharply with the Puritanism of the previous century; it succeeded where the other had failed; it bridged the gap in the life of the country people, where the other had crumbled. Puritanism was an appeal to the reason; its writers, Morgan Llwyd, Rowland Fychan, Edward James and others, presented their facts in reasoned arguments, in the works of prose that are the literary contributions of the Puritan movement. Methodism on the other hand took root in Wales by appealing to the emotional aspect of the people's character; it presented none of the arid theological doctrines of the earlier dissent, but swept the people into a wave of ecstasy, inflaming their minds with fervour and enthusiasm, obsessing their thoughts with promises of a world to come, and with hell fire. Its armament was not the prose and the reasoned arguments of the Puritans, but the oratorial *hwyl* of the Revivalist, and the melancholy hymns of Pantycelyn. Puritanism prospered in those border areas where the people, because of their whole background, were forced to think for themselves. To them religion was something that was intimately concerned with their daily lives; it was a part of their very existence in this world. Methodism on the other hand was a product of the mountainous core of Wales, of Trefecca, of Llanddowror, Llangeitho and Pantycelyn. Unlike Puritanism, Methodism was not to the same extent concerned with the life of the people, but rather it lifted their minds to a plane far higher than that of their rather humdrum and prosaic rural existence. It demanded no deep thought and no reasoning, but a feeling of salvation, a feeling of communion with the Almighty.

Yet, in essence, Welsh Methodism was but a return to medieval Catholicism, and it has been suggested that one reason for its success in the rural areas was the fact that it reflected the age-old tradition of the countryside, rekindling the dormant flame that Anglicanism and Puritanism had dampened, but failed to extinguish. Powerful preachers dominated the people, keeping them in servile dumbness much as the priest centuries previously had dominated the minds and behaviour of their forefathers. Once again the chanting of those priests could be heard in the *hwyl* of the Revivalist, as by sheer oratorical power he moved his congregation into alternate moods of misery and ecstasy. At one moment he was raising their hopes to the highest pinnacles of glory, with vivid descriptions of white angels sitting on the right hand of God in the World hereafter; at the next he was shattering all their dreams with equally vivid descriptions of the hell awaiting them with its fire of burning sulphur. Welsh Methodism, like its Catholic predecessor, appealed therefore to the higher emotions of man, to pity, sorrow, sympathy, remorse, reverence and humility. Even today no Welsh religious service is considered complete or satisfying unless there is some manifestation of feeling or emotion; the best sermon being that which reaches the highest emotional level; the most popular hymns being those theologically fatalistic lines in a minor key, so popular in the singing festivals of Wales.

11 Food and Drink

By no stretch of the imagination could rural Wales be regarded as a gastronomic paradise, for much of the diet consisted of salty home-cured bacon, home-grown vegetables, especially potatoes and other root vegetables, and oat-based food. A monotonous diet characterized the life of many Welsh countrymen in recent years. For example, an elderly informant in north Pembrokeshire mentioned a typical day's menu on a farm on which he worked in the nineteen-thirties. Breakfast of tea and oat bread was taken at 6 a.m. before milking. This was followed by ten o'clock tea (*te deg*), known as *bite* in parts of mid-Wales. This consisted of bread, cheese and tea. The midday meal, daily, consisted of *cawl*, a broth of mixed vegetables in bacon stock, followed on two or three days of the week by an apple or plain suet dumpling cooked with the vegetables in the *cawl*. Fresh *cawl* was made on Tuesdays, Thursdays, and Saturdays, but on the other days the broth of the preceding days would be reheated. Tea was often taken in the fields and consisted of bread and cheese with tea, with the added luxury of wheat bread and jam on Sundays. Supper on most days consisted of bread and tea or bread and milk, and occasionally the cold meat from the *cawl* of midday.

In the diet of country people oats were important, and oatmeal formed the basis of numerous dishes, such as *llymru, uwd, bwdram* as well as oatcakes. The oatcakes, in turn, were often ground with a wooden roller and the crushed cakes formed the basis of such dishes as *picws mali* (or *shot*) and *brywes*. There were two types of oatcake: the thin type that was spread with butter and eaten with or instead of bread, and a thicker variety of oatcake intended for crumbling. Recipes for oatcakes varied from district to district, but the most common was as follows:

> 3 tablespoons of boiling water
> 1½ tablespoons of bacon fat
> 4 tablespoons of fine oatmeal
> pinch of salt

Melt the bacon fat in water, mix with oatmeal. Spread out and knead well;

roll out thinly and cut into circles. Bake on a moderately hot bakestone or a thick frying pan for ten minutes.

The equipment necessary for making oatcakes consisted of a rolling pin (although in some areas it was believed that better oatcakes were made if the rolling out were done with the palm of the hand, or bare forearm); a wooden slice (*rhawlech*) for turning oatcakes on the bakestone; and a wooden or metal rack (*diogyn* or *car bara ceirch*) (Pl. 116) for drying the oatcakes in front of an open fire. This could be anything up to twenty-four inches wide and twelve inches high, and stood on four short legs. The oatcakes after cooking were stacked upright on the rack and allowed to dry in front of the fire.

Food based on oats varied tremendously, but the following are examples of the most commonplace recipes.

CAWL LLAETH (Milk broth)
>
> 2 bowlfuls of skim milk
> 1 tablespoon of oatmeal
> cold water
> salt

Boil the milk. Mix oatmeal and water to a fine paste and add to the milk. Bring to the boil, add salt and eat.

In many districts this was eaten for breakfast.

Sucan, which was oatmeal with the husks included, was widely used in some parts of the country in a number of recipes. One of them was *bwdram*, made with a bowlful of *sucan* with a quart of lukewarm water. Water was poured on the *sucan* and the mixture was allowed to steep overnight. For supper the following night, the mixture was sieved and had to be of such consistency that its colour would be seen on the back of a wooden spoon, when the spoon was removed from the mixture. If it was too thick, then cold water was added. The *bwdram* after heating for five minutes was then ready to be eaten with salted herring and barley bread. *Bwdram* was regarded in west Wales as a winter supper delicacy.

Fig. 11. BREAD AND OATCAKES
1. Bakestone; Bethel, Merioneth. 2. Pot crane; Llanfyllin, Powys. 3. Hanging bakestone; Cardiff. 4–6. Bakestone stands: 4, Cardigan; 5, Pembroke; 6, Llanwrtyd, Brecknock. 7–13. Oatcake slices (rhawlechi): 7, Bethel; 8, Monmouth; 9, Llandovery, Carmarthen; 10, Llangamarch, Brecknock; 11, Anglesey; 12, West Glamorgan; 13, Nelson, Glamorgan. 14. Oatcake rack (diogyn); Llanllyfni, Caernarvon. 15–18. Rolling pins: 15, Denbigh; 16, 17, Glamorgan; 18, Caernarvon.

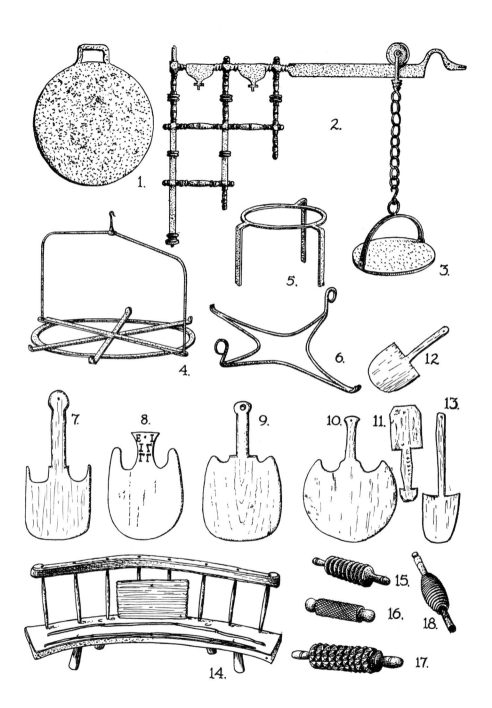

The so-called *bwyd sucan* (sucan food) of west Wales was a thicker version of *bwdram*.

BRYWES

Oatcakes and *cawl*.

Cawl was reheated a third or fourth time and mixed with crushed oatcakes.

This was regarded as a breakfast food.

LLITH

3 dessertspoons of oatmeal
1 bowlful of buttermilk

This was especially popular in the harvest field. In rural south Cardiganshire in the late nineteenth century, for example, it was customary for the farm women-folk to carry a jug of buttermilk and a jug of oatmeal to the fields, between tea time and supper time. Each harvester would take two dessertspoonfuls of oatmeal in a bowl and add the buttermilk from the other jug.

SHOT

6 oatcakes
6 bowls of buttermilk

Oatcakes were rolled with a rolling pin and placed in a bowl. The mixture was allowed to steep with added buttermilk for an hour or more and then eaten, usually for supper.

SOPAS

3 gallons of skim milk
1 tablespoon of rennet

Heat the milk to blood temperature. Add rennet and cover with cloth. Leave for some hours and mix.

This was regarded as a summer breakfast food.

To produce the essential ingredients of so many rural foods, every locality in Wales had a corn mill. In 1923 the county of Cardigan had 77 working corn mills, Brecknockshire had 44, and Pembrokeshire 54. All these mills were water-driven, but in some areas—Anglesey and the Vale of Glamorgan in particular—windmills were very common. In other districts, notably in the Milford Haven district of Pembrokeshire, tide mills were known; the Carew mill is now pre-served in that area.

Corn milling was undoubtedly the most widespread of all rural industries, for there was hardly a river or stream in Wales without a mill along its banks. Undoubtedly considerable quantities of cereals were grown in Wales, for not only may the remains of corn mills be seen in fertile valleys suitable for cereal crops, but they may also be seen in the narrow valleys of the moorlands, areas that must be regarded as completely unsuitable for cereal growth. In the past, it seems, it was considered obligatory for even the moorland sheep farmer to grow his quota of oats, rye and barley to feed both man and animal, even though the land may have been completely unsuited to tillage.

A re-erected mill at the Welsh Folk Museum is typical of the small corn mills that once dotted the Welsh countryside. Melin Pontbren, from Llanllwchaearn, Ceredigion, operated on the banks of the tiny River Soden until the early nineteen-sixties. Like most other west Wales mills it is a stone-built, hip-roofed building on three floors with a lower building containing a kiln for corn drying attached. The mill is built on a slope, so that at the back only two floors appear above the ground, while at the front it has three floors. A narrow doorway at the back leads to the first floor, or 'stone floor', of the mill, while at the front another door, located on the end of the building, is wide enough to admit a cart to the ground floor. The all-iron, over-shot water wheel was made by S. F. Kelly of Cardigan, and a wooden trough, whose angle may be controlled by a lever on the first floor, leads from the mill race (*pinfarch*) and pond. The flow of water along the mill race is controlled by a wooden trap door. Not only does the wheel drive the machinery but it also provides power for the chain hoist, by which sacks of grain were lifted from the ground floor, through two pairs of hinged trap doors in the other floors to the top of the building, or 'bin floor'.

The top floor itself was for storing grain and it contains the entrances to four chutes leading to the milling machinery on the first or 'stone' floor. The first of the pieces of milling machinery is a pair of French burr millstones, usually preferred for milling barley, a cereal crop that was especially important in south Cardiganshire before 1914. Millstone Grit stones were preferred for wheat and oat milling and Melin Pontbren has a pair of such stones of this type. The quality of a millstone is of vital importance to the miller and both the fixed bed stones and the revolving runner stones had to be dressed at regular intervals with a special hammer known as a 'mill bill'. Deep grooves of a regular pattern had to be cut in the stones to ensure that they ground the corn efficiently and distributed the flour at the periphery of the stone. A home-made gauge consisting of a piece of wood with a feather pattern for testing the true running of the stones was also essential for stone dressing. Both pairs of stones are enclosed in a wooden casing with hoppers above for feeding in the grain. Also on the first floor of the building is the grain cleaner, for when seed was brought into the mill for grinding, it was hauled from the ground floor of the building to the top floor by means of the chain hoist. Before it could be milled, impurities had to be removed and the grain had to be passed through the cleaner, then the series of oscillating sieves to remove all the materials that could not be milled. The cleaned grain came out of the seed cleaner through a chute to the ground floor of the building, where it was sacked and hoisted again to the top floor. The other piece of equipment on the first floor is a flour bolter (*mashin fflowro*), which with its series of revolving brushes was used for refining flour and ensuring that the best and finest-grained flour was separated from the bran and inferior flour (*blawd coch*). On the first floor, too, is located the mill's main driving gear, which has apple-wood cogs on cast iron wheels, together with the revolving shaft connected to the water wheel.

On the ground floor are the chutes and troughs for the milled flour and husks, together with a winnower (*mashin nithio*), mainly used for winnowing oats. In this oats were sieved to separate the husks from the flour. The room adjoining the mill is the kiln where oats were gently heated for some hours before milling. The kiln has a grate underneath a metal-bottomed, perforated grain container, the walls of the kiln being of stone. The oats were placed on the metal, a fire of culm was lit underneath and the oats were gently heated; the grain was carefully mixed every twenty minutes or so with a long-handled wooden rake known as a *corloc*. Usually oats were roasted for three hours, and after cooling for twelve hours or more, the grain was milled. It was then winnowed and the oat kernels were again milled.

Of the other items of diet, not based on oats, broth (*cawl*) was the mainstay of most rural districts, especially in the southern half of Wales. The north Wales equivalent was *lobscows*. The usual method of making *cawl* was to place salty beef, salty bacon or some other meat in a boilerful of about four gallons of water. This was boiled for about an hour and a half; potatoes, swedes, carrots, parsnips, cabbages and leeks were added. Sometimes a herb would be added as well. Two tablespoons of oatmeal were mixed with the water and added to the *cawl* to thicken it. In west Wales, the *cawl* itself was eaten first, usually from a wooden

Fig. 12. BUTTER MAKING (i)
1. Plunger (knocker) churn; Salem, Llandeilo, Carmarthen. 2. Plunger for churn. 3. Plunger (knocker) churn; Peterstone Wentloog, Gwent. 4. Box churn; Llansteffan, Carmarthen. 5. Table barrel churn; Pentyrch, Glamorgan. 6. Swing churn; Montgomery. 7, 8. Rocker churns: 7, Cribyn, Cardigan; 8, Radnor. 9. End-over-end barrel churn by Llewellin of Haverfordwest, Pembroke.

1.

2.

3.

4.

5.

6.

7.

8.

9.

bowl or basin and almost invariably with a wooden spoon. This was followed by a second course of meat and vegetables with a certain amount of the liquid to moisten it.

Cawl, especially in winter, would be followed by apple dumplings or plain dumplings. To prepare apple dumplings flour was mixed with a spoonful of *cawl* into a thick paste. This was applied to an unpeeled and uncored apple and each dumpling was placed in the boiling *cawl*.

Butter was made on most farms and smallholdings weekly, and the butter was often stored in casks ready to be taken every few weeks to the nearest market town (Pls 117–121). Large quantities of butter were produced in the spring months, for many of the old farmers believed that calving should be limited to the months of April and May. Milk was poured into a slate or wooden trough in the farm dairy and allowed to stand, so that the cream could be skimmed off its surface. Since churning took place on only one day a week, the cream could be slightly sour before it was converted into butter. Skimming was usually undertaken with a sycamore skimmer, produced by one of the many bowl turners that sold their wares in Welsh markets. By far the simplest type of butter churn was the swing churn: a two-hand, coopered bucket with two of the staves extended to form a couple of handles. To make butter, cream was placed in the churn, the handles were grasped and the churn was swung to and fro in front of the body; this method was extremely slow and laborious. The plunger churn (*fuddai gnoc* or *fuddai dwmp*) was a more common type of churn, and this consisted of a near conical, coopered container, anything up to a yard high, with a vertical plunger or knocker, equipped with a perforated metal disc on the bottom, passing through a central hole in the churn lid (Pl. 117). Rectangular box churns of various sizes were widely used, while until recent times barrel churns of the horizontal or end-over-end type occurred widely. While most barrel churns were hand operated, dog-wheels, horse turnstiles, and even water power were used in some districts for churning. Butter churns like cheese vats were the products of the white

Fig. 13. BUTTER MAKING (ii)
1. Dogwheel and churn; Llanwnda, Caernarvon. 2. Milking pail (stwc); Llanfyllin, Powys. 3. Milk straining frame and funnel; Llanwnen, Cardigan. 4. Milk pen; Bethel, Merioneth. 5, 6. Cream skimmers: 5, Flint; 6, Pembroke. 7, 8. Cream stirrers: 7, Pwllheli, Caernarvon; 8, Carmarthen. 9. Butter working table; Llanddarog, Carmarthen. 10. Buttermilk ladle made by William Rees of Henllan, Cardigan, 1930. 11. Butter tub; Cardigan. 12. Butter scoop; Cribyn, Cardigan. 13. Butter scoop and print; Llanrhystud, Cardigan. 14. Butter print; Llandeilo, Carmarthen. 15. Butter clapper; Llanrhystud. 16. Scotch hands; Rhydlewis, Cardigan. 17. Butter mould; Llanllyfni, Caernarvon.

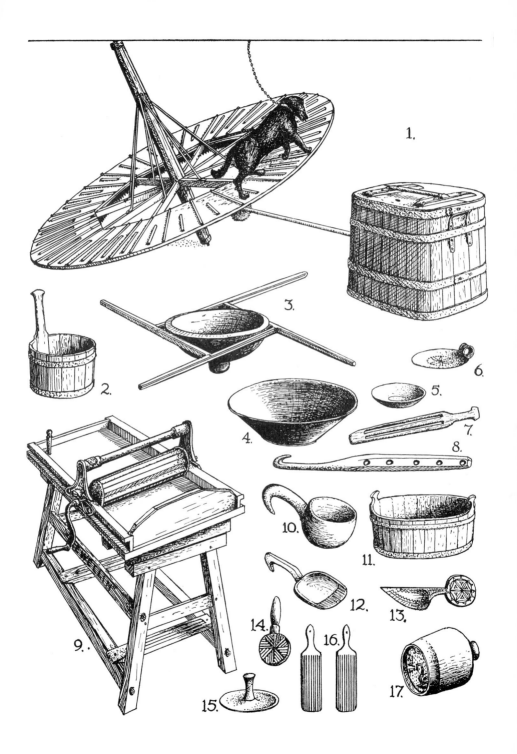

cooper's workshop and in many districts white coopers were familiar craftsmen until recently. Most of them lived in market towns and the last, Charles Parry of Welshpool, Montgomeryshire, only stopped working in the early nineteen-sixties.

The skimmed milk was usually fed to calves, but in most districts was also used to make cheese. In some parts sheep were milked after the spring lambing and their milk was mixed with the skimmed cow's milk. The usual recipe was:

> 1 gallon of ewe's milk
> 4 gallons of cow's milk
> calf's caul or rennet (2 tablespoons)
> salt

The milk was heated in a brass pan to blood heat. It was then removed from the fire, the rennet was added, and the mixture was left standing for a few hours. A wooden spoon or bowl was used to cut it up and the whey was poured away. The curds were then mixed and pressed with the bare hands, salt was added and the curds were placed in a cloth ready for pressing. Most farms possessed wooden, metal or stone cheese presses and a cheese had to be pressed for two days before it was considered ready. The cheese had to be turned three times each day: for the first two turnings a hole was bored in the cheese to allow the whey to run out. Usually a cheese was kept for at least two years before it was considered fit to eat.

In some households the whey would be used to make a dish known as *gwyneb maidd*. About three gallons of whey were heated to near boiling point and fresh milk and buttermilk were added. The milk curdled; bread was added, and the dish was eaten, usually with bread and cheese.

It seems that the monotonous diet of rural communities in Wales was a diet of poverty; of using everything that could be grown or made at home to produce food that in most cases was not the tastiest. In communities that lived in close proximity to the sea, however, fish provided some variety. In many parts of Wales, especially in the Llŷn peninsula and in the south-west, herrings were particularly popular. In the autumn it was customary to buy a 'meise' of herrings, consisting of five hundred fish, and salt them. The herrings were not washed, but salt was placed in a cask and a layer of herrings put on top. This was followed by another

Fig. 14. CHEESE MAKING
1. Brass pan; Pontardawe, Glamorgan. 2. Curd knife; Brecknock. 3. Curd mill; Llangadog, Carmarthen. 4. Cheese vat; Llancarfan, Glamorgan. 5. Cheese vat follower. 6, 7. Cheese presses: 6, Gower; 7, Montgomery. 8, 9. Cheese testers: 8, Clwyd; 9, Caernarvon.

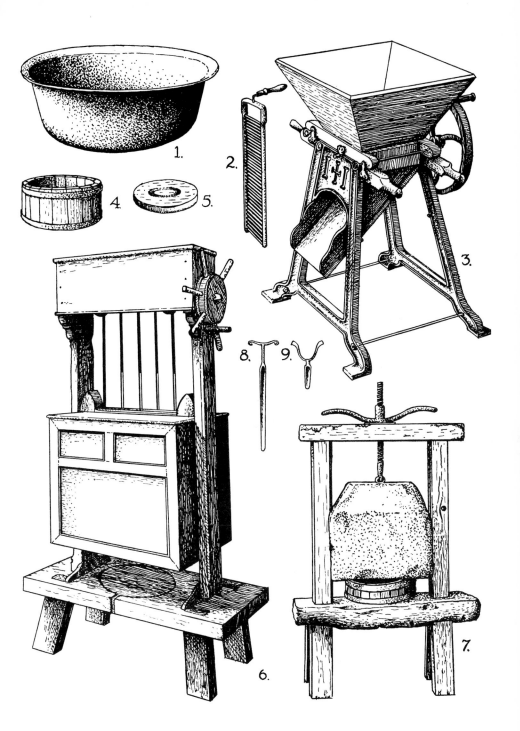

1.

2.

4.   5.

3.

8.   9.

6.

7.

layer of salt until the cask was full. This was stored in a dark, cool corner for two months. When the salted herrings were required, dozens were washed in cold water and they were allowed to steep in the cold water overnight. On the following day a stick was passed through the eyes and the herrings were hung inside the open chimney to dry.

In some riverside communities salmon was preserved by smoking in the chimney, but smoked salmon was not regarded as a luxury at all, merely as a last resort to preserve fish that could not be sold on the open market when fresh. In rural Carmarthenshire and Gower, cockles from Llanrhidian beach sold by the cockle women of Pen-clawdd, in north Gower, were popular (see Chapter 12). These were boiled or fried with bacon and laver bread but, in much of Wales, shellfish was not popular.

DRINK

In a land famous for the militancy of its temperance leaders in the nineteenth and early twentieth centuries, one of the oddest institutions that ever existed in Wales was a distillery that operated for a few years between 1887 and 1905. This was established at Frongoch, near Bala in Merioneth, a town that was a notable centre of Calvinistic Methodism and all that that implied. It was an idea propounded by a certain R. J. Lloyd who thought that Wales could become as important a centre of whisky distilling as the Scottish Highlands. Samples of water from various rivers in north Wales were sent to a laboratory and the Tair-felin river was chosen as the ideal place for the establishment of a distillery. A Scotsman, a certain Mr Colville, was engaged to run the new venture that started production on the banks of the stream and near the railway in 1889. A great advertising campaign was launched and soon bottles of Welsh whisky, with a painting of Jenny Jones in Welsh costume on the label, began to appear everywhere. Every label carried the verse:

> *Why with capers so many*
> *John Jones, gay you are*
> *Welsh whisky, dear Jenny*
> *From Bala*, bur dda.

Despite the extensive advertising campaign, Welsh whisky never became the success that its manufacturers hoped for, and with the closing of the distillery in the early twentieth century, it was the fish of the River Tryweryn that suffered the greatest loss. For a decade or more the fish had flourished on the mixture of barley and hot water that emanated from the distillery. It was certainly not 'the best whisky that drove all skeletons from the feast: or that painted pictures on the mind of man'. According to the distillery's advertisement it was 'a mixture of the soul of peat and barley, washed white in the waters of the Tryweryn. In it is found sunshine and cloud following one another over a wave-crested field, the breath of June, the carol of larks, night dewdrops, the wealth of summer, the harvest of autumn.' To those that drank Welsh whisky the verdict was that it resembled hot, stagnant water, boiled for a week over a peaty fire.

There is perhaps no national Welsh drink, although in many parts of the country, notably Brecknockshire, Radnorshire and Monmouthshire, cider was widely drunk; indeed so widespread was the drinking of cider on Brecknockshire farms that, as has been said, in the nineteen-thirties a certain Calvinistic Methodist preacher attending a *sasiwn* (preaching session) at Trefeca in 1934 described Brecknock as 'a cider besotten county'.

Cider making was widely practised on many farms until recent times, and cider orchards containing such varieties of apple as Golden Pippin, Redstreak, Kingston Black, Old Foxwhelp, Perthyre and Frederick were well distributed throughout the border counties. Many public houses, too, had their cider house containing milling and pressing equipment, and in the border counties cider seems to have been the most popular drink amongst the countrymen.

The method of making cider in Brecknockshire was as follows:

Harvesting of apples was carried out in October and November, but the fruit was not picked; the trees were shaken so that the ripe apples fell to the ground. They were then piled into heaps in the orchard to mature for a week or two.

The apples were then carted to the cider house, usually a brick or stone building, but occasionally an open-sided thatched shed. This contained a horse-driven stone cider mill for crushing the apples into a pomace, or 'must', and a press for pressing the pomace to extract the juice.

The stone mill consists of a massive circular trough, from six to ten feet in diameter, made of a number of shaped stone blocks fixed together with leaded iron cramps. The actual trough or groove in which the crushing wheel runs is known as a 'chase' and can vary in depth from six inches to a foot. An example of a cider press from Llanigon, preserved at the Welsh Folk Museum, is made of Forest of Dean Millstone Grit and is seven feet in diameter; the press is made up of three separate parts clamped together, and the chase, which is eighteen inches wide, is hollowed out to a depth of nine inches. The rim is capped with elm and the mill is built on a rubble base. Every mill has a massive runner stone, weighing up to two tons and measuring three to four feet in diameter; the runner of Llanigon mill is forty-five inches in diameter and with a rim of eighteen inches. The axle passes through a square hole in the centre of the runner stone and is secured to a revolving post, pivoting between the centre of the trough and one of the roof beams of the cider house. The central core of the mill, known as the 'nut', is solid stone, capped with wood, and has a hole in the centre to accommodate the bottom of the pivoting axle. 'The chase encircles the nut, its inner side being perpendicular and its peripheral side sloping outwards towards the lip of the stone; on this lip a wooden curbing rises to the same height as the wooden covering of the nut and prevents the pomace from being spilt through the action of the runner.'

Attached to the post is a wooden framework that extends beyond the side of the mill and carries the shafts to which the horse or donkey is harnessed. The horse was led into and harnessed head first into the shafts and the frame was pushed, not drawn, usually in a clock-wise direction. In many cases, as in the example from Llanigon, a small board measuring fifteen inches by eight inches was attached horizontally to the shafts. This extended over the chase and its object was to prevent the horse from eating the pomace and to scrape the runner clear of any pomace adhering to it.

It is notable that cider mills of this type were introduced some time during the seventeenth century, for 'before this, apples were pulped in large mortars with long handled pestles: a laborious job which it is estimated took three or four men a whole day to manage twenty or thirty bushels'. Hand methods of cider making persisted in Brecknockshire until the mid nineteenth century despite the widespread occurrence of horse-driven mills. At the Welsh Folk Museum is a wooden trough from Ty'nllwyn, Partishow (Partrisio), measuring some four feet long in which worked a stone runner propelled by two men, one on either side holding the projecting ends of the stone's axle.

Another crushing device, used in Brecknock from the mid nineteenth century, was the 'breaker'—a mangle with toothed iron rollers into which the apples were fed. This was originally turned by hand or by horse gear 'and later by a pulley driven by a steam donkey-engine. This method is used by the itinerant cider makers and until a few years ago produced excellent cider for the New Inn, Talgarth, claimed to be the last Welsh public house at which cider was made' (Pl.124).

The most common method of crushing apples, however, was the stone mill, and as soon as the chase had been filled with apples, the horse began walking and the runner crushed the fruit. Since a mound of pomace would build up against the runner, it had to be levelled with a wooden scraper called a 'pusher' or 'reever'. This was specially made to fit into the chase of the mill and had a wooden handle

97. 'Market Day in Wales', by R. Griffiths, 1851.

98. 'Cardiganshire Costume', a drawing by Lady Llanover, c. 1830.

99. A late nineteenth-century posed photograph of egg gathering and sock knitting. Pictures such as this were the tourist photographs of late Victorian Wales.

100. The open-air prayer
held annually near Llyn E
Cardiganshire. Meetings
type became common af
religious revivals of 18
1904.

101. Capel Penrhiw, a
ian chapel of the eighteenth
from Dre-fach, Felindre
marthenshire, now at the
Folk Museum.

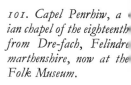

102. A quoits match in
at Llandysul, 1970.

Drying oak bark for tanning
e Forest of Dean, 1970.

. The Rhaeadr Tannery in the
os.

105. *Tanning tongs used for removing hides from the tan pits.*

106. *The beam house, where unhairing and fleshing are carried out.*

107. *The roller used for 'sammying' tanned hides.*

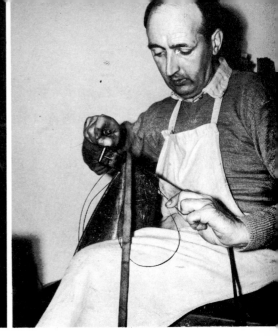

108. *Geler Jones, Cardigan saddler, in 1970.*

109. *Country clog maker: Thomas James of Skyfog, near St Davids, at work in 1970.*

110. *Itinerant cloggers: John Weaver and David Pugh at Tal-y-bont, Cardiganshire, c. 1920.*

111, 112. Carew Tide Mill, Pembrokeshire. Below, the secondary drive wheel undergoing restoration.

113. 114. HEARTHS

    113. Penrhos, Maenclochog, Pembrokeshire.

114. Kennixton farmhouse, from Llangennydd, Gower. The hearth is level with the floor, and at the left is a cupboard bed.

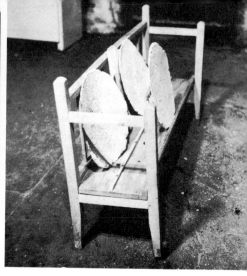

115. *Baking an oatcake on a bakestone at Erw Deg, Bala, 1970.*

116. *Oatcakes drying on a rack (car bara ceirch*

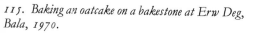

117. *Working a plunger churn, Carmarthenshire, c. 1880.*

118. *Butter working on a clapper at Brechfa, Carmarthenshire, c. 1880.*

119–121. *Mr and Mrs Thomas of Arosfa, Maes-Llyn, Cardiganshire, making butter, 1969. Extracting air from the churn; butter working; printing.*

122. *Domestic beer brewing at L[*
boidy, Carmarthenshire, 1969.
gorse in the churn acts as a f[

123. *Goffering stack for crim[*
lace; from Glamorgan.

124. *Travelling cider makers[*
Brecknockshire farm, c. 1950.

125. Miss Hannah Jones and two assistants making candles at Abergorlech, Carmarthenshire, 1895.

126. Making rushlights at Cwmhesgen, Abergeirw, 1953.

127. *Charcoal burners in the B[*
counties*, c. 1910.*

128. *A charcoal clamp in a B[*
nockshire wood*, c. 1930.*

129. *Coastal vessels beached[*
Llangrannog, Cardiganshire, c. 1[*

Llangwm fishwives depicted on [a] nineteenth-century postcard. [They] were regarded as being very [good] and were able to fish as well as [sell] the catch.

'Inkwell' lobster pots on the [shore] near St Davids, Pembroke-[shire], c. 1930.

Eddie Williams of Aberdaron [mak]ing the traditional Llŷn lobster [pot,] 1965.

133. *Glyn Morgan of Llangwm waiting for a catch on the River Cleddau, 1972. This type of net is called a compass net on the Cleddau.*

135. *Drift netting on the River Dee, 197... Members of the Bithell family of Flint are t... only legal users of the traditional three-wal... Dee trammel net.*

134. *Stop-net fishing... Wye above Chepsto...*

136. Elwyn Brown of Laugharne, Carmarthenshire, with a wade net used for catching salmon on the River Taf, 1972.

137. A smoke house for salmon at Porton, Monmouthshire.

138. A putcher weir in the Severn Estuary

139. A blacksmith-made salmon spear (tryfer) from West Wales.

140. Coracle fishing, Monmouth, 1890.

141. Teifi coracle men, c. 1934.

142. Coracle and net making at C arth, c. 1947.

forty inches long. The pomace after being crushed thoroughly was transferred with wooden shovels into wooden buckets and then to the press, usually a massive oak-framed apparatus at the base of which was a heavy stone slab. This was grooved near the outer edge and had a lip projecting above a semicircular stone trough, tub or vat. Through the upper beam of the frame ran a heavy metal screw, and at its bottom was a horizontal wooden pressing beam or shooter, running in grooves on the vertical members of the frame.

Although oat straw, coarse-meshed manila or goat hair could be used in the press, in Brecknockshire horse-hair mats, called 'cider hair', were used in the pressing process. A mat was 'placed upon the slab, within a square wooden frame called the guide which was manipulated by two staves placed through slots made to receive them. The pomace is now shovelled into the cider hair, which when full is called the cheese, the staves serving to hold down the sides of the cider hair in position. Another cider-hair is placed above the first, filled with pomace and arranged into a cheese in the same manner.' With the pressing beam exerting its full pressure on the layer of cheese, the juice filtered through the cider hairs and dripped into the groove of the stone and thence over the lip to the receptacle below.

The cider was then racked. Casks were filled with the liquor and allowed to ferment for two or three weeks before the casks were sealed. Usually casks were sealed with mixtures of clay, cow dung, chaff and ashes, and the cider was left untouched for up to a year before it was considered fit to drink. In some cases cider makers liked to use casks that had been used for sherry, rum, port or whisky, and some placed pieces of fresh meat in the fermenting casks. The flavour of cider, it is said, is considerably improved by these methods. It required seven to ten hundredweights of apples to produce a hogshead (52 gallons) of cider.

In the past it was quite a common practice to boil the spent pomace in water to produce an inferior fermented drink called 'ciderkin', while pomace was often used as pig swill and even for fuel.

The art of cider making has virtually disappeared from Monmouthshire, Brecknockshire and Radnorshire farms, though some of the apples from the cider orchards of these counties are still sent to Herefordshire cider factories. In the past, one of the main uses of the thick-planked farm wagons of the area was to carry apples from the orchards of Hereford, for local supplies of suitable apples were insufficient to meet the demands of cider makers. The constant preaching of temperance by Nonconformist ministers, the depletion of the farm labour force, and the disappearance of draught horses for driving mills, have all contributed to the decline of this once-important rural industry.

Although beer making was widely practised in Welsh households in the past, the impact of temperance leaders and a number of religious revivals between 1859 and 1904 put an end to this traditional domestic occupation over the major part of Wales. In rural Wales, temperance sprang from the experience of the eighteenth-century Methodist Revival, whose leaders taught the people to sacrifice all worldly pleasures and desires to seek the spiritual ideal. The nineteenth century, its revivals and puritanical outlook on ethical and sexual problems, strengthened and deepened the austere pattern laid down by the early Methodist leaders. Until recently in many parts of Wales, total abstinence from alcoholic drink was regarded as the kingpin of correct social behaviour; until recently too, Calvinistic Methodism, the most widespread of Welsh denominational affiliations, still required an affirmation of total abstinence from all its newly elected elders.

In some districts, notably the Gwaun valley in Pembrokeshire, the temperance movement never caught the imagination of the population as it did in the major part of Wales, and domestic beer brewing has always been important in that remote valley.

The basis of good beer is malted barley, and although in the Gwaun valley today this is bought from the shops, in the past the malting of barley on the farm, or in special malthouses, was widely practised. In Haverfordwest in 1870 there were ten maltsters and in Pembroke there were eight; in addition, the art of malting was known to many Welsh farmers. The remains of farm malthouses are still evident in many parts of the country; in Brecknockshire, for example, there may be seen many farm buildings with perforated tiled floors, where malted barley was dried over a wood fire. Malting usually took place in winter; the barley, after being steeped in water for approximately five days, was drained and spread evenly on the dry floor of the malthouse. It was left there without being touched for a period varying between twelve and forty-eight hours, depending on the temperature, until the appearance of small roots emanating from the base of the corn. From that stage, great care had to be taken; the temperature had to be controlled and the sprouting grain had to be turned at frequent intervals with wooden shovels and rakes. No one was allowed on the growing floor unless he was bare-footed, in case the barley was damaged. The process of flooring went on for about ten days; occasionally water was sprinkled on the grain. The green malt was then taken to the kiln, placed on the perforated tiles and gently dried by the wood fire lit in the chamber beneath. The heating arrested growth and gave the malt the characteristically 'biscuity' taste.

To make the strong beer of Christmas, eight or nine gallons of clean spring water were required for every bushel of malt, but to make the weaker brew of the hay harvest or corn harvest, the amount of water was increased to fourteen or fifteen gallons. The water was boiled and poured on the malt in the wooden brewing vessel. A bunch of gorse or wheat straw was first fitted over the bung hole at the bottom of the vessel to act as a filter when the liquid was drained (Pl. 122). The mixture was covered with an old blanket or coat and allowed to stand in a warm place for at least three hours. More water was added, the liquid was transferred to a boiler and a half-pound of hops and six pounds of brown sugar were added. After cooking overnight, two ounces of yeast were added and the beer left to ferment for two days before being casked or bottled.

Oddly enough in many parts of Wales mead did not join beer as one of the deadly sins and in those districts caskfuls of mead were made in late summer. The ingredients of mead were honeycombs with the honey removed, cold water, hops and yeast. Cold water was poured on the honeycombs, and the mixture was allowed to steep overnight. On the following day it was strained through a fine sieve into a boiler to be boiled very slowly. The surface of the liquid was skimmed frequently, a handful of hops was added and after boiling for another quarter of an hour the liquid was allowed to cool to blood temperature. A pint of brewer's yeast was then added and left for some hours. Usually the mead was bottled in stone jars that had to be buried in a marshy field for at least six months before it was considered fit to drink.

12 Fishing

As befits a country with a long indented coastline and numerous swiftly flowing streams, well blessed with fish, fishermen have been important in Wales throughout the centuries. Methods of fishing that have remained virtually unchanged from prehistoric times may still be seen in parts of Wales, and pieces of equipment used by present-day fishermen on Welsh rivers and in coastal waters have not changed in any important detail for two thousand years or more. For example, the coracles that are still used for salmon fishing on three west Wales rivers are direct descendants of the skin-covered boats described in such detail by Caesar, Pliny and other Roman writers. Fishing weirs that are used for catching salmon on the Conway and other Welsh rivers are said to have been used continuously for nearly two thousand years. Gatherers of shellfish on the shores of Carmarthen Bay have been operating continuously on the same beaches from prehistoric times. The persistence of traditional fishing methods is a characteristic of the Welsh fishing industry, but nevertheless these are methods and equipment that are likely to disappear soon, swamped by the standardizing influences of the twentieth century. For example, 1971 saw the end of the coracle as a fishing craft above Llechryd bridge on the river Teifi; until that year one pair of coracles operated by the last two elderly licensees ceased to be used on this section of river, and a local by-law forbids the issue of any more licences to coracle fishermen on the non-tidal reaches of the Teifi. Thirty years ago there were thirteen pairs of coracles in use in the village of Cenarth alone, of which in the early nineteenth century one writer said: 'There is scarcely a cottage in the neighbourhood of the Tywi or the other rivers in these parts, abounding with fish, without its coracle hanging by the door.' Within the last fifty years coracles have disappeared completely from the Dee, Severn, Usk, Wye, Monnow, Cleddau and Conway, and those in use today, with rigid legal limitations, are found on three rivers only: Teifi, Tywi and Taf.

Other methods of fishing that are likely to disappear soon include that of wade-net fishing, practised by one sole survivor at Laugharne, Carmarthenshire (Pl. 136). Armed with a net thirty yards long, the fisherman and his partner actually wade in the waters of the river, often with the water up to their necks, and attempt to catch salmon on the ebb tide. Fishing weirs of stone and of wattle have disappeared by the dozen and the once ubiquitous hazel salmon trap of north Wales is to be found in one place only—on the River Lledr near Betws-y-coed. In this age of affluence even poachers are rarer than they were, and the days when many rural blacksmiths shaped iron gaffs and spears for local poachers are rapidly passing (Pl. 139).

HERRINGS

Until the end of the nineteenth century, inshore fishing was carried out around all parts of the Welsh coast, and was particularly important in Cardigan Bay. More often than not, inshore fishing was carried out by part-time fishermen, part-time farmers who operated in small rowing or sailing boats; pastoralism seems to have been the main occupation of the inhabitants of the Welsh shores, who were also engaged in off-shore herring fishing in late summer and autumn. It seems unlikely that fishing in medieval Wales was much more than a subsidiary occupation, contributing to the economic self-sufficiency of each rural neighbourhood. Nevertheless in one part, Aberystwyth, fishing did develop into an important commercial venture in the Middle Ages. Salted herrings were an important item of export from this Cardigan Bay seaport. In 1206, it was said in *Brut y Tywysogion* that there were great quantities of fish at Aberystwyth; 'Y roddes Duw amylder o byscawt yn Aber Ystwyth ac nabu y Kyfryw kynno hynny' ('God provided more fish in Aberystwyth than ever before'). The fishermen of Aberystwyth were expected to hand over a proportion of their catch of herrings to the lord of the manor and an extant Court Roll of the Borough of Aberystwyth gives an interesting glimpse of local fishery conditions. It seems that in one year 'there were between twenty and thirty cases connected with the fishery. Some of the delinquents persisted in selling their herrings on the sands below high water mark in order to escape paying market tolls; others would seem to have taken part in the herring industry without obtaining properly accredited licences for their fishing boats. Heavy fines were sometimes imposed, and led to heated altercations between the mayor and fishermen.'

Inshore fishing, particularly off the shores of Cardigan Bay, developed phenomenally in the sixteenth century and every creek and bay had its fleet of herring boats. The requisites of fishing, nets for catching and salt for preserving, were imported from Ireland in Irish-owned vessels that for centuries had been engaged in trading along the Welsh coasts. Casks for preserving were produced in most coastal neighbourhoods by the large number of coopers that lived and worked in Wales. An indication of the growing importance of fishing is given in George Owen's *Description of Pembrokeshire* of 1603, where he describes the coast of the county as if it were 'inclosed in with a hedge of heringes, which being in great store and sold in parts beyond sea, procureth alsoe some store of money'. Large quantities of fish were sold at Haverfordwest, Tenby and Pembroke markets and 'the fish at Tenby, where there was a daily market for it was held in special estimation'. The Welsh name Dinbych-y-Pysgod (Denbigh of the fish) is in itself an indication of the importance of fishing in the local economy.

The coast of south Wales, from Caldey Island to the mouth of the Wye, was of no great significance as a centre of commercial inshore fishing and this section of the coast had to wait until the late eighteenth century before Swansea, and to a lesser extent Cardiff, developed as important fishing ports. The north Wales coast from the Llŷn peninsula to the mouth of the Dee, on the other hand, did develop its inshore fishing industry, particularly from Nefyn and Caernarvon and Hoylake in the Wirral, but on the whole the fishing industry was less important than that of Cardigan Bay.

In sixteenth-century Wales, herrings were sold by the 'meise' of five hundred herrings. The 'hundred' was nevertheless one hundred and twenty herrings, and

'as every two score were counted a herring was thrown to one side, this being apparently to keep in mind how many score had been dealt with; another herring was thrown out at the end of every hundred, so that the meise of five hundred herrings finally consisted of 120 × 5 = 600, plus 15 "warp" (the herrings thrown aside to keep tally of the number of score) and 5 "tale", one for each "hundred"— a total of 620 herrings.'

During the seventeenth and eighteenth centuries the fisheries of Wales developed substantially, especially after the enactment of the Bounty Act of 1705 and the subsequent Act of 1718. Bounties of 'a shilling were paid on every barrel of shotten red herring exported beyond the sea; one shilling and nine pence on every barrel of full red herring and two shillings and eight pence on every barrel of white herring'. The Act of the Encouragement of the British White Herring Fishery of 1750 resulted in a phenomenal increase in fishing. By this Act a bounty of thirty shillings per ton was paid for every decked vessel of thirty tons to eighty tons built specifically for herring fishing. Since these ships had to rendezvous at Brassa Sound in the Shetlands, or Campbeltown in Argyllshire, the 'barrel bounty' system did lead to the development of a fishing industry that was not based on offshore fishing grounds alone. An Act of 1787 granted a bounty on every barrel of herrings taken by open or half-deck boats of less than twenty tons burthen. For the earlier part of the eighteenth century Aberystwyth still reigned supreme as the most important fishing port in Cardigan Bay.

'What it is chiefly resorted to for and contributed to its wealth', said one eighteenth-century writer, 'is its Fishing Trade of Cod, Whitings but principally Herrings . . . the Herring Fishery here is in most so exceedingly abundant that a thousand barrels have been taken in one night. . . . In addition to herring they have such an abundance of Cod, Pollack, Common Whiting, Ray and other fish that they set but little value upon them. Bottlenoses and porpoises sometimes run on shore in shoals and blue sharks are frequently caught upon the coast, from all of which they make considerable quantities of oil.'

Inshore fishing developed rapidly during the course of the last decade of the eighteenth century. In the Llŷn peninsula, for example, Pennant speaks of the abundance of herrings taken 'from Porte Ysgadan or the Port of Herrings to Bardseye island', while Swansea developed rapidly as a fishing port and fish market after 1790. Not all parts of Wales continued to share in the prosperity, for the herring became much rarer in Cardigan Bay and, speaking of Aberystwyth, one writer says 'that fish is now a stranger to the coast'. Donovan, writing of Tenby in 1804, says that although the inshore fishing grounds were as productive as ever, the fishermen were incapacitated by poverty, their property consisting only of 'a few open boats, with nets and dredges . . . quite unsuitable for venturing to sea and capable only of working in the bay or just outside the pier'. Tenby waters were, however, visited regularly by Torbay and Brixham trawlers and the fish taken to the Bristol market.

Deep-sea trawling based on Milford and Swansea developed during the nineteenth century, particularly with the growth of the railway system and the consequent ease of taking fish to market, but in most parts of Wales fishing was still largely carried out by part-time fishermen who operated in small open boats. In Cardiganshire, for example, the small boats of coastal villages such as Aberaeron, Llangrannog and Aber-porth were used for inshore trawling and lining. Aberaeron had in the 1830s 'a lucrative herring fishery in which about thirty boats, with seven men to each are engaged'. Aber-porth was a scene of great activity between August and December, as a fleet of small boats left for the local herring fishery, while nearby New Quay had 'fish of very superior quality . . . soles, oysters and turbot being taken in great numbers'. The Teifi estuary had its fleet of offshore herring boats, with the village of St Dogmaels regarded as

'one of the principal stations for the herring industry . . . where the boats engaged in it are commonly of from eight to twenty tons burthen, with masts and sails, but mostly open, without decks and manned by six or eight men; the herrings generally make their first appearance on the neighbouring coast between the middle and the end of September which is considered the best period of the season, as they will then bear carriage to distant markets, and the harvest being commonly over, the fishermen can be better spared from agricultural labours'.

Seventy per cent of the inshore harvest of fish is caught by trawl nets at the present time. The earliest form of trawl net was the beam trawl where the mouth of the net was kept open 'by a rigid bar or beam of timber, supported at the ends by iron trawl heads'. The beam trawl was in the form of a large, elongated pocket and was pulled behind a boat as it fished. Nevertheless, the other trawl, where the mouth of the net is kept open by two other boards or doors, has superseded the beam trawl and is widely used today, especially by Conway and Milford trawlers. Trawling is, of course, the most effective method of catching the demersal species of fish, that is, those which unlike the herring or mackerel live on, or near, the bottom of the sea.

Since in the past a large proportion of fish caught off the Welsh coasts was herring, fished usually between September and December, drift nets were widely used by fishermen. In Aberystwyth

'the drift nets used in the open and half-decked boats were 30 yards long, about 4 fathoms deep and had a $1\frac{1}{4}$ in. mesh. The top of the mesh was attached to a line called the *upper tant* which was suspended below the buoy rope by lines, perhaps $2\frac{1}{2}$ fathoms long, but varying according to the depth at which they expected to find the fish. Along this rope and spaced at about 1 fathom intervals, were the cork floats. The foot of the net was secured to the *lower tant* and stones were sewn in at intervals to act as weights to keep the net upright in the water.'

The larger Aberystwyth boats carried

'fifteen to twenty to twenty-five nets each, while the smaller gigs and double-ended beach boats only carried between six and eight nets. During the season fifteen to twenty boats or more would sail in company to the fishing grounds in time to shoot their nets at sunset. After a boat had lain to her nets for an hour or so, the first net was brought in-board, and if the catch seemed satisfactory all the nets were hauled aboard and fish and nets were dumped in the bottom of the boat.

The boats were so small and the working space so restricted that no attempt was made to take the fish out of the nets, until the boats had returned to port.'

The modern drift net of cotton or synthetic fibre is fifty to fifty-five yards long and is suspended by a 'strap' some two fathoms long from a buoy. The bottom of the net is attached to a stout manila warp which takes the strain when hauling (Pl. 135).

Seine nets, 'movable nets ... which are shot in position so as to enclose a definite body of water or a shoal of fish', are more widely used in Wales today for salmon fishing in river estuaries such as the Teifi, Tywi, Conway and Dee, and are rarely used for inshore fishing. In the past they were widely used, as for example at Tenby, where in the nineteenth century both herring and mackerel were caught with seine nets—each seventy fathoms long and eight to ten fathoms deep; in 1864 eight Tenby boats were concerned in this trade. Fixed nets may still be seen in a number of places, notably Carmarthen Bay, and fishing lines are widely used for inshore fishing, particularly mackerel fishing. Lines may be divided into two types: hand-lines on which there are generally a few hooks that are attended to continuously, the line being hauled in as soon as the presence of fish is felt; and secondly there are long-lines, which are not attended to while fishing. They are periodically hauled and the presence or absence of the fish is not known until they are raised.

In many parts of Wales thorn hooks survived until fairly recent times. They were used in the Ferryside district of Carmarthen Bay and at Conway until 1939. Blackthorn hooks were placed in an oven for some days to harden the points and were fitted to hand-lines or long-lines that were particularly effective for catching flatfish. In 1923 F. M. Davis noted that

'the lugworm which is used as bait is threaded from the bottom upwards and over the point of the thorn as near as possible to the snood. When the flatfish ... takes the bait and sucks it and the hook into its mouth, the hook, owing to the angle at which it is set to the snood, jams across the mouth of the fish.'

In some districts, notably the Conway district, horsehair snoods with thorn hooks at eight-inch to fifteen-inch intervals were widely used for long-lines.

LOBSTERS

Lobster fishing is one of the most important activities on the western coast of Wales today, and the total value of lobster landed at Welsh ports in 1968 amounted to £75,000. A rugged coastline with extensive areas of rough ground is the ideal environment for lobsters and crabs, and both species occur profusely along the coast of Wales. Little lobster potting has been practised east of Caldey Island, with the exception of a limited amount along the Gower coast; while in north Wales there has never been lobstering on any scale east of Llandudno. Today appreciable quantities of lobster are exported from such villages as Aberdaron in Llŷn and New Quay in Cardiganshire to France and other parts of western Europe. Although some fishermen, notably those operating in large boats from Milford Haven, set lobster pots throughout the year if weather conditions are favourable, to most fishermen lobster fishing is a seasonal occupation, extending from mid March or early April to early October. Today the European market is the main avenue of sale for Welsh lobsters, for few are sold within Wales itself; indeed traditionally crabs are preferred to lobster for consumption at home by fishermen and their families. The Cardigan Bay lobster, found along rocky sections of the coast, is regarded as the best possible type; the best weighing from $1\frac{1}{2}$ lb. to 2 lb. George Owen, the Pembrokeshire historian, writing in 1600, noted that the lobsters caught off the coast of that county were 'very sweete and delicate meate and plentie taken'.

Nevertheless, lobster catching was not practised on any scale until the late nineteenth century, with the exception of Bardsey Island and the Llŷn coast, where the fishing of lobster and crab has been carried on for many centuries. Writing in 1800, Bingley noted that 'collecting lobsters and crabs occupies most of the time of the inhabitants of Bardsey Island'. The pots used for the capture of lobsters, Bingley adds, were 'made of willows exactly in the shape of a wire mouse trap, with the cone inverted'. These pots, similar to many that are still used in Llŷn today (Pl. 132), were fished singly and were weighted down with stones attached to them on the outside. The catches were sent by boat from Bardsey to Liverpool, a regular service from the island to the Mersey continuing until 1914.

There are few other references to lobster fisheries in Wales during the nineteenth century. Pennant in his *Tours of Wales* in 1810 makes a passing reference to the lobster fishermen of Pwllheli, who made pots 'of pack thread . . . baited with pieces of lesser spotted shark'. Holdsworth in his comprehensive survey of sea fishing in 1874 does not even mention lobster and crab fishing on the Welsh coast, nor is there a reference in Buckland and Walpole's equally comprehensive survey of 1877. Davies in 1884, however, noted that in north Pembrokeshire and around Caldey Island in the south of the county, lobsters and crabs abounded. Commercial exploitation of the lobster supplies had not developed, for the few that were caught by hand and hook amongst rocks at low water, and by a certain amount of potting from open boats, were 'disposed of locally'.

Elsewhere on the Welsh coast lobster potting was largely an innovation of the present century that developed as transport facilities improved to ensure the rapid carriage of the fish to the market. The end of the First World War marked the beginning of a period when lobster fishing, from Caldey in the south to Anglesey in the north, developed steadily. The fishing was almost exclusively done from small open boats propelled by sail and oar, but in the mid twenties larger boats fitted with outboard engines and even larger motor boats were introduced. By 1924 in Pembrokeshire, for example, Marloes had 9 lobster boats employing 17 men; Angle had 6 boats employing 12 men; St Davids, 3 boats and 7 men; Porthgain, 3 boats and 6 men; Solva, 2 boats and 4 men; Dale, 2 boats and 4 men; Little Haven, 2 boats and 2 men; St Brides, 1 boat and 2 men; and Abermawr, 1 boat and 1 man. In the twenties part-time lobster fishermen were to be found for the first time operating from such seaside villages as Aber-porth, Llangrannog and New Quay in Cardiganshire, and from Amlwch, Church Bay, Moelfre and Cemais in Anglesey.

As marketing facilities improved and as the demand for lobsters increased, the period since 1945 has seen a considerable increase in the number of both full-time and part-time fishermen. Although small open boats manned by one or two men are still widely used, there has been a tendency in recent years to use larger motor boats, often converted ships' lifeboats, for lobster fishing. In many cases fishermen sail for considerable distances from their home ports to fish: in 1969 more lobsters were landed at Barmouth in Merioneth than at any other Welsh fishing port, but the boats concerned were based on Milford Haven and not locally.

MUSSELS

The gathering of cockles and mussels is of considerable antiquity in Wales, for the shells of these molluscs have been excavated from a number of prehistoric and Roman sites. The most important centre of commercial mussel gathering today is the Conway district, where the total annual value of mussels landed amounts to £40,000. At Portmadoc in Gwynedd the annual value of the mussel catch is £20,000, while near Bangor mussel farming, where the mussels are artificially bred, is gradually becoming far more important. At Pen-clawdd in Gower appreciable quantities of mussels are gathered by the cockle women of that village, while before 1939 mussel fishing was of considerable importance in the Menai Straits, Pwllheli, Barmouth, Aberdyfi, Cydweli, Ferryside and Laugharne.

At Conway today there are eight boats at work compared with a total of seventy-two before the war. Mussels are caught on the ebbing tide in shifts of three or so hours of back-breaking work. The season extends from the middle of September until the end of April, and some of the fishermen for the remainder of the year are concerned with seine-net salmon fishing on the Conway, sparling fishing at Tal-y-cafn or with running pleasure boats from Conway quay. Most of the mussels taken at Conway are obtained from the sea bottom at a depth of twelve feet of water or more. A long-handled *cram*, or rake, is required and this may have a handle as long as thirty feet. The cram has ten or more prongs each some six inches long, and on the back of the iron rake head is fitted a fine-meshed net or purse. When at work, the gatherer moors his open boat above a mussel bed and drops the head of the *cram* into the water, as far as possible from the boat. The tines of the cram actually rest on the sea bed. The top of the long handle is placed against the fisherman's shoulder and he draws the *cram* towards him, at the same time exerting some downward pressure so that the mussels are torn off the sea bottom and are caught in the net purse. When the handle of the *cram* is nearly vertical the *cram* is turned over, lifted and the mussels tipped into the boat. The harvest is then sorted according to size and the mussels taken back to the shore to be washed thoroughly in specially constructed tanks. This process of sterilization and purification is vital and the necessity of installing mussel washeries may have retarded the commercial development of mussel fishing in Cardigan Bay and elsewhere in Wales.

Mussels that are exposed at low water are detached from rocks by a knife, and in Carmarthen Bay this is the usual method of gathering. Nevertheless, mussel gathering is in that area subsidiary to cockle gathering.

One important aspect of mussel gathering at Conway was pearl fishing, that was well-known in the Middle Ages.

'The pearls found in these mountain rivers are plentiful and commonly large', says Meredith Owen in a letter in 1690; '. . . several ladies of Denbighshire have collections of good pearls found in the river Conway.'

A local historian in 1835 gives details of the pearl fishery at the time. He says:

'There are two kinds of muscles [*sic*] found on the Conwy, from which pearls are obtained; *mya margaritifera* (*cragen y diluw*) and the *mytilus edulis* (*cragen lâs*). Those of the former species are procured high up the river above Trefriw, and pearls scarcely inferior to the oriental ones are occasionally found in them. . . . The other variety, the *cragen lâs*, is found in abundance on the bar at the mouth of the river, and great quantities of the muscles are gathered by numbers of industrious persons. At ebb tide, the fishers, men, women and children, may be observed busily collecting the muscles, until they are driven away by the flood. They then carry the contents of their sacks and baskets to *Cewnwro*, the northern extremity of the marsh, where the muscles are boiled; for this operation there are large *crochanau* or iron pots, placed in slight huts; or rather pits as they are almost buried in a vast heap of shells. The fish are picked out and put into a tub, and stamped with the feet until they are reduced to pulp; when water being poured in, the animal matter floats, which is called *solach* and is used as food for ducks, while the sand, particles of stone and the pearls settle in the bottom. After numerous washings, the sediment is carefully collected and dried, and the pearls, even the most minute are separated with a feather on a large wooden platter.'

The industry lingered on till the eighteen-sixties, for 'The mussels are found in considerable abundance at low water all along the shore at the entrance to the river and are dredged by boatmen along the course of the river as well as collected on the mussel banks.'

COCKLES

The main occupation of the women and a few of the men of Pen-clawdd and the adjacent villages of Crofty and Llanmorlais on the north coast of Gower is gathering cockles from the beaches of the Burry Inlet. Today there are seventy-nine licensed cockle gatherers concerned with the commercial exploitation of the cockle beds at Llanrhidian beach, with a further twenty-two licensees on the north shore of the inlet around Llanelli. Although cockle gathering is practised in other parts of Carmarthen Bay—at Laugharne, Ferryside and Llansaint, for example—the Burry Inlet which 'lies to the east of a line drawn from the eastern bank of the Llanrhidian Pill in the south, true north until it meets the western extremity of the Great Western Dock, Llanelli in the north', is the true centre of the shellfish fishery. To understand something of the character and personality of the seaside communities of the Burry Inlet, one must know something of the cockle gathering industry that employs so many of the inhabitants.

The history of cockle gathering in Carmarthen Bay is shrouded in mystery, for the origin of the industry is not known. Undoubtedly cockle gathering was widely practised on the Welsh coast in Roman times, for many excavated sites have yielded vast quantities of cockle shells, which suggests that the shellfish was extensively used as food in those times. In addition 'in almost every midden, cave and churchyard have cockleshells been found'. In later centuries, cockle gathering was widely practised throughout Wales. George Owen, for example, in 1603 notes that cockles were taken in most parts of the Pembrokeshire shore. In 1804 Donovan remarks on 'the partiality of the Glamorgan peasants for these molluscs for which they would dig in the sand'. The Rev. J. Evans on his Tour of 1803 describes the cockle fishery carried out in Carmarthen Bay at the mouth of the Tywi; he describes how the wives and daughters of the fishermen and others collected the cockles, put them into sacks and carried them 'to the boats which plied for this purpose at high tide, between Carmarthen and the river mouth, at a fare of 2d. per person. The cockles were commonly sold at the rate of 6d. per bushel.'

In 1929 Matheson surveyed the Welsh sea fisheries and he describes the cockle fishery as being 'centred mainly at Penclawdd, Ferryside and Laugharne. The cockles and mussels taken at Penclawdd and near Llanelli about 1884 are stated to have been worth over £15,000 a year. . . . In 1925 the quantity collected was 20,952 cwts. valued at £5,235'. On the other side of Carmarthen Bay, the villagers of Laugharne landed 9,949 cwts of cockles valued at £1,741 in 1925, while at Ferryside 29,505 cwts valued at £4,532 were landed. A certain amount of cockle gathering was found at Llanstephen, Llansaint and as far south as Tenby and Saundersfoot. In Cardigan Bay 102 cwts of cockles was landed at Aberdyfi, while in north Wales 560 cwts were landed at Bangor and 302 cwts at Caernarfon.

Today, the cockle-gathering industry is of little importance in Wales except in Carmarthen Bay. The Laugharne, Llanstephan and Ferryside cockle beds have declined in importance and there is little commercial exploitation of the fisheries in those districts; indeed no licence is required for cockle gathering in districts other than the Burry Inlet. Llanrhidian beach on the south shore of the Inlet has a profusion of cockles despite the heavy toll taken by oystercatchers, which are regarded as a menace by the fisherwomen. A licence fee of three pounds per annum is payable by the commercial fisherwoman and no equipment but a hand rake (*cram*), scraper (*scrap*) and riddle is allowed to fish for cockles. The riddle has apertures of ¾-inch square, for it is an offence to gather cockles less than eleven-sixteenths of an inch in diameter. Cockle gathering is forbidden on Sundays and 'between half an hour after sunset on any day and half an hour before sunrise on the following day'. There are limitations on the quantity each fisherwoman may collect, '[not] more than two cwts of cockles in any one day . . . except as permitted by the provision of a licence in that behalf or by the written authority of the Clerk of the Committee or by the appointee of the Clerk present at the time of the removal'. In effect, this means that each licensed cockle gatherer is limited to a quota of seven cwts per day, whereas until 1967 each person could collect ten cwts of cockles per day. An officer of the South Wales Sea Fisheries Committee is present on the beach at all times to ensure that the regulations are carried out.

The life of a Pen-clawdd cockle woman is not an easy one, for she has to leave her home, often at an unearthly hour, to travel across the inhospitable, windswept marshland to the cockle beds. Until recently, donkeys equipped with panniers were used for transporting cockles, but today horse-drawn, two-wheeled carts are used. At the appointed hour a long line of carts leaves the village, the fisher-woman with her sacks, basket, riddle, scraping knife and rake, sitting on the front of each cart. Occasionally the convoy has to stop at Salthouse Point to await the ebb before venturing across the wet sand to the cockle beds. This can be a journey of considerable peril at night or in foggy weather, for a number of rapidly flowing streams, or 'pills', can prove a hazard to anyone who ventures on the beach. Each fisherwoman after arrival on the cockle beds takes her allotted section of beach and with her *scrap* scratches the surface of the sand to expose the cockles a few inches below. The cockles are then gathered together with the *cram* and placed in a sieve, which is shaken backwards and forwards and from side to side to ensure that all under-sized cockles fall through the mesh. The cockles have to be boiled in one of the 'boiling plants' in the village. In the past boiling was performed on an open fire on the beach, but now each cockle gatherer has to take cockles either to a communal 'factory', or to a privately owned plant found in the gardens of many Pen-clawdd houses. Although some cockles are sold to bottling factories, it is a custom for Pen-clawdd cockle women to take cockles to market themselves. Some attend Swansea market on Fridays and Saturdays; some travel to Pontypridd and the Rhondda valleys; while some travel as far as Hereford or Gloucester, selling cockles from door to door. Custom has dictated that most of the cockle gathering should be completed on Monday, Tuesday and Wednesday mornings. Boiling takes place on Wednesdays and Thursdays, and the produce is sold on Fridays and Saturdays.

SALMON

By far the most important fish caught in Welsh rivers is the salmon. For many centuries Welsh rivers have been renowned for the quality and quantity of their salmon and fishing has provided a livelihood for many generations of riverside dwellers. For example, Giraldus Cambrensis in the twelfth century described that notable salmon river, the Teifi, as 'the noble river Teivi that abounds more than any river of Wales with the finest salmon'. George Owen in 1603 spoke of the 'Ryver fishe, whereof the saman shall have the first place, partely for the plentie and store thereof taken in manie partes and places of the countrie, but chiefly for the excellencie and daintyness thereof, wherein yt exceedeth those of other countryes'.

Travellers to Wales in later centuries were all impressed with the quality and abundance of salmon and sewin in Welsh rivers. Writing of Cardiff during the first decade of the nineteenth century, Donovan was greatly impressed with the abundance of sewin in the river Taff where he 'observed fishermen taking them in vast numbers in their nets'. To Malkin, another early nineteenth-century traveller, the Teifi was the best of all Welsh salmon rivers and the 'salmon . . . esteemed the most excellent in Wales. There is scarcely a cottage in the neighbour-hood of the Tivy, or the other rivers in these parts, abounding with fish, without its coracle hanging by the door.'

The rivers of north Wales, especially the Dee, Clwyd and Conway, were equally important salmon rivers and fish were caught by a variety of methods ranging from coracle nets to basket traps and from seine and sling nets to stone weirs. The quantity of salmon taken in the nineteenth century must have been con-siderable: on the Dee in 1882, for example, 10,935 salmon and 650 sewin were taken, while on the Severn in the same year the catch amounted to 15,500 salmon. Salmon fishing, said Abraham Rees, the Montgomeryshire encyclopaedist, was 'of great national importance, furnishing a constant and copious source and supply of human food'. 'The fisheries', he adds, 'may be said with propriety to rank next to that of the cultivation of the land in utility in this intention.'

CORACLES

The use of the coracle as a fishing craft has declined very rapidly in recent years and today coracle fishing is limited to three rivers only—the Teifi (Pl. 141), Tywi and Taf in west Wales. In the nineteen-twenties and thirties coracles were to be found on many other rivers, such as the Dee, the Severn and the Cleddau; at the turn of the century, other rivers such as the Usk, Wye and Conway had coracle fishermen. Each river had its own specific type of coracle, and the customs and rules relating to fishing were those that could be traced back for hundreds of years.

Coracle fishermen were described in 1861 as 'a numerous class, bound together by a strong *esprit de corps*, and from long and undisturbed enjoyment of their peculiar mode of fishing have come to look on their river almost as their own, and to regard with extreme jealousy any sign of interference with what they consider their rights'. The coracle fishermen of the Teifi were, therefore, almost a closed community. The river was divided into four sections amongst four riverside villages, and custom dictated that only fishermen from one of these four villages might fish in those sections of the river. The four villages concerned were Cilgerran, Cenarth, Aber-cuch and Llechryd. Each section of the river was known as a *bwrw* (cast), and each *bwrw* was divided into three parts, each of which was called a *traill* (trawl). At Cilgerran, for example, the principal trawl (*y draill*) was that side of the river nearest the village; the second trawl (*yr ail draill*) signified the middle of the river; and *yr hawel* or *tu'r dre* signified a third trawl on the opposite side of the river from the principal trawl. According to local tradition, each of the eight casts that belonged to Cilgerran coracle men had its own characteristics, expressed in a doggerel verse passed down over many generations to the present day.

> ' *Bwrw byr hyfryd, Brocen ddryslyd,*
> *Gwegrydd lana, Nantyffil lwma.*
> *Crow'n rhoddi, Pwll du'n pallu,*
> *Bwmbwll yn hela, Draill fach yn dala.*'

> ' *Lovely Bwrw byr, complex Brocen,*
> *Cleanest Gwegrydd, poorest Nantyffil.*
> *When Crow gives, Pwll du refuses,*
> *When one hunts at Bwmbwll, you may catch at Draill fach.*'

Each of these main casts had minor casts attached, but there were also seventeen other minor casts, that were not attached to the principal *bwrws*.

'In or about the month of April', said a writer in 1867, 'the town crier used to convene by a public cry a meeting of all the fishermen. Formerly none were permitted to fish in that part of the Teivi which borders on the confines of this parish, save those who had previously been admitted burgesses of the ancient borough of Cilgerran, so that the river being entirely monopolised by them, strangers were effectively excluded from participating in the fishery.'

At the annual April meeting of the fishermen, the turns or casts for the first night of the fishing season were allocated. For this purpose, slips of paper on which were written the names of the eight principal casts and of the minor casts were deposited in a hat, from which every fisherman in turn picked out a slip, and whatever name or position might be written on that slip would be his station for the opening night of the salmon fishing season. This arrangement of course 'only held good for the first night, for he that would have the best chance on the first trawl . . . would be the last on the next cast on the following night, and so on until he had gone through all the subdivisions in each *bwrw*'. If a fisherman should absent himself from his station on any one night, no one could take his place, for the allocation of casts was very rigidly enforced at all times. The starting point of every station was termed *pen bwrw* (the head of the cast), where the coracles were placed in order of precedence. The two leading coracles were required to be with their keels on the ground, in the same position as when on the water, with the paddle resting on the seat. If this rule was not adhered to, the owners of the leading coracles were deprived of their trawl.

The rigid rules of precedence and privilege were undoubtedly framed by the fishermen themselves and were invaluable in that disputes were avoided. They were oral laws passed down from father to son in a closely knit village community and were practised with little variation by the coracle men of Llechryd, Abercuch and Cenarth, as well as those of Cilgerran. Before the eighteen-sixties the close season for salmon fishing on the Teifi was also a matter of unwritten law rather than of legislation, and the closed season extended from August to February. One fisherman in each village was responsible for locking up the coracles during the close season.

The eighteen-sixties saw the end of the rigid rules of precedence that had been practised on the river from time immemorial. At Cilgerran, for example:

'before a person has any certainty of a draw, he must need place himself at the starting point and then remain with his coracle from the morning till the evening sets in and the darkness enables him to spread his net to advantage, and even this patient watching does not always now secure a first position. In fact there is no regulation whatever adhered to, everybody scrambles for the first chance, and everybody spreads his net wherever he thinks it likely to obtain a fish.'

Nevertheless, even in the nineteen-seventies this is not quite true, for among the half dozen pairs of coracles that operate in Cilgerran gorge, vestiges of the older system still remain. The first coracle on the river during a fishing session is still referred to as *yr ergyd*; the second as *yr ail draill*; and the third as *y trydydd*. Only three pairs are allowed on the river at the same time. Fishing is still practised in strict rotation and the first net may not enter the water a second time until the first trawl by all the other coracles is complete.

On the Tywi too, the coracle men by tradition have a strong sense of community.

The first *Report of her Majesty's Inspectors on Salmon Fisheries* in 1863 described the Tywi coracle men as

'lawless and often aggressive . . . he uses violence if he is strong, he threatens if his opponent be not so much weaker than himself as to make violence safe. A man of some property in this part told us that they had encroached upon his water and taken possession of it; that he did not dare to interfere for they would burn their stacks. This year on the Towy they went in a body to Ferry-side, where the long net men mostly live, attacked the men and destroyed their crops.'

There are still twelve pairs of coracles on the Tywi who fish at night during the season. The beginning of each fishing session is described as *clyfwchwr*, when the seven stars appear in the sky. The men start from the fishing station at intervals of two hundred yards and use a net that is weighted according to an exact mathematical formula, the position of the lead weights on the lead line of the net varying according to the flow of the river. It is interesting to note that although many of the Tywi coracle men are not Welsh speaking, all the technical terms relating to coracle, net and fish are always in the Welsh language.

SEINE NETTING

The shore seine is widely used around Britain, particularly in river estuaries, and it is a simply constructed plain wall of netting two hundred yards or more in length and of a depth suitable to the water in which it is used. It is important that the net should extend as far as possible from the surface of the water to the bottom and should stand as nearly vertical as possible in the water. The head-rope is fitted with corks or plastic floats and the foot-rope weighted with lead or stones. The net is carefully stowed on the flat transom of a small boat. One of the crew stands ashore holding a rope attached to the end of the net. The boat is then rowed out into the stream from the shore on a semicircular course, with the net being paid out over the stern. When all the net has been shot, the boat returns to the shore whence it set out. The crew then lands, the boat is made fast, and the net is hauled in. The landing place is usually downstream of the shoreman, but the net is occasionally shot upstream if the boat—as on the Teifi and Dee—is equipped with an outboard motor. The hauling of the net is rapid and smooth, and the two ends of the net are brought close together 'thus making a narrow bag of the middle of the enclosed space, where the fish are concentrated and can be hauled ashore. The foot-rope is hauled faster than the headline, thus making a more pronounced bag of the centre of the net.' The whole net is drawn in; the salmon or sewin caught in its mesh are killed with the knocker and the net has to be re-arranged on the boat transom again ready for the next shot.

Despite its occurrence in estuarine waters throughout Wales, there are local variations in the dimensions and techniques of using the seine net. On the Teifi, for example, nets are usually 180 yards to 200 yards long and 3 yards deep with a 2-inch mesh. On the Tywi, a 1½-inch mesh is allowed. The Gwynedd River Authority, responsible for such rivers as the Conway, Mawddach and Dyfi, specifies seine nets not more than 150 yards long and 6 yards deep, but the mesh of net is not specified. On the Dee, on the other hand, nets may be up to 200 yards long, 5 yards deep, with a mesh of not less than 2 inches.

Seine nets are used in the Teifi estuary below the village of St Dogmaels for catching salmon and sea trout. The *rhwydau sân*, as they are known locally, measure 200 yards in length, have a mesh of 2 inches from knot to knot and are 12 feet in depth. Rowing boats equipped with outboard motors are used; in the past, these boats were referred to by the fishermen as *llestri sân*.

Undoubtedly seine net fishing has been well known on the Teifi for many centuries. George Owen, writing in 1603, for example, describes the 'great store' of salmon 'as allso of sueings, mullettes and botchers, taken in the said Ryver neere St dogmells in a sayne net after everye tyde'. Until the present century salmon and sewin fishing in the spring and summer and herring fishing in the autumn and winter seem to have been the main occupation of the inhabitants of St Dogmaels. 'It affords employment', said one nineteenth-century author, 'to such of the inhabitants that are not engaged in agricultural pursuits.' It is difficult to estimate the extent of seine net fishing on the Teifi in the past, but in 1884 there were sixty-two licensed netsmen on the Teifi and large quantities of salmon and sewin were taken. During the summer of 1883 'as much as half a ton of salmon was caught in the lower reaches of the river and sent to London and other places in one day'.

During the course of the present century, and particularly since 1939, there has been a steady decrease in the number of seine net fishermen operating in the Teifi estuary. In 1939 there were thirteen boats, each one manned by a team of five fishermen; today the number has decreased to six boats, each manned by four men only. In the nineteen-twenties, each team consisted of seven fishermen and it has been estimated that twenty boats were engaged in seine net fishing at the time. The twenty-four full-time fishermen of St Dogmaels are all members of the St Dogmaels Seine Net Fishermen's Association, whose headquarters are at the Netpool in the village.

There are a number of reasons for the decline of seine net fishing in the estuary of the Teifi. The fishermen themselves tend to blame the River Authority for severely curtailing their activities. The season extends from 1st March to 31st August, but before 1939 it commenced on 16th February. There are limitations too, on the mesh of the nets, for it has to be '4 inches when wet, or not less than 2 inches from knot to knot', and they have to be 'unarmoured nets without bags or pockets and consisting of a single sheet of netting measuring not more than 200 yards in length'. There are also limitations on the period of legal time for fishing, for no netsman may operate between 6 a.m. on Saturday and mid-day on Monday. High licence fees of £28 per annum are also blamed for the decline in the numbers of fishermen. Undoubtedly, too, one of the main reasons for the decline has been the gradual silting up of the river estuary and a change in the course of the river. Silting has followed the decline of Cardigan as a sea port, for when the wharves of Cardigan flourished, a navigable channel was kept open to the sea; sand from the estuary was also used as ballast for the ships. As a result of the decline of trade, the river has silted up and there would literally be no room for the twenty seine nets of the past. Pools that yielded appreciable quantities of salmon have silted up and the seine netting today is concentrated in four pools only—Pwll Nawpis, Pwll y Perch, Pwll y Castell and Pwll Sama. Until 1935 other pools such as Pwll Nhiwcyn, Pwll y Cam, Pwll Pric, Pwll Parchaus, Pwll y Brig, Pwll Rhipin Coch and Pwll Wil-y-gof were all well known salmon pools, but have now virtually disappeared.

To decide which fisherman goes to which stretch of river, lots are always drawn before each tide at the Netpool (*Pwll y Rhwyd*), by picking numbered stones (*cymryd shot*) from a hat. For that period of fishing a particular stretch of the river, a *bwrw*, belongs to the team that has drawn the stone with a number corresponding to that of the pool. No fisherman is allowed to fish any portion of the river other than the 'cast' or 'station' which fell to his lot before leaving the Netpool. The stretch of river surrounding the deep pools, where fishing is allowed, is known as *traill* (trawl) and those of the estuary below Cardigan Bridge are known as Traill y Brain, now never used; Traill Fach below Pwll y Castell; Traill Pwll Nawpis, and Traill y Rhyd above Pwll y Perch.

Fishing takes place on the ebb tide and each team proceeds to its allotted station in the river. The team or teams that have drawn Pwll Sama have a journey of over a mile to the bar of the river, while those that have drawn Pwll y Castell have little way to travel. The sailing down river from St Dogmaels is described as '*mynd i'r sân*' ('going to the seine').

The teams wait at their allotted station until the tide is considered right for the first cast, or *ergyd*. With the net carefully folded on the stern the boat, which is equipped with an outboard engine, is steered out to the centre of the pool, the net being paid out to a half-moon shape from the shore. The regulations state that 'One end of the head-rope of a draft or seine net shall be shot or paid out from a boat, which shall start from such shore or bank, and shall return thereto without pause or delay, and the net shall thereupon forthwith be drawn into and landed on the shore or bank on which the head-rope is being held.' One member of the team, usually the least experienced (*y bastynwr*), acts as a shoreman and holds the head-rope on the bank; another is concerned with steering the boat, while the other two pay out the net from the stern. One, often the owner, is concerned with the head-rope and its cork floats, the other with the bottom rope and its lead weights. Each section of net has its specific name: the centre is known as *rhwyd got*, which is made of thick twine, and on either side of it are three pairs of other nets—*rhwyd nesa'r got, rhwyd ganol* and *rhwyd fastwn*; the mesh of each section is slightly different. The net must always be cast to starboard.

Slowly the boat makes its way downstream, and after the whole net has been extended, the boat is steered towards the shore, anchored, and the three fishermen together with the shoreman pull in the head-rope and net. If a salmon or sewin is caught in the net, it is knocked on the head with a wooden *cnocer*. The net is then rearranged on the gunwale of the boat and is cast again. The process is repeated until the tide makes it impossible to continue; a single *ergyd* takes approximately fifteen minutes. On the return of the fishermen to the village, the catch is weighed and packed ready for market. The fishermen are paid a piece-rate wage and the share of each team is divided into five equal parts—four for the fishermen and 'one for the boat'. The fifth share is designed to pay the expenses of the boat owner, who is, in most cases, a member of the fishing team.

In the seine netting pools of the Teifi it is believed that if a parson or preacher is seen on the shore, that is an omen of ill luck. In 1965 an old ceremony of blessing the fishing harvest was revived on the Netpool at St Dogmaels. Many of the fisher‐men believe that the poor salmon seasons experienced since then are due almost entirely to the revival of this religious ceremony and that the presence of gentle‐men of the cloth at that ceremony has contributed to the absence of fish from the river. Someone appearing on the bank in red clothes is also an omen of bad luck, but someone dressed in white would be very welcome. The cry of a bird, known locally as the 'Welsh parrot', that screeches the words *Dim byd, dim byd* (nothing, nothing) also signifies that the particular fishing season when it appears will be without a catch, particularly if that bird flies across the river and over the fishing team. It is also considered bad luck to grasp the *cnocer* from the bottom of the boat until the net has been hauled in.

Select Bibliography

ASHBY, A. W., and EVANS, I. L., *The Agriculture of Wales and Monmouthshire*. University of Wales Press, 1944.

DANIEL, GLYN, *Who are the Welsh?* British Academy, 1954.

DAVIES, ELWYN, and REES, ALWYN D. (eds), *Welsh Rural Communities*. University of Wales Press, 1960.

DAVIES, SIR LEONARD TWISTON, and EDWARDS, AVERYL, *Welsh Life in the Eighteenth Century*. Country Life, 1939.

DAVIES, MARGARET, *Wales in Maps*. University of Wales Press, 1951.

DODD, A. H., *Life in Wales*. Batsford, 1972.

DODD, A. H., *The Industrial Revolution in North Wales*. University of Wales Press, 1933.

EMMETT, I., *A North Wales Village*. Routledge and Kegan Paul, 1964.

EVANS, NESTA, *Social Life in Mid-Eighteenth Century Anglesey*. University of Wales Press, 1936.

FISHLOCK, TREVOR, *Wales and the Welsh*. Cassell, 1972.

FITZGIBBON, THEODORA, *A Taste of Wales*. Dent, 1971.

FOX, CYRIL, *The Personality of Wales*. National Museum of Wales, 1947.

FOX, SIR CYRIL, and RAGLAN, LORD, *Monmouthshire Houses*. National Museum of Wales, 1951–4.

FRANKENBERG, R., *Villages on the Border*. Cohen & West, 1957.

FRAZER, MAXWELL, *Wales*, 2 vols. Robert Hale, 1952.

GRIFFITH, WYN, *The Welsh*. University of Wales Press, 1964.

JENKINS, DAVID, *The Agricultural Community of South-West Wales at the Turn of the Twentieth Century*. University of Wales Press, 1971.

JENKINS, J. GERAINT, *The Welsh Woollen Industry*. National Museum of Wales. 1969. *Nets and Coracles*. David & Charles, 1974. *Traditional Country Craftsmen*. Routledge & Kegan Paul, 1965.

JENKINS, R. T., and REES, WILLIAM, *A Bibliography of the History of Wales*. University of Wales Press, 1931.

JONES, E. D., *Victorian and Edwardian Wales from Old Photographs*. Batsford, 1972.

JONES, R. BRINLEY (ed.), *Anatomy of Wales*. Gwerin Publications, 1972.

JONES, T. GWYNN, *The Culture and Tradition of Wales*. Hughes, Wrexham, 1927.

LLOYD, D. M. and E. M., *A Book of Wales*. Collins, 1953.

MORGAN, GERALD, *The Dragon's Tongue*. Triskell Press, 1963.

MORGAN, PRYS, *Background to Wales*. Christopher Davies, 1968.

OWEN, TREFORM., *Welsh Folk Customs*. National Museum of Wales, 1968.

PARRY, THOMAS, *A History of Welsh Literature*. Clarendon, 1955.

PAYNE, FF. G., *Welsh Peasant Costume*. National Museum of Wales, 1964.

PEATE, IORWERTH C., *Guide to the Collection of Welsh Bygones*. National Museum of Wales, 1929. *The Welsh House*. Cymmrodorion, 1940. *Tradition and Folk Life: a Welsh View*. Faber & Faber, 1972.

REES, ALWYN D., *Life in a Welsh Countryside*. University of Wales Press, 1950.

RHYS, JOHN, and JONES, D. BRYNMOR, *The Welsh People*. Fisher Unwin, 1909.

ROBERTS, R. ALUN, *Welsh Homespun*. Welsh Outlook Press, 1930.

RODERICK, A. J., *Wales Through the Ages*, 2 vols. Christopher Davies, 1956.

STEPHENS, MEIC (ed.), *The Welsh Language Today*. Gomerian Press, 1973.

THOMAS, HUGH, *A History of Wales 1485–1660*. University of Wales Press, 1972.

TIBBOTT, S. MINWEL, *Welsh Fare*. National Museum of Wales 1976.

TWISTON-DAVIES, L., and LLOYD-JOHNES, H. J., *Welsh Furniture*. University of Wales Press, 1950.

Index

Numerals in italics indicate page numbers of drawings; photographs are indicated by plate numbers at the ends of entries.